TOWERS
OF
GOLD

◆

FEET
OF
CLAY

TOWERS
OF
GOLD
·
FEET
OF
CLAY

THE
CANADIAN BANKS

Walter Stewart

A Totem Book
Toronto

For my wife, Joan.
Sometime banker.

First published 1982
by Collins Publishers
100 Lesmill Road, Don Mills, Ontario

This edition published 1983
by TOTEM BOOKS
a division of Collins Publishers

© 1982 by SHRUG Limited

Canadian Cataloguing in Publication Data

Stewart, Walter, 1931-
Towers of gold, feet of clay: the Canadian banks

Includes bibliographical references and index.
ISBN 0-00-217109-0

1. Banks and banking – Canada. I. Title.

HG2704.574 1983   332.1'2'0971   C83-098723-1

Design: Marg Round

Contents

The Background

1 My, What Big Vaults You Have *1*
2 An Eye For An Eye — Plus Interest *15*
3 The Founding Finaglers *26*

The Innards

4 Step Into My Cage *43*
5 The Collectors *59*
6 Nearer My Bank To Thee *69*

The Network

7 The Unity Bank Caper *83*
8 The Club Of The Worthy *105*
9 The Boys In The Bank *117*
10 Big Daddy *130*
11 Watch Out For The Watchdog — He Bruises Easily *152*

The Long Arm Of The Banks

12 Clout *165*
13 There Is Some Corner Of A Foreign Field
That Is Forever Mortgaged *185*
14 Whose Balloon? Inflation And The Banks Abroad *206*
15 Whose Balloon? Inflation And The Banks At Home *220*

The Prospects

16 Stick 'Em Up. This Is A Recording *236*
17 The Balance Sheet *251*

The Data

18 Appendix I — The Tables *270*
19 Appendix II — Glossary *291*
20 Notes *296*
Index *305*

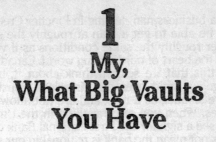

1
My,
What Big Vaults
You Have

"I object to the claim that banks are a rip-off. They're part of the monetary system. Sure, there is hocus-pocus in the money game, but people know that. It's an acceptable fraud."

A middle rank Canadian banker

The good news is that the Canadian banking system is as secure as any in the world, that it is generally honest and reasonably business-like. Even if your bank were to go bankrupt, which is highly unlikely, your funds are secure; they are protected by a government guarantee of up to $20,000 per account through the Canadian Deposit Insurance Corporation.[1] It would take a tremendous upheaval across the entire world of finance to shake the Canadian banking system, or our confidence in it. The possibility of such an upheaval exists; indeed, as we shall see, there are perils overhanging the financial structure of the entire world. But there are no particular perils aimed at Canadians. If the whole globe's economy blows up, we will be involved inevitably, but in the short run we have greater security in our banking system than most nations.

We have other advantages in the Canadian banking system, too. We have what is called "full-branch banking," which is to say that our large banks – and they are all that count – reach from coast to coast, and provide roughly similar services wherever they go. If your car breaks down in Ecum Secum, Nova Scotia and you write a cheque on your Vancouver bank, the money will be cleared out of your account before you can say "overdraft." Similarly, if you are a businessman dealing in Pincher Creek, Alberta, you will be able to get a loan at roughly the same price and under roughly the same conditions as if you lived in Toronto, the heart of our banking world. Canadians are so used to this that we seldom think about it, but it is an advantage we hold over our American cousins, whose banks are smaller, as a rule, and are not allowed to span state lines. When you are travelling in the United States and you see a sign for the First National Bank of Kokomo, that does not mean the bank is national in our sense.[2] It is national only because it holds a federal charter; actually, it can't stir a step out of Kokomo, and if you choose to settle down there and go into business, you may find that your choice is between dealing with that bank, under whatever conditions it chooses to create, or dealing with another bank fifty miles away.

Our banks have a large measure of uniformity, which means, depending on your view, that they are uniformly appalling or uniformly efficient or uniformly in-between.

Finally, our banks have the advantage of size. They are world-class institutions. They can compete abroad with the largest banks of Britain, the United States, Japan, France, West Germany or Switzerland, and that is a real help to Canadian business.

The bad news is that the Canadian banking system is one in which, as economist John Chant wrote, "Competition has yet to be tried."[3] It is efficient enough, but it is efficient for the banks, not for their customers. Recently, the Bank of Nova Scotia lost $1,400 of mine — it just disappeared into the old computer. I found out about it when I tried to take out some money and discovered that the cupboard was bare; so I spoke to the savings supervisor, and warned her not to send any cheques back. She promised she would keep an eye on the account herself. That same day, the bank bounced my mortgage cheque, which I discovered when I got a five dollar overdraft charge in the mail. When I went bellowing into the office of the manager, Wayne Haley, he said that it was "the darndest thing." He couldn't understand how it happened. Nor could he. Nor could anybody find out what had gone wrong. It remains, to this day, one of life's mysteries. The mortgage company billed me ten dollars for the returned cheque, so we had a lot of fun about that, too. It took the bank six days to get the money back into my account, during which time I was financially immobilized. The day after I became solvent again, the same bank lost another cheque on me. I would have shifted my account to the nearby Bank of Montreal except that the Bank of Montreal did exactly the same thing to me last summer, and then tried to make me pay the overdraft charge anyway, arguing that, however caused, I did have an overdraft, and the rules demanded that somebody pay for it. The Bank of Nova Scotia graciously forgave its five bucks. I can't even use this story at cocktail parties, because it pales beside the stories that immediately interrupt mine. This same Bank of Nova Scotia, this same Bank of Montreal, can blip money over to Saudi Arabia in an instant, write complex deals with real-estate developers in Hong Kong, or foreclose a mortgage in Nassau – even getting the right mortgage – without turning a hair, but they can't keep my account straight. Or yours.

They are in the Inflation Business

Banks are massive bureaucracies, and behave as such. This should not surprise us. When we learn that the Ministry of Transport has 21,000 employees, we nod our heads and say, That explains why those jokers are always screwing up. Bureaucracy, what can you do? The Royal Bank has 36,928 employees[4], as rigidly regimented as the faceless wonders of the Ministry of Transport. More so. They can be fired more easily.

The uniformity of the banks, which becomes an advantage on some occasions, is a drawback on others; their large size has negative as well as positive aspects, but these considerations pale in importance beside the overwhelming concern Canadians should have about their banks, which is that they are in the inflation business, and that they are very nearly beyond our power to control. Strong words. I hope to justify them before this book is done, but first we need to set the stage by understanding just what it is that banks do, and how our banks, in particular, work.

Spreading the Spread

Banks buy and sell money. That's all. They do it in a

number of ingenious ways, but that's the job in a nutshell. They make a profit on the difference between what they pay for the money and what they can sell it for. If they pay bank depositors 12% and charge borrowers 15%, they make three per cent. That three per cent is called "the spread". It's exactly the same as the "markup" on a can of peas. Obviously, the less the banks pay for their money and the more they get for it, the more profit they make. In addition, the more money there is in the system, the faster they grow, and growth is at least as important as profit to any business. The banks like to tell us that inflation will be the ruin of all of us. Not all of us; not the banks. (In runaway inflation, yes, but not with the ordinary variety.) Inflation gives them more money to play with, and allows them to grow faster and sometimes, not always, allows them to "widen the spread."

Historically, "real interest" has hovered around 3%[5]. That is, people would put money out for rent if they could get a real return of three per cent on it. With no inflation, interest of 3% is a good investment; with inflation at 10%, interest at 13% is the same thing. When inflation gets really soaring, two things happen to help the banks. The first is that there are many more dollars in the system for them to work with; the second is that they can widen the spread without much fuss — a 4% spread with interest at 18% (you borrow at 18%, and earn 14% on bank deposits) isn't as noticeable as it is at 8% (you borrow at 8% and earn 4% on deposits). In Table 3 of the Appendices you will see how, in 1981, the banks effectively doubled their spread as interest rates rose, and then kept it constant as they fell, earning more in the process. Ergo, despite their loud and repeated denials, banks are in the inflation business.

Greed, Zeal and Imagination

You wouldn't believe a car salesman if he tried to tell you that what he wanted was to sell fewer and cheaper cars; why should you believe a banker who tells that he wishes he didn't have to charge you so much? If you do, it is because bankers and banks have always held a special place in society; they have surrounded themselves with mystery and their work with an aura of reverence that neither deserves. Banking is a business like any other, motivated by the same forces, marked by the same greed, driven by the same ambitions and, when it works well, illuminated by the same zeal and imagination as, say, manufacturing motor-cycles or selling men's suits. Seen as a religion, it is mysterious, holy and worthy. Seen as a trade, it is straightforward, profane and useful.

If banking is a trade, we need to know how it obtains the commodity that is the subject of its transactions — money. The answer is straightforward. Some of the money it raises from investors, some it borrows from the public and most it manufactures on the premises. It will help if we look at these three sources one by one.

The invested money comes from the bank's stockholders, the people who own its publicly-traded shares. There are a great many of these people; none of our banks is closely-held. In 1980, 214,265[6] people owned stock in Canadian banks, and they were overwhelmingly — 96% — residents of Canada. Banks stocks are not expensive — shares in the Royal Bank of Canada, our largest, ranged from a low of $24.13 to a high of $32.25 during 1981[7].

The bank may also issue debentures, which are bonds backed by the entire credit of the bank — as opposed to a mortgage bond, secured only by a real estate asset. Debentures are one way a bank gets money to increase its capital; the other way is to plough back retained earnings. The money accumulated through stocks, debentures and retained earnings constitutes what is called the "paid-in capital" of the bank: its equity. There is a rough relationship between the equity of a bank and the amount of money it can loan out. For a bank, a loan is an asset — because it is going to get the money back, with interest — just as, to a bank, a deposit is a liability — because it owes that money to a depositor. The capital-to-assets ratio is the measure used to link together the bank's equity and its reach; this is called its "leverage." The normal leverage for Canadian banks is about 32-to-1[8]; that is, for every dollar they have in capital, they have about thirty-two out working, and earning interest. Or, to put it another way, real dollars are very thin on the ground compared to the assets on any bank's books. (Don't worry about all these terms; there is a Glossary at the back to define them for you.)

The borrowed money is money that the bank takes in across the counter, as deposits in savings or chequing accounts, or in term deposits, which may have maturities of anywhere from twenty-nine days to five years. These borrowings (deposits) are the bank's major liabilities, just as its loans are its major assets. Again, there is a relationship between the amount of money on deposit and the money the bank has available to loan, and again, it is lopsided. Canadian banking law provides that for every dollar of deposits, the bank is required to hold, on reserve with the Bank of Canada, a fixed amount of cash or securities. This amount varies with the kind of deposit under consideration. Money deposited in a chequing account for immediate use is more likely to be called on than money invested in a notice deposit. A savings account is a "notice deposit"; if you look at your bank book, you will see that, technically, you could be required to give the bank seven days notice – at the Bank of Nova Scotia, ten days – to take money out of your savings account. In fact, you will be able to collect any reasonable amount at once, but the precaution is there. Other notice and term deposits carry other requirements. There is little chance that everyone who has dollars in the bank is going to want them at once, so the bank doesn't keep anything like as much cash on hand as it has on deposit. The banks have a term for the rude process of people wanting to take their money back out in cash instead of the civilized way, by writing a cheque. It's called "leakage." The amount of leakage at any bank is only a small portion of its assets, and the law recognizes the fact by requiring the bank to keep in reserve an amount equal to ten per cent of its "demand deposits" and four per cent of its "notice deposits."[9]

So, for every dollar the bank has in reserve, it can loan either ten dollars – in the case of a 10% reserve – or twenty-five – in the case of a 4% reserve – out to earn interest.

But, if the bank really only has one dollar on hand, where does it get the extra money that it puts out to loan? It makes it up, creates it out of thin air. Indeed, that is the only magic there is to banking – its capacity to create cash out of nothing, to manufacture, with the stroke of a pen, or now, with a few keystrokes of a computer, money that can be spent, used, wasted or lost. Again, there is nothing really mysterious about the process. When you go to the bank to borrow money – let us give you a really impressive loan of $100,000 – there is none of this crude business of passing 100,000 one-dollar bills over the counter. No sir. The bank writes down your name and, beside it, a dollar sign, a one, and five zeroes. That's all there is to it. You can spend this money, by writing out cheques; they in turn will be deposited in other banks. Then, because these other banks have some of your $100,000 loan on deposit, they, in turn, can create more money.

If someone is rude enough to come back to your bank for actual dollars – leakage – they will be paid out, but that will not represent more than a tiny fraction of the ghostly glitter the bank created in your name. When the money is actually taken in the form of cash, it is called "monetizing the debt,"[10] a phrase which, like "leakage", sounds faintly sinister, and correctly conveys the impression that something untoward has taken place.

To put it at its flattest, when you borrow $100,000, what you are getting is a bank entry, and you will go on paying back, for years, not only that manufactured money, but interest charges that can run to more than the original amount of the loan, and all for a few strokes of a pen.

The banks cannot create money forever; they are limited by reserve requirements and by capital-asset ratios. Reserve requirements are established by law, capital-asset ratios by banking practice. Within these limits, the banks can and do create and control currency, and then sell it at a profit.

Banks did not always have reserve requirements, which is why they developed an unfortunate habit of going broke when the customers called around for cash, and they are not at all happy with the reserve requirements they have now. Indeed, we will see as this book winds on how the banks spend much of their time and effort trying to get out of all the curbs that have been placed on them, and to what extent they have succeeded. Briefly, they have managed to lower the reserve requirements at home and to escape them entirely abroad, with incalculable consequences for us all. They are forever manufacturing more money to trade, while denying that this is what they are about. The one aspect in which banks differ from any other business is that there is no other industry extant that spends so much of its time denying that it does what it does for a living. The possible exception is street-walking.

Most of what I have said so far applies to banks

everywhere — money manufacturing is universal. It is time now to look at Canadian banks in particular.

The Giants and the Gaggle

Although there are fifty-eight chartered banks in Canada[11] — and the number is rising constantly under the new Bank Act — only eleven of these amount to anything much. These are the eleven created by acts of Parliament, the original chartered banks. The gaggle of foreign banks beginning to crowd the scene comprise, in total, about five per cent of the business. We will learn more about them later, but we can ignore them when describing the main elements of Canadian banking, and concentrate on the eleven parliamentary chartered banks, the ones that were set up under special acts, each with its very own law, in the business of banking. And what is the business of banking? It is whatever the banks do. They have never had their occupation defined; instead, the Bank Act says:

"'bank' means a bank to which this Act applies."[12]

And, under the section on "Business and Powers of a Bank," this little gem:

"A bank may engage in and carry on such business as generally appertains to the business of banking."[13]

So, a bank is a firm that does banking, and banking is what a bank does. All clear so far?

In addition to the eleven parliamentary banks, we have forty-seven banks created (so far) by letters patent. The new Bank Act, passed in 1980, changed the rules for bank creation. The rationale was that, to increase competition, more banks should be allowed, and the easiest way to do that was to open the process by having banks established through letters patent — as many other companies are — instead of going through the laborious process of parliamentary charter.[14] That is the way the story was put out, anyway. What actually happened was that foreign banks were operating in Canada but not calling themselves banks, in exactly the same way that Canadian banks are operating in other countries.

These agencies, as most foreign banks were called, didn't have to put up reserves and could do things our banks couldn't.[15] They were brought to heel. The new Bank Act required them to turn themselves into banks by letters patent, and to hold reserves. Then they were squeezed into one tiny corner of the banking business by the stipulation that the assets (loans) of all foreign banks could not exceed eight per cent of all the assets in domestic banking. The foreign agencies operating here already held five per cent [16] of our banking assets, so, in effect, they have been required to turn themselves into banks for the privilege of squabbling over three per cent of the market. Foreign agencies can in theory refuse to become banks, but then they will not be allowed to use the guarantees of their parents to back loans in the Canadian money market. Refusal to apply for a charter is not within the realm of practical politics for the interlopers. They will fill a role as commercial bankers, helping to finance business transactions. They believe they will do well in this role, because they think our banks are slow and unenterprising, but they will never be full-service banks in more than a few locations across the country.

Foreign banks are satellites on the edge of a system consisting, for all practical purposes, of eleven institutions. Among them, they controlled assets of $343.97 billion as of October 1981.[17] They are rich, and getting richer, huge, and getting huger. They dominate our economic landscape and reach into every corner of Canadian life. Virtually everything we do, from the food we eat – financed by a farm loan – to the houses we live in, the cars we drive, even the clothing we wear – and bought on VISA or MasterCard – comes under the sway of the eleven.

But even eleven is a misleading number; there are really only five banks that dominate the country. For the eleven chartered banks are divided into two groups, the Big Five and The Rest. Here are the Big Five and their assets as of October 31, 1981:[18]

1. The Royal Bank of Canada, $87.51 billion.
2. The Canadian Imperial Bank of Commerce, $66.84 billion.
3. The Bank of Montreal, $63.78 billion.
4. The Bank of Nova Scotia, $50.14 billion.
5. The Toronto-Dominion Bank, $44.86 billion.

And here are The Rest.

6. The National Bank of Canada, $19.16 billion.
7. The Mercantile Bank of Canada, $4.10 billion.
8. The Bank of British Columbia, $2.99 billion.
9. The Continental Bank of Canada, $2.52 billion.
10. The Canadian Commercial Bank, $1.53 billion.
11. The Northland Bank, $517 million.

Among them, the Big Five hold $313.13 of the $343.97 billion in the system, or ninety-one per cent. The smallest of the Big Five, the Toronto-Dominion, holds one-and-a-half times as many assets as every one of The Rest rolled into one. Among them, these five hold more assets than the top 250 non-financial corporations in the nation put together.[19] Banks always find this comparison invidious because, they say, their assets are not the same as, say, the assets of General Motors of Canada. GM's assets consist of accounts receivable, cars, buildings, real estate and so forth, while much of the Royal Bank's assets consist of loans — money owed to them. By the same token, GM's liabilities consist mainly of bank loans, while the Royal's consist of its deposits — the money it owes others. So what? What we are measuring is heft, financial impact, call it what you will, and the banks' assets contain more heft than any tangible object — as anyone can tell you who has had a demand note called.

In terms of assets, then, the Royal Bank is twenty-two times the size of General Motors Canada, the Commerce is four-and-a-half times the size of Bell Canada, and little T-D is almost two-and-a-half times the size of Canada's top four oil companies — Imperial, Gulf, Texaco and BP — lumped together.[20]

Between October 1980 and October 1981, the chartered banks increased their assets by 27.5%, from $269 billion to $344 billion (after a 21% jump in 1980).[21] That $75 billion increase amounted to about six times the federal deficit for 1980.[22] Or, to put it another way, while the rest of the Canadian economy was in the doldrums, the banks were stashing the stuff away and moaning all the while that it wasn't enough.

Our banks are so overblown that they not only dominate our own landscape, but compete effectively abroad. The Top Five are on the list of the sixty-five largest banks on the planet.[23] In the United States, 15,000[24] banks struggle for supremacy; in Canada, eleven. Not surprisingly, under the circumstances, the Zurich gnomes who smile and rub their hands when the bigshots from Bank of America or Chase Manhattan pop into town are just as quick to fall on the necks of the lads from the Royal Bank or the Bank of Montreal.

Over-banked and Under-served

As anyone would expect in an oligopoly, our banks are non-competitive and over-bearing. They spend a lot of time and money on television advertising, but as little as possible serving customers. They treat each other with deference, and their customers like retarded, but boisterous, children. They worship at the shrine of free enterprise, but pull on the public teat. They compete -- as other oligopolies compete -- mainly in the array of services they offer and the number of branches they build. Price competition, once all the gimmicks are winnowed out and balanced against each other, is practically non-existent. We are one of the most over-banked nations in the world. We have 7,374[25] bank branches, one for every 3,230 Canadians; we have 26,174,907[26] savings accounts -- more than we have men, women and children -- and 20,888,554 other bank accounts.[27] The banks have 151,140 employees[28] and more slogans, advertising tags and gimmicks than we know what to do with, but I defy any Canadian, once he is inside a bank, to tell what distinguishes it from any other bank. The slogans differ, the tellers change, the degree of cheer or surliness on the other side of the counter runs through variations, and there are perceptible differences in the shades of condescension we meet at the loans desk and the levels of incompetence we meet in the handling of our accounts, but these vary from branch to branch, not bank to bank. They are a factor of personality, not competition.

At the same time, the closeness of the system, and the links between the big banks and big business, almost guarantee that individuals and small firms will be ignored by the mainstream banks. This has been institutionalized in the prime rate. Large companies, whose presidents sit on the boards of the banks, can borrow at prime; the rest of us pay from one to two per cent more. The theory is that the larger firms represent a lower risk, and therefore are entitled to a lower charge. But wouldn't it make more sense, economically and socially, to set a uniform rate and spread it across a broader spectrum? Does it help you that General Motors can borrow more cheaply than a small Canadian entrepreneur?

The Big Five have done such a bad job serving small and medium-sized businesses that governments have had to create banks of their own to take up the slack. The Federal Business Development Bank exists because the chartered banks don't do the job.

The charge that Canadians have lacked the courage to develop our magnificent heritage does not belong to the nation as a whole — we are not, after all, measurably different from our American cousins — it belongs to our banking institutions. Send not to ask for whom the mouse squeaks, it squeaks for the Royal, the Commerce and the rest of the gang.

If our banks were not so huge, they might be less arrogant. When a Toronto man went to close out his account at the Toronto-Dominion bank, he was given $600 too much by mistake. He hung onto it. The bank had him charged with theft. If your bank takes too much away from you, do you think you can get its officers charged with theft? In this case, the bank got rapped on the knuckles. County Court Judge Lloyd Graham dismissed the charge, noting, "This case represents a classic example of what could happen ... If you can afford to pay in the civil context, you avoid a criminal prosecution; but if you cannot, you face prosecution in the criminal courts." The bank was not very contrite. Its lawyer explained that Toronto-Dominion doesn't usually use the criminal courts to chase money; usually, it sues as well.[29]

If our banks were not so sheltered, they might be more efficient. Jack Weldon, head of the Economics department at McGill University, once advised me to "compare our banks with the Russians. I'm almost sure you'll find they have more competition." Close, but no cigar. It could be argued that the Russians have four huge banks where we have five, so it should be noted that our banks are marginally more competitive than those in the Soviet Union.

If our banks were truly competitive, classical economics

tells us that we could expect their profits to be lean, their growth uneven, and their efficiency a marvel to behold. In fact, between 1960 and 1970, the banks tripled in size; then inflation soared and between 1970 and 1980, they multiplied six-fold (the figures are in Table 2 of the Appendices). Between the end of 1960 and the end of 1981, they grew 2033%, multiplying twenty-fold in twenty-one years.[30] Their profits grew from the comfortable to the astonishing, and they moved upwards in lock-step. As to their efficiency, they carve off a fatter slice of profit and service charges than their counterparts in the United States.

Our banks are efficient in one respect, however – they are terrific at dodging taxes. The Top Five banks paid lower taxes, not merely in proportion, but in absolute dollars, in 1979 than they did in 1970, although they made two-and-a-half times as much in profit in 1979.[31]

Banks make this money in good times and in bad; they are shock-proof, inflation-proof, depression-proof and watertight. The last time a Canadian bank went under was in 1923 when the Home Bank bit the dust. The Canadian Bankers' Association likes to point to this as a sign of the stability of the system. Stultification would be a better word. Think of it for a moment; throughout the last sixty years, through depression, inflation, expansion, retraction and damnation, not a single Canadian bank gave up the ghost. Industrial empires toppled, trust companies caved, developers went belly-up, even oil companies occasionally took a nose-dive, but throughout it all, the banks went on making more and more and more money. Does that suggest that they are marvellously efficient, that, by some happy chance, no blunderers have ever taken over a Canadian bank? Or does it suggest that competition is lacking?

The Mystique that Blinds

I raise these rude questions because I think it is time, and well past time, for Canadians to take a critical look at the most important business in this nation. It is a business dominated by a group of five companies, closely linked to a network of major corporations yet isolated from the chill winds that shake the rest of the economy. It is a business that shapes our lives, buoys our hopes and – just as often – shatters our dreams. It is a business that makes large

2
An Eye For An Eye, Plus Interest

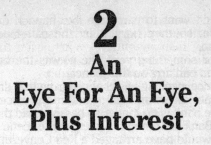

"Make money and the whole nation will conspire to call you a gentleman."

Bob Edwards, *1920*

We are in a sylvan glade in Mesopotamia. The year is 11,000 B.C., give or take a decade. Along the pathway comes our Remote Ancestor, bearing a haunch of ibex. He encounters a family moving the other way, making its way towards the water-hole. They are One Eye, his wife Bird-Lips, and their nubile daughter Rosy Dawn. Remote Ancestor, a sociable sort, stops to chat, leaning on his ibex-haunch and casting an appreciative glance at Rosy.

"Awrk," grunts Remote Ancestor, which is to say, "Sir, I am no trifler. I will not conceal from you the fact that my feelings towards Rosy Dawn, even upon such hasty acquaintance, are stronger and deeper than those of ordinary friendship."

"Erk," puts in Bird-Lips, by which she means, "How much?"

The introduction of this sordid commercial note marks a new aspect to the encounter. Remote Ancestor offers half his ibex-haunch for the girl. One Eye notes that he sold his last daughter for half an ibex-haunch six moons ago, and since then, the price of everything has gone up. But One Eye, being a reasonable man, will throw in three flints, and the remains of a decaying squirrel, if Remote Ancestor will give him the entire ibex-haunch for his daughter.

"Ork," says Remote Ancestor, meaning, "You drive a hard bargain, sir, but I acquiesce." It turns out that One

Eye doesn't want to carry the ibex-haunch down to the water-hole, so they bury it by the path-side, for later excavation.

That, or something very like it, was the beginning of money and banking on this planet.

In essence, nothing has changed from that day to this in the conduct of commercial transactions, except that the role of the bank is no longer so passive. Had the Canadian Imperial Bank of Commerce been on the scene in Mesopotamia, it would have arranged a Red Convertible loan for Remote Ancestor, taken over One Eye's accounts receivable, traded the ibex-haunch around the countryside ten or fifteen times, given everybody a lot of bum advice along the way, and then foreclosed on the lot of them. Things were not so well organized in Remote Ancestor's day.

However, even in his day, money was important, because money is simply any agreed-upon medium of exchange, from ibex-haunches to coconut-shells, from strings of beads to dollar bills. And money, by its very presence, creates price. Remote Ancestor was able to strike a tough bargain with One Eye because ibex was in short supply that year. If a herd had moved into the area, the value of his haunch would have plummeted immediately.

Mattress Economics

Because Remote Ancestor's was a barter economy, money was not, as it is now reputed to be, a "standard unit of account." An ibex-haunch was worth what you could get for it on the open market, no more and no less. To make a transaction work, you had to have what the economists call "a double coincidence of wants" — Remote wanted Rosy, One Eye wanted the ibex-haunch, so they had the makings of a deal. But money was, even then — to use another economist's phrase — "a store of value." In fact, it was a better store of value then than it is now, because prices were not as variable, even in the recent past, as they are today. In 1582, the man who buried his small store of value in his mattress for a decade or so and then took it out would find that, while it had not gained anything — mattresses don't pay interest — it hadn't lost, either. It was worth precisely the same as it was when he put it away. Today, a man who stuffs his money in a mattress will find that, within a decade, it will have lost at least half its value, because its purchasing power is less. Indeed, economists, who are faster with phrases than they are with ideas, have enshrined this notion in the phrase "constant dollars" to salute the fact that there is nothing constant about them. Today's dollar, minus the inflation rate, is the constant dollar.

Just as money has always implied prices, so has it always implied banking. Indeed, we had banking before we had exchangeable coins. In ancient Egypt, grain was a common measure of exchange[1] and people paid their taxes in grain, which was deposited in granaries run by the state. In many early civilizations, the royal palace and temple were both a centre of distribution and the place where people of wealth deposited it for safekeeping. Usually, that meant depositing crops and getting back a receipt. It was a short step from the piece of papyrus that said "Ptah of Memphis has 5,000 bushels of wheat in the royal storehouse" to the piece that said "Please turn over 2,000 of my 5,000 bushels to Ptush of Chaldee, as I tried to draw to an inside straight last night." The cheque was born.

Hammurabi, the king of Babylon from 1792 to 1750 B.C., set down one of the earliest codes of law. Inevitably, this code dealt with banking, and in fact contains 150 paragraphs on the subject.[2] Hammurabi has gone into the history books as a hard nut because of some unfortunate references in the Code. Every time it comes up, somebody drags out the "eye for an eye" line, which actually reads, "If a man destroy the eye of another man, they shall destroy his eye." In the banking business, he was on the side of the customer, as witness his provision that "If a man owe a debt and a flood shall inundate his field and carry away the produce ... in that year he shall not make any return of grain to the creditor." How many Canadian farmers would like to work out that kind of arrangement with the Friendly Folks of the Royal? In our day, if a man owe a debt and a flood – or wheat rust or locusts or high mortgage rates – shall wipe out his take, they shall destroy his holdings unto the last sou until the bank is repaid. An eye for an eye, plus 22.5% interest. This is known as progress.

By about 1,000 B.C. the practice of transferring bank deposits to a third party was well-established in Babylon, and then the palace or temple began making loans from its own assets, or from deposits on hand, to be repaid with interest after the harvest.[3] That is, a farmer could borrow seed-grain to be repaid, with interest, when the crop came in.

The Greeks, too, established banks which accepted deposits for safekeeping and acted as agents in the settlement of debts. These were private banks, not arms of the state, and Pasion of Athens,[4] one of the most famous of these bankers, who operated in the fourth century B.C., used to invest his own funds, and those of depositors to whom he paid interest, in commercial ventures. Usually, these were maritime ventures. You got your money back when your ship came in.

The Romans took the business a step further, although it is notable that banking developments were centralized, by and large, in the capital of the empire, Rome, and remained rudimentary in the provinces. The Romans became, of necessity, expert money-changers.[5] The tribes they conquered had advanced past the stage of mere barter, or of measuring all wealth in cattle, grain and hides, to the business of exchanging coins of set value. The first record of this process goes back to Gyges, the king of Lydia, who had electrum – an amalgam of silver and gold – cast into ingots of uniform weight, with his effigy stamped on them, as a guarantee of value.[6]

Debasing the Coinage

With the development of coinage came, inevitably, the development of debasing the coinage, and counterfeiting. Who was to know if a little less than the usual gold went into the electrum, or if a little had been shaved off the side? (You would know the latter today, because our coins have ridged sides, but it was not always thus.) It became important to commerce not only to have some assurance that the coins were what they seemed to be, but to have an exchange rate by which the value of coins from, say, Gaul, could be measured against those of, say, Britain. As the Roman Empire spread, its bankers took on this vital function. They became money-changers, auctioneers, discounters and creditors. They evaluated the exotic currencies gathered during the conquests, and the jewelry that formed a part of the loot. In turn, they became speculators in these articles. It also became common for Roman bankers to accept deposits, mostly non-interest-bearing deposits such as jewelry and precious objects, and to pay out sums on behalf of their depositors. The Roman banks did many of the things our modern institutions do, including paying debts for clients in other cities by exchanging liabilities.[7] They formed their own banking association, kept careful accounts, and could be required to produce those accounts on demand for a client, or even for a third party. They didn't have savings accounts, in our sense of the words, but they did have what we would recognize as current accounts.

The decline of the Roman Empire, which had nothing to do with its banking system, brought further development to an abrupt halt. The barbarian invasions, as it were, foreclosed on the early bankers, although they retained their role as money-changers, specialists in the value of coins from the bewildering variety of states and realms that sprang up in the ruins of Europe. The word "bank" comes from the Italian word "banco," describing the bench where the money-changers sat to conduct their business.[8] From the end of the western Roman Empire — with the deposition of Romulus Augustus by the Goths in A.D. 476 — until the eleventh century, bankers were primarily money-changers.

They began to make a comeback as bankers in our sense of the word with the onset of the Crusades. It costs money to fight wars, and while kings didn't always have money, they commanded armies, which are marvellously persuasive instruments when you are looking for donations, so financing military ventures became a profitable, though sometimes chancy, affair. The Lombards, from northern Italy, became active in this business.[9] They were merchants who operated out of Italy into the Rhineland to the north, forming themselves into companies to deal with the merchant guilds. They would set up only where they could get special favours — chiefly, where they were not required to pay taxes — and they were regarded as superior to the Jewish money-lenders who were in the same sort of business. The Jews had become active because they were not bound by the Christian injunction against usury, and the Lombards were not fussy. Like the Lombard merchants, the Jewish bankers would accept deposits, grant advances and make payments in other towns for a consideration. The Lombards also became active as tax collectors, usually as a discount-house; that is, they would collect taxes and turn part of the proceeds over the state, retaining the rest.[10]

From the thirteenth century onwards, Italian city-states levied forced loans on their people, to provide the funds with which to slaughter each other. Citizens were required to pay into a special fund, called a "monte," which collected revenues from taxes and duties to repay the forced depositors.[11] The most famous of these monti was one set up in the thirteenth century to allow Florence to war against Pisa. Later, the monti became voluntary, and were established to raise capital for joint ventures such as trading associations. The depositors would share in the profits, while losses were limited to the money originally deposited – the limited, joint-stock company was born.

From raising money for city-states to fight wars, it was a natural development for Italy's budding bankers to make loans to Christian kings who wanted to lead Crusades to the Holy Land and massacre the infidels in the name of brotherly love. Then, as now, the bankers said that what was done with the money they put up was none of their concern. The Lombards were at the centre of this business. They were merchants and lenders, not money-changers, but the custom grew of entrusting money and valuables to them.[12] They became "goldsmith bankers" – lending money on the basis of funds deposited with them. From there it was a short step to lending out several times as much money as was held on hand for redemption.

The role occupied by Jews and Lombards in Europe became the preserve of the Lombards alone in England after 1290. The Jews were as well out of it, probably, because loaning money to kings tended to be a risky business for any group of people that could be readily singled out for a pogrom. Henry III borrowed from the Jews to finance his wars, but limited the interest to two pence per pound per week,[13] which is to say, 43% per annum. The reason such high rates were required was that times were so unsettled. It became something of a routine for kings to get up to their hips in hock to the money-lenders, and then to declare that the glory of God demanded a pogrom, upon which the debts would be renounced and the debt-holders disposed of in various unpleasant ways. In 1290, Edward I, deeply in debt, expelled the Jews from England, and the Lombards moved in.[14] Because they were in a nefarious business, they were required to live together on a single street in London, Lombard Street, which has been, from that day to this, a symbol of financial power.

Bankers, first in their role of money-changers, and later in more complex roles, were vital to the operations of the fairs which were the major marketplaces of Europe for centuries. They were on hand to change money, advance funds, and accept deposits. Because coins weighed so much, were so hard to lug from town to town, and so attractive to the element that preferred to take out its loans with the aid of a dirk, it became simpler for merchants to have current accounts with the bankers as they moved from fair to fair. The banks became clearing-houses, and transactions were accomplished through bills of exchange, originally called "policies of exchange," which were promises to pay that became negotiable instruments – paper money. Bankers were still mainly merchants, however; while they handled funds for others, they traded on their own account, bought and sold stocks, bought the right to collect taxes, and ran lotteries. Modern banks no longer buy the right to collect taxes, but their close connections with the operations of government, and merchandising go back a long way.

One of Britain's famous early bankers was Sir Thomas Gresham, who was born somewhere around 1519 and died in 1579. He was a merchant, and the royal financial agent in Antwerp after 1551. "His methods," one author notes, "were frequently more effective than ethical."[15] He is generally credited with what is known as "Gresham's Law," although it turns out, typically, that he didn't formulate the law, he just repeated it. It is worth repeating:

"Bad money drives out good."

What this means is that at the trade fairs that Gresham attended, he noticed that whenever two different coins were in circulation, one of which was solid and certain, the other of which was dubious, it was inevitably the bad money that was proffered in a transaction, and the good retained. The law holds true today, whether the money spoken of is Libyan dirhams, Ghanian pesewas or Iraqi dinars; all will be spent before Swiss francs and American dollars. Gresham's Law is the only economic rule that has never been challenged.

Bad money was given an especial opportunity to drive out good when the flood of treasure from Europe's overseas possessions began to pour in after the discovery of the New World and the expansion of trade into the Far East. Much of this wealth was swiftly converted into gold and silver coins, and just as swiftly debased and counterfeited. A Dutch parliamentary manual of 1606 listed 846 different coins then in circulation in the nation and its territories.[16]

To minimize the chaos, in 1609 the city of Amsterdam created the Bank of Amsterdam, which became, in effect, the guarantor of coinage, since it would accept coins only at what it considered to be their real value.[17] It was not a lending bank; deposits were left in its vaults to the credit of those who made them. There was a run on the bank in 1672, when an invading French army heaved over the horizon and local merchants descended on the bank to take out their money. When they found that it was all there, they left it in.[18] The first run on a bank had been survived.

The Bank of Stockholm, founded about the same time as he Bank of Amsterdam, gave receipts for deposits which were then circulated as cash at their face value, both for buying goods and as bills of exchange.[19] These receipts were the bank's promises to pay, the first true bank notes.

The Bank of England, founded in 1694, issued bank notes. It was a private bank (and remained so until 1946), set up under a royal charter to raise money to help King William III fight France.[20] The Tonnage Act authorized the bank to levy a tax on the tonnage of British ships. The promise of money forthcoming from this tax allowed the bank to advance credit to the king, with a promissory note as its only security. Then the bank printed notes, backed by the royal promise to redeem the paper, and these notes were loaned out, at interest, to merchants who used them the way we would use any bank note. Had the king tried to collect a straight royal tax on shipping, he might have had a problem, but that isn't what he did; he gave that right to the bank, got a loan in return, put up a piece of paper to secure the loan, and the bank issued loans based on his paper. The king got money, the bank got money, the public got loans and the whole thing was floated on the basis of revenues that might or might not ever be collected under the Tonnage Act. Money was being created out of airy nothing, a technique that was to be refined as time went on, and greatly expanded.

When the time came to pull this trick in France, it was a Scotsman, John Law, who brought it off. Law, the son of a jeweler, had fled his native country on a charge of murder after he killed a man in a duel, and went to live in Amsterdam.[21] In 1700, when things had quieted down at home, he returned to Scotland where, in 1705, he published Money And Trade Considered, an essay in which he proposed the founding of a national bank whose notes would be secured by the value of land. This notion was rejected as far too radical by both the Scots and the Dutch, so Law left for France. He had met the Duc d'Orleans some years earlier,[22] (both were inveterate gamblers) and the duke was taking over the reins of the nation, as regent, after the death of Louis XIV. The Sun King had left France on the verge of bankruptcy, and Law persuaded his mentor that an expansion of credit would promote and restore prosperity. His reasoning was sound. In 1716, Law was given a charter to form the Banque Generale with a capital of six million livres and the right to issue notes as currency, which it did, mostly in the form of loans to the government. The government then used the notes to pay off its creditors, and in turn accepted them as legal tender for the payment of taxes.[23]

Workable Hocus-Pocus

Hocus-pocus, of course, because the notes had nothing of value behind them but workable hocus-pocus. Whereas Louis XIV kept himself solvent by constantly debasing the coinage or simply refusing to pay his debts, the new government had notes of the Banque Generale in the exchequer, and the bank promised, on the face of the notes, to redeem in metal on request. Trust me, the notes said, and all will be well. So it was, for a time. The infusion of credit did exactly what Law said it would. Trade prospered, prices rose (as they always do in times of prosperity), and employment increased. In 1718, the bank became a royal institution, as the Banque Royale, and the government became a direct guarantor of its notes. In 1719, Law had another brilliant idea. He would form a company to exploit the riches of the burgeoning colonies, and finance it through his bank. He was given a monopoly of trade into the Mississippi region of North America, and launched an extravagant promotion to sell stock.[24] Frantic speculation ensued, share prices shot through the ceiling as Frenchmen counted the value of (non-existent) Louisiana gold. The proceeds of the stock sale, however, were not going to develop Louisiana, but were being loaned to the government for expenses. Law became the Comptroller General of France and the Duc d'Arkansas, but his titles didn't put any cash in the bank's coffers and when creditors began to try to redeem their notes, there was nothing in the till. There was a run on the bank in 1720, and fifteen people were squeezed to death in the crush of customers who besieged the institution in Paris, trying to turn their notes into the promised metal.[25] The bank came crashing down, and Law fled to Venice, where he made a living as a gambler, and died ten years later.

Law's experiment provided a number of lessons. The first was that money had become not merely a standard unit of account and a store of value, but a measure of faith. It could be created out of thin air, and its creation would stimulate trade, expand the economy, provide jobs and drive up prices. A measure of inflation is not the product of mismanaging financial expansion, it is the inevitable product of that expansion. The notion of stable prices and prosperity linked together is a chimera of even less substance than John Law's Mississippi gold. I point out this obvious fact because, although it became apparent in 1720, Canadian financial policy has been based on ignoring it for the past seven years.

The French experience also showed how easy it is to abuse the public trust in any enterprise which shows even modest success. And it showed how swiftly the fabric of any enterprise based on simple faith — such as banking — can be shredded.

Finally, Law had shown how a bank can be used as an arm of state policy, how, indeed, the creation of money out of thin air can work miracles for the national economy. It is a lesson that has been underlined many times since. The French Revolution was fought and won on the back of paper money whose value went up and down with bewildering speed. The American Revolution, similarly, was financed on hope and ignorance, in roughly equal amounts. Paper money was issued; it wasn't worth a damn, but it was accepted — at least often enough to keep the armies of discontent going — and being accepted, it became real. The Russian Revolution repeated the process and, in between, the American Civil War showed how, when the fortunes of battle flow against the note-issuing side, and paper money is left to fend for itself, it becomes as useless as, well, Confederate notes.

We have seen how banks developed from the grain hoards of ancient Egypt through the money-changers and goldsmiths of the Middle Ages into the hocus-pocus of John Law. Developments from that day to this have not added much. Great state banks have sprung up to stand beside the private institutions, central banks have developed to curb the excesses of these institutions, refinements have been added to banking practice, and a number of dodges have been thought up that might have excited the awed admiration even of a high-roller like John Law, such as credit cards and automatic overdrafts.

But these developments, which we will see in other chapters in more detail, are essentially refinements. By John Law's time, the basis of modern banking had already been established. That basis was the creation of paper money to replace ibex-haunches, the establishment of credit and interest, and the infusion of faith into the barter system to make it into a modern, commercial system.

In the next chapter, we will see how these developments worked themselves out in Canadian history.

3
The Founding Finaglers

"It was the day of strong rather than scrupulous men."

B. E. Walker,
A History of Banking in Canada

One way to think about the traditional Canadian banker is to conjure up an image of a large gent with a paunch, a cigar, a gold ring, a blue suit, shiny black shoes, and a general air of comfortable probity. But when I think of the traditional Canadian banker, the image that flashes into my head is that of Samuel Zimmerman, a palpable rogue who carved his initials on the backside of posterity before he went to his untimely death in 1857, at the age of forty-five.

Zimmerman was born in Huntingdon County,[1] Pennsylvania, in 1815, and came to Upper Canada in 1842, when he was twenty-seven, to set himself up as a contractor. He lived in the Niagara district, at Thorold, and built four locks on the second Welland Canal, the first suspension railway bridge over the Niagara gorge, and the Great Western Railway from London to Windsor and Sarnia.[2] He also founded his own bank, the Zimmerman bank, which issued its own handsome bank notes and helped to finance his schemes. In 1852, he became involved in a scam known as the Great Southern Railway project, which somehow never got built but managed to make its promoters a lot of money anyway.[3]

The idea was to build a railway across the rich agricultural belt of southern Ontario from the Niagara River to the Detroit and St. Clair Rivers. Zimmerman got the contract to build the eastern part of this railroad in a straightforward manner — by slipping a bribe of $50,000 to Henry de Blaquiere, one of the railway company directors. Then Zimmerman and his friends set out to raise the cash from municipalities along the way, sometimes by bribery but more often by simply lying to them. They were told that the railway's stock had been paid up, when it had not (that is, there was nothing behind the company); they were told that there was no way their money could be lost, when it not only could be, it was; they were told that the money they were being asked to put up in the form of loan subsidies represented only half the cost of building the railway, and that wasn't true, either. It was a nice touch, I think, that a clergyman was one of the official company agents used to put this codswallop across.

The railway raised $750,000, a lot of money in those days, much of which was spent buying land the railway directors owned, and had obtained either free, or at very low cost. In 1854, when construction was suspended, about $160,000 worth of work had actually been done, for which $435,000 was paid. In the meantime, Zimmerman got himself involved in another railway, the Great Western. It, too, was marked by bribery and corruption, but it was finally built. Alas, the way it was built did Zimmerman in. The company persuaded the legislature to lift a provision of the Railway Act that required trains to stop before crossing the Desjardins Canal near Hamilton, Ontario. The crossing was made on a wooden trestle bridge, on the building of which Zimmerman, as an almost routine matter, violated the conditions of the contract — it was to had been built of oak, and he built it instead of pine, pocketing the difference in cost. On March 12, 1857, a Great Western train, neglecting to stop at the edge of the canal, sped onto the trestle, which collapsed, and plunged through to the river. Sixty passengers were killed, among them Samuel Zimmerman.

Zimmerman's death did not finish the railway, but it did finish the bank, in time. All that remained was to transmogrify Zimmerman into a stalwart citizen, and that was done. If you look him up in the Encyclopedia Canadiana, you will find nothing of his bribes or the real cause of his death, only a note about his contracting career, with that non-starter, the Great Southern Railway, left out, and the comment that "The success of these enterprises brought him a large fortune and enabled him to contribute generously to many worthy causes."

The Myth of Banking Stability

The comforting thing about traditional histories of the Canadian banking system is that they are so reassuring. Our bankers are men of probity; our banks are bastions of stability. The discomforting thing about the reality of our banking history is that it has nothing to do with that tradition. In reality, our early bankers were rogues and rascals, almost to a man; in reality, our banks were sinkholes for looting and corruption until comparatively recently; in reality, they were anything but stable until a few banks gained such a strangle-hold on the system that it became well-nigh impossible for them to fail. Nothing our bankers have done is more impressive than the image they have burned in our memories of their own immaculate past. In large part, this awesome performance has been brought about by the elementary prudence of the banks in making sure that banking history was written, by and large, by bankers themselves. For the rest, we have only ourselves to blame. We have raised our bankers into a priesthood; our financial reporting has been generally free of the taint of critical analysis − it is more theology than reporting, more public relations than journalism − and we are a nation that likes to think the best of itself.

The real history of our banking past is far more interesting than the pap we have been fed. That history contains four themes that mark the periods of our past. First, there was the outright rascality of our early banking tycoons, the men who used the government as a cash-box, the railways as a jam-jar and the public as sucker-bait. These men were mostly successful, and were accordingly heaped with honour. Secondly, there was the imperialism of early banking. It was formed in imitation of British traditions to suit the needs of British finance, with results we still live with. Thirdly, there was the instability that marked our banking until the 1920s, and which could be traced, in large measure, to the rascality of the bankers. And finally, there was the peace, blessed peace, that settled on the system once it had been turned into an oligopoly. The removal of real competition made it failsafe. Today, Canada's largest bank, the Royal, has a slogan that says, "When you succeed, we succeed." I can't understand why they don't put in the second half, which is, "And when you go belly up, we still succeed."

In Canada's early days, under the French regime, skins were currency, and barter the usual method of trade. With the Indians, of course, booze was also currency. B. E. Walker, a banker, noted in his History of Banking in Canada that "A decree was not necessary to make brandy a most satisfactory medium of exchange with the Indians." Actually, the French used brandy, the British rum; the Indians preferred rum as a general rule, a fact that helped the British. Such coins as arrived from France rapidly returned there to buy imports, since what we now call our balance-of-trade was perpetually tilted against the colonies. The colonial exports were worth no more than thirty per cent of imports.[4] The custom was for a supply of coins and merchandise to arrive a year ahead of actual use, and to be held by the authorities for release. In 1685, this annual shipment failed to appear, but the Intendant, who grasped the first rule of banking — if you don't have it, make it up — simply created his own money by cutting up playing cards, signing them, and turning them into money, in denominations of four francs, forty sols and fifteen sols. He paid his soldiers with these pieces of card, and ordered them colonists to accept them as money, to be redeemed in goods and coin when the fleet eventually arrived. The scheme worked so well that thereafter France made no attempt to provide supplies a year in advance. Cards would do just as well. Off and on, cards were used as money up until Wolfe's victory at Quebec; they were exchanged for drafts on the French Treasury or for specie. Inevitably, the crooked intendant, Francois Bigot (whose partners in the systematic looting of the colony were a firm of French bankers), abused the system, issuing due bills which were not redeemable in specie but in card money. When the British took over after 1760, the Canadian colony was in debt to the tune of 80,000,000 livres, much of it in the "ordonnances" created by Bigot. They became worthless, and hundreds of people saw their hard-won savings wiped out at a stroke.[5]

After the conquest, the British used Mexican coins,

Spanish, Portuguese, French and German coins, anything that would pass as money, with which to pay their troops, and this money became, along with trade goods, the coin of the realm. But there were still no banks, as such, in the British colonies, until the Bank of North America of Philadelphia was chartered in 1781.[6] A year later, Montreal merchants moved to establish their own institution and founded the Canada Banking Company.[7] It strikes me as significant that this First Canadian Bank (one of the slogans used by today's Bank of Montreal) promptly crashed. The bank was to accept deposits, discount bills, and eventually open branches in "every part of the two provinces (of Canada) where an agent may be judged necessary."[8] However, the key to the scheme was that the bank would have the right to issue notes. Money at this time still consisted of the collection of coins issued by other nations that were acceptable to merchants, along with whatever notes could be exchanged for coin or goods. There were no bank notes, and the new venture proposed to issue them. But consent could never be obtained from the legislature. Too many Canadians had been burned by the repudiation of Bigot's ordonnances, which left a bitter distaste for paper money. The bank was abandoned, as were two other attempts, one in 1807 – in Quebec City – and another in 1808, a joint Montreal-Quebec venture.[8] This last venture died when the legislature refused to issue a charter for fear that bank-issued notes would drive out specie, foster speculation and lead to fraud, because "the people were too ignorant to understand the denominations of notes or guard against counterfeits, etc."

When the War of 1812 broke out, it became necessary to create paper money with which to fight the Americans, and that was done. A war, like the prospect of hanging, concentrates the mind wonderfully. The governor was authorized to issue "Army Bills" with which to pay the army, in denominations ranging from $100 down to $4. Notes from $100 down to $25 were really like Treasury bills of today; they bore interest, and could be exchanged for cash, government bills of exchange in London, or more Army Bills.[10] Lower denominations did not pay interest. The money was readily accepted and proved a great boon, not only to help finance the war but to aid commerce, which had been struggling by with foreign coins in a bewildering variety of denominations. There were new issues of these bills, and all were eventually redeemed. Paper money was established in Canada, and the way cleared for the creation of our own banks.

These were joint-stock banks, private institutions with limited liability, owned by a handful of men, as opposed to the banks of today, which are privately, but widely, owned, with their shares traded on stock exchanges. The first of these joint-stock operations to get off the ground was the Bank of Montreal, which arrogantly opened its doors in August 1817, and only afterwards applied to the legislature for a charter to go into business. The charter was refused, and continued to be refused, until three banks, the Bank of Montreal, the Bank of Canada and the Bank of Quebec, were given charters in 1822.[11]

A Rich Pageant of Corruption

Canada was now launched into the era of bank-creation, land frauds and railway speculation that made our nineteenth-century history the rich pageant that it was.

Enos Collins, a Nova Scotian who became a privateer during the Napoleonic Wars, added to his booty during the War of 1812, and used some of his money to finance other privateers. Then he started the Halifax Banking Company, in 1825, and died the richest man of his time in British North America. Many of our other early bankers were, if not outright privateers, at least colourful characters.

The Bank of Upper Canada was controlled by the same men who made up the Family Compact, and they hit on the device of simply having the legislature refuse charters to any group that looked as if it might compete, unless, of course, its owners included some of the Compact. This technique proved enormously profitable for the bankers, but constraining to the rest of the community. The Compact members were not interested in promoting industrial competition for their own firms. When the Bank of Upper Canada became the mortgagee of the first machinery works in the nation in 1836, it foreclosed on the mortgage, broke up the foundry and disposed of the pieces at a sheriff's sale.[13] People went back to buying their machinery in England as God, and the British, intended. Complaints of this sort of abuse were part of the ferment of the Rebellion of 1837.[14]

The year of the rebellion also brought a business panic, and a run on some of the privately owned banks. One history of the time notes that "The private bank of Truscott, Green & Co., known as the Agricultural Bank, failed, the partners leaving the country."

Actually, the more bankers that left the country, the better off Canadians should have been. They were rapscallions. Take Francis Hincks, for example. Born in county Cork, in Ireland, he emigrated to York in 1830, and became a cashier, and later manager, of the Bank of the People. He went into politics, and, with the backing of the business interests he represented, became Prime Minister of the united Province of Canada. In that post, he helped with the stock manipulation of the railway companies whose major financing came from the government. He was a land speculator, swindler – he pushed through a swindle on City of Toronto bonds with the help of the city's mayor – and the cheerful recipient of bribes.[15] For helping to sell the charter of the scandal-ridden Grand Trunk Railway to an English firm, he received a payoff of £50,400 in Grand Trunk stock. He was caught at this, and publicly charged by George Brown, then a Liberal MP. Hincks was unable to deny receiving the stock, but said he was merely holding it "in trust for allotment in Canada to parties who might be desirous to take an interest in the Company." The Prime Minister wasn't an outright crook, he was just a stock-tout.

Eventually, Hincks was forced to resign as more tales of his speculations came to light, but the Governor-General, Lord Elgin, who had also profited in the Grand Trunk scheme, arranged his appointment as a Caribbean governor, and he left the country for a few judicious years. When he returned in 1869, he became Sir John A. Macdonald's minister of finance, and was soon back at the trough, selling off the Canadian fishing industry for personal gain, to raise money for more railway speculation. He also steered Canada's first Bank Act through the House of Commons – which seemed suitable, since he was still in the banking business on the side – and then capped his career by arranging the Canadian Pacific Railway contract that led to the Pacific Scandal. Ousted from office – but not from Parliament – by that scandal, he was able to devote more of his time to banking, and was named president of the Consolidated Bank, a merger of two shaky institutions, the City Bank and the Royal Canadian. In due course, the Consolidated failed, taking with it the fortunes of a great many ordinary investors – but not Hincks', of course; he had sold off his stock while the selling was good, so much so that when the scandal eventually broke, it was discovered that he didn't even qualify to be a bank director, although he was. Hincks, and some of his colleagues, were charged with fraud for, among other things, falsifying returns to the federal government.

Despite the parade of witnesses who came to testify on his behalf – including the general manager of the Bank of Montreal, who testified that Hincks' manipulations, although illegal, were standard banking practice – Hincks was found guilty of fraud. Then – have you already guessed – the conviction was reversed on appeal. By this time, the usual apologists had gone to work, and Hincks was restored to virtue. The influential financial newspaper, The Monetary Times, concluded that he must have been temporarily insane when he committed his undoubted crimes.[16] He died full of riches and honour, with a knighthood.

Then there was Sir Hugh Allan, who founded the Merchants' Bank in 1861. He became one of the central figures in the Canadian Pacific Railway and a wholesale briber of legislators (one of his letters to a colleague lists thirteen MPs – including the ubiquitous Francis Hincks – who were to be given stock totalling $850,000 in the CPR in return for their help in Parliament).[17] Allan was also president of the Allan Line, a steamship company that made large sums of money by the systematic ill-treatment of steerage-class passengers being brought from Europe to Canada where, if they survived the trip on Allan's ships, they stood to be cheated by the CPR on their way to the prairies.[18]

Allan, it need hardly be said, was given a knighthood, and saluted by the press of his time as a man who, however busy, "still could find time to lecture in church."

Peter McGill, president of the Bank of Montreal, was involved in the notorious British American Land Company[19] along with the finance minister, Sir Alexander Galt, who liked to put things clearly – "I am all for objects of material advantage," he wrote.[20] McGill and Galt were part of the Grand Trunk Railway scam, too, which, in brief, used government money to build a railroad, and siphoned off the take to its private backers. Galt also started up his own bank, the Eastern Townships Bank, which helped him in his main career, which was to divert public funds to his own private use.[21]

Another Bank of Montreal president given to railway speculation was George Stephen, who took $8,000,000 out of the bank without the knowledge or consent of the board of directors, to invest in the St. Paul and Minneapolis Railway, which he managed to get at a knock-down price by having a fraudulent report prepared for the company's bondholders and stockholders in Holland, purporting to show that the line was in grave difficulties. The American who produced this ersatz report then sued, because he felt he was entitled to a share of the loot. The first court to hear the case dismissed it on the grounds that it should not be called upon to decide "how plunder should be divided among different members of a gang,"[22] but the suit dragged on for thirteen years. In the end, it failed, the railway made money, Stephen was able to restore the missing funds, continued to rule the Bank of Montreal and was knighted. He eventually became Lord Mount Stephen.

Plunged into Insolvency

In the years immediately preceding and following Confederation, the fraud merchants, railway speculators, bankers and government ministers were one and the same. It became common practice for a group of politicians to join together, found a bank, give it a charter, and then arrange to have the government deposit money, free of interest, in their own bank. The Bank of Montreal was particularly good at this, along with the Bank of Ontario, and the Montreal and District Savings Bank.

The Molson's Bank, one of the nation's richest for many years, was put together by a group of Montreal notables and MPs — including William Molson and John Molson — in a way that caused the American social critic, Gustavus Myers, to complain bitterly. He wrote:

"Politicians in the United States have long since so well appraised the value of bank charters that as early as the years 1799, 1805, 1811 and 1824 bribery had been used to wrest from the legislators charters for the Manhattan, Mercantile, Merchants' and other New York City banks. But in Canada, with many of the bank incorporators themselves leaders in legislative councils, bribery was, in general, superfluous."[23]

Although they had some characteristics in common — mainly that both were run, in the main, by rascals — the Canadian and American banking systems grew up quite differently. Thomas Naylor, the economic historian, puts this down to the fact that "Canadian banking was a branch plant of English commercial banking."[24] It was a system based on the financing of staple crops, to be shipped to Britain. The Mother Country would provide whatever portfolio financing was required, and our banks would concentrate on keeping the trade flowing. That is, there would be money for moving Canadian resources to market, but not to set Canadian entrepreneurs up in business. Naylor contends "It was the model least suited to promoting industrial development in the colony."[25]

It was also a model that did very little for regional development. Until very recently, Canadian banks have always been run from the centre of the country, and for the benefit of the centre of the country. The argument always was that local control would lead to instability in the banking business, an argument that Naylor says "hardly follows from Canada's appalling record of banks plundered into insolvency by their own directors at head office."[26] Attempts to found local banks, for example, in the Maritimes, were not successful, because of the manipulations of the centralized commercial banks, but the local banks at least had the merit that when they went under, they had done their best to promote local business, while the commercial banks, Naylor notes, "left nothing but criminal charges behind them."[27]

The great virtue of a banking system that consisted of a few large companies, each with many branches across the country, was supposed to be that funds would be transferred readily from areas of surplus to the regions where money was needed for development. It didn't work out that way. In one Maritime town, by 1912, the ratio of deposits to loans was running at twenty-to-one[28] — that is, for every dollar collected locally, only a nickel was loaned locally, and the surplus was transferred down to central

Canada, for development there. When the locals complained, their comments were dismissed by the head of the Bank of Montreal, who described them as "local grievances against what we regard as the interests of the country as a whole."[29] And who knew what was in the interests of the country as a whole? The Bank of Montreal, of course.

The Maritimes were once touted as the future cradle of a Canadian industrial revolution, but as savings were drained from the area to finance development in central Canada, this hope became a bitter joke.

In the West, too, complaints about the sacking of local savings to build up central Canada were dismissed with scorn. The Bank of Vancouver was established in 1911 after claims that the area was being drained to fulfill the needs of the East, but it made little headway. At the same time, agitation for provincial banks in Alberta and Saskatchewan began, but came to naught. It was easy to see why the westerners were upset. Grain farmers were faced with a banking system designed to force them to dump their crops onto the market for whatever it would bear. When they went to borrow money, the notes were dated to become due just before harvest-time. If they didn't sell, they could lose everything, but if they did, they would have to take whatever was offered on a market crowded by other farmers doing the same thing. Requests for loans to finance holding onto crops against a price-rise later in the season were rejected.[30] In addition, loans for farm improvements, or for mortgages, were rare. What the banks were interested in was putting out money for three months to finance the crop — and in nothing else. That had the gratifying side-effect of driving down prices in eastern markets.

When the westerners tried to get together to found their own bank, they were balked; the Canadian Bankers' Association had a right to veto bank charters, and exercised this veto against a western regional bank.[31]

Interest rates were set by law at 7% per annum, but the eastern banks collected as much as 14%, compounded every three months. They got around the law buy discounting the loans in advance. A farmer borrowing $5,000 wouldn't receive that amount; instead, the interest on $5,000 would be taken off the loan — he might get $4,400, although he paid interest on $5,000, effectively doubling his interest rate. The bankers met openly in Winnipeg every year to fix the discount rate. It was a gang operation. All the banks were in on it, but Tom Naylor notes that "The Bank of Commerce seemed to win the prize for extortion and usury."[32]

Grain dealers who wanted financing to buy the crop met no difficulty, but farmers who wanted to gain a measure of control over their own markets, and western businessmen who wanted to promote secondary industry, which would inevitably compete with the eastern firms backed by the same gang of bankers, were out of luck.

U.S. Banks Opened the West, Ours Closed It

In the United States, quite a different development took place. Their banking system, equally marked by rascality, was at least their own. Banks were, from the start, fiercely competitive, regionally oriented, and happy to plunge into the venture-capital financing that our banks have always eschewed as if it were a social disease. American banks, like Canadian ones, found themselves in a basic conflict as the nation began to develop. Eastern banks preferred stable prices and gradual expansion, while the people of the west needed, and demanded, such rapid expansion that it was bound to lead to rapid price increases.[33] In effect, the American system split itself into two, as John Kenneth Galbraith, the Canadian-born American economist, has shown. Western banks were expansionist and venturesome, while those in the east followed much more conservative policies. The Americans had the best of both worlds at the time of their greatest expansion, while the centralized Canadian banking system remained tied to policies that stultified both development and growth, but made a whale of a lot of money for the bankers. Over time, we shook off the British colonial ties that marked our early banking industry, only to replace them with ties attached at the business end to bank counters in Montreal and Toronto.

What made the process richly comic, unless you happened to be a victim of it, was the fact that our repressive approach was sanctioned on the grounds of the rectitude of our bankers – which was non-existent – and by the stability of the system they designed. That didn't exist, either. The period from Confederation to 1923 was punctuated by bank failures, often marked by the sudden disappearance of both the cash and the principal officers of the bank. Ordinary depositors were left holding the (empty) bag. The collapse of La Banque Ville Marie was perhaps typical. The bank was founded in 1872 by a group of Quebec businessmen, and was in trouble as early as 1876.[34] English Canadians moved in to take control, but the bank remained in difficulty, and began to manipulate its own stock to try to raise money. This illegal action was known to the federal government, and finance department officials advised that, at least, government funds should be withdrawn from the bank, but nothing was done. Then, in 1899, a teller made off with $58,000, and when word of that leaked out, there was a run on the bank by anxious depositors who found, sure enough, that there was no money on hand to meet their demands. The bank was suspended. A subsequent investigation revealed that the bank had issued notes far in excess of its legal limit, that the president had extracted $300,000 from the till by means of promissory notes signed on behalf of firms that were in bankruptcy, and that an accountant had used $173,000 for stock gambles that failed. The accountant was charged with theft, but no one from the bank would testify against him.

Between 1867 and 1914, twenty-six Canadian banks failed, of seventy-two that had gone into operation – a failure rate of 36%. During the same period, the failure rate in the United States was 22.5%. Tom Naylor has calculated that "in per capita terms, even taking only the unambiguous failures, Canadian losses to shareholders ran at three-and-one-half times the rate of American."[35] Bank failures were much more common than failures in other areas of business, and accompanied by even greater larcenies – of the twenty-six failures in this period, nineteen led to criminal charges against bank officers or employees. Naylor concludes, "The record of stability of the Canadian banking system is alarming, and the myth of stability sheer propaganda."[36]

Inspections Would Thwart God's Will

Because they were so busy looting the till, Canadian bankers developed a reluctance, which they retain, to submit to the ministrations of bank inspectors, and they even had a rationale for it. Inspection systems might cut the number of failures, they said, and that would impede the efficient operation of the banking system, by interfering with the survival of the fittest. It was God's will that some banks should go under,[37] and who were mortals to trifle with the intentions of the Divine? (God's will has since been redefined to provide for the immortality of financial institutions, and to make that immortality the sign of divine favour.)

Just the same, a certain nervousness began to develop on the part of the general public, and the revisions of the Bank Act which took place every ten years gradually imposed restrictions on the banks. The revision of 1890 required them to become guarantors at least in part of the notes of failed banks. (In one spectacular failure, bank agents fanned out to exchange the notes of the defunct institution for other bank notes at whatever they could get before the word got out.) That same revision contained a proposal to require the banks to put up reserves, but the bank lobby went to work, and defeated the proposal.

The lobby turned itself into the Canadian Bankers' Association (CBA) in 1891, and quickly gained a veto over bank charters. That veto was used to dash the dream of a western bank easily enough, but the CBA's real function was, and remains, to ride herd on the Bank Act of which its members, the chartered banks, are alleged to be the subjects. They are, rather, its designers, and they were able to keep a reserve off the statute books for another two decades, by which time they had decided it was a good idea. The reserve provided for a proportion of bank deposits to be held by four trustees (there was no central bank to fill this function). One trustee was appointed by the minister of finance, and three by the Canadian Bankers' Association itself.

A more rigorous auditing procedure was established, to give the shareholders a better chance to see what was being done with their money. It wasn't much – and it still isn't much – but it was some improvement.

Other changes began the rudiments of a central banking system by giving the department of finance the power to advance Dominion of Canada notes to the banks, in return for a pledge of securities. Credit control was within the hands of the federal government, because these notes would set reserve levels.

Canada's last bank failure, that of the Home Bank, occurred in 1923. The Home Bank had been established in 1903 in Toronto, and subject to twenty straight years of graft, manipulation and mismanagement, all carefully concealed from the public. It was effectively bankrupt in early 1914, but the federal government refused to act because it didn't want to put a bank under during wartime. It struggled on for nine more years, until the general manager died and the bank's shortage of funds became a matter of public knowledge. The subsequent investigation followed the usual path. It was shown that the president, five directors, the accountant and auditor had been cooking the books.[38] All but the president, who died before his case came to trial, were charged and convicted. Then the conviction was quashed on appeal. The depositors did get partial restitution from the federal government, however, because it had been so negligent in acting to straighten out the bank's affairs over the past decade.

The Home Bank case led to agitation for some kind of regular bank inspection and, in 1924, an Inspector General of Banks was established. We will meet his successor and learn something of the operations of his branch in Chapter Eleven.

The collapse may also have helped to pave the way for the establishment of a central bank, the Bank of Canada, in 1935, although it is more likely that that was a reaction to a number of visible blunders the banks had made. In 1920, for example, in the midst of an inflationary boom, the banks abruptly cut back on credit to control prices, and brought on a ruinous recession.[39] Sound familiar? Historian W. L. Morton notes, "The banks who had imposed the deflationary measures for the general good did not suffer perceptibly at all ... No doubt that is why they administered so drastic a medicine with such philosophic calm and such unflinching courage."[40]

Then again, as the Great Depression began its ruinous roll across Canada in 1929, the banks raised interest rates and cut back on credit just in time to make things that much worse.[41] They did not endear themselves to many Canadians, and their behaviour helped induce a climate of acceptance for the idea of a central bank. We will be looking at that central bank again; for now, the point to note is that it became, from the start, not the adversary of the banks, but their handmaiden. It did, however, take on two important functions. The first was responsibility for control of the money supply, through reserve requirements clearly spelled out. The second was responsibility for issuance of bank notes. The private bank notes were gradually removed from circulation over the next ten years.

The Canadian banking system became more and more consolidated. The large commercial banks succeeded in destroying, in turn, the "free" banks (one bank, one branch, like most of those in the United States), the private banks, the regional banks and the savings banks. This was accomplished, as often as not, by extending and suddenly withdrawing credit to smaller banks, or by simply manipulating the Bank Act to eliminate competition. Sir Edmund Walker, a president of the Bank of Commerce, once boasted proudly that every change in the Bank Act between 1871 and 1913 had been initiated by the bankers themselves.[42]

At Confederation, the federal government assumed control over provincial savings banks, where many ordinary Canadians had channelled their savings. Many of these banks were in the Maritimes, and the federal government used them, not to promote local industry, but to finance projects like the CPR. Then the chartered banks moved in and the savings banks were closed down. The Social Credit government of Alberta set up the Alberta Treasury Branches in 1938, and these have evolved into full-service banks, with 117 branches and 100 agencies in 195 Alberta communities. But they were, until the founding of the Bank of British Columbia in 1968, our only regional bank. (There is a Province of Ontario Savings Bank, but its sole function is to take in deposits and pass them on to the Ontario government, to use as it sees fit.) We had regional names, but not regional banks. The Bank of Nova Scotia, which started in Halifax, moved to central Canada and its most evidence connection with its native province today consists of a swiped coat-of-arms. The savings bank, regionally based, was garrotted by the central Canadian giants.

We also had a number of private banks, but they, too, have gone under. They were done in, sometimes, by their own stupidity or cupidity but, more often, by the activities of the chartered banks.[43] These small institutions usually grew up in response to a need to finance local industry — a woollen mill, a canal, or a tannery might have its own locally-held banking institution behind it. These banks peaked in 1895, when there were 202 of them in the country. Then the bankers' lobby went to work. First, the private bodies were required to state on their literature that they were not incorporated, which made investors nervous; then, they were denied the right to call themselves banks.[44] By 1914, their numbers were down to sixty-one, mainly stock-brokers functioning as banks. Now they are gone. By and large, the record of these private banks in financing local business and agriculture was commendable; they were, after all, part of the community. But they were, in the long run, at the mercy of the charter-holders, who had the right to issue currency, and to extend credit, which could be withdrawn at any time.

In 1901, there were thirty-six chartered banks in Canada;[45] eighty years later, we were down, for all practical purposes, to five big ones and six little ones. In fact, the banking business had been unchanged — except in a minor way — since the Bank of Commerce and the Imperial Bank merged in 1961. In 1914, Gustavus Myers wrote, "Perhaps nowhere in the world can be found so intensive a degree of close organization as among the bank interests of Canada."[46] At that time, we had twenty-six banks; now we have eleven that matter., It is some comfort to know that the process can't go much further.

Bankers no longer tend to decamp with the proceeds, and we have deposit insurance to protect us if they do. The bribery and corruption of MPs by bankers is no longer a matter of routine. It is possible to hope it no longer happens at all. Public reporting processes exist — they are far from perfect, but they exist — to alert shareholders when things start to go wrong. But the intertwining of other business interests with banking has proceeded apace, government is still, to far too large an extent, the passive servant of the banks, and the banking system still has larceny in its heart.

4
Step Into My Cage

"You're not dealing with the Salvation Army."

Alix Granger,
Don't Bank on It, 1981

At the corner of Laurier and Kent Streets in downtown Ottawa stands one of the 1,592 branches[1] of the Royal Bank of Canada, Canada's largest bank (in terms of assets). It is a medium-sized branch, with sixteen fulltime employees plus another three who are called "fulltime-partime," because they come in regularly to help out on government paydays. This is not a typical branch — I had asked the public relations people at the Royal Bank to put me into a typical branch to work, but they are no fools, and instead put me in one of the best-run branches in the system. The manager is a woman, Mrs. Pat Cobus, and so is the Branch Administration Officer, and that is unusual. Still, the main features of the branch are shared with every one of the 7,374 chartered bank branches[2] across the country, and a tour through here will tell us all we need to know about how a bank actually operates.

As we approach the bank, note the large posters in the window, designed to sell us money. There is a picture of a young couple standing on what seems to be a tropical island, and a picture of a sailboat, and a house and a shiny new car, and a lot of bumph designed to make us believe that all we need to attain consumer's paradise is a bank loan or a mortgage note. This should be a reminder to us that the banks are great kidders; they are always issuing dire warnings about the profligacy of the Canadian public.

We must restrain ourselves, they say. Meanwhile, back at the branch are all the inducements they can think of to make us spend. If a call-girl were to issue a warning that sex is bad for you, we might have difficulty taking her seriously, but when banks work a similar wheeze, we are impressed. That is because we regard money as a religious system, requiring faith, not logic, from the practitioner.

The door is open. We will note, if we look carefully, that it is thick, and is wired to an alarm system. The alarm system is not all that good but knowing it's there makes everybody feel better. Inside the bank, we are faced with one large rectangular room, pleasant, open, and lit by the large windows that form two sides of the branch, which is situated on the ground floor of a large office building. Straight ahead of us is the manager's office, a room about fifteen feet by twelve feet, functional rather than ostentatious. Just outside this sits the manager's secretary, on guard for people trying to see the manager without an appointment. There is an aisle next to the manager's office, for access to the rear of the bank, and then the main tellers' counter, stretching down most of the length of the office. There are eight tellers' wickets and, in front of them, the usual tango line of customers waiting for a wicket to come open. Please Line Up Here, the sign says, so you do, joining the snake. In the past, you just took pot-luck, falling in in front of whichever teller had the smallest line to deal with. Then it turned out that the guy in front of you was banking for seventeen relatives; you would have done better to pick the line with six standees, because they were just cashing cheques. Today, thanks to the marvel of the computer, and the new, fairer lineup system, you can get to wait longer, but your agony is shared by everyone else. In front of the lineup area are the writing tables with slots containing the forms for deposits and withdrawals, and pens that don't work but are chained to the desk just as if they did.

Doing Sappy Things Cheerfully

Note that the people behind the counter are wearing badges that say Can Do, the current Royal Bank slogan. At the Bank of Nova Scotia down the street, they have to wear T-shirts that say Excel, and there are little pennants on the wall bearing the same message. This material is supposed to make the bank employees enthusiastic, and convey a sense of achievement and fun to the customer. The employees have not been asked what they think of the notion. They are expected to do sappy things cheerfully, or take up another line of work.

Where the tellers' counter ends, another counter starts, at right angles to it. It is open, not divided into little sections like the tellers' area, and behind it are the desks of the junior bank officers. Behind the tellers' counter there are the computer terminals, one to each two tellers, an aisle and a wall. The wall is the wall of the room containing the bank-vault, accessible from the aisle. Off this same aisle, opposite the vault, is a proof-room, where machines buzz and click. There is a luncheon room behind that. The aisle behind the computers, if we follow it to the left instead of to the right, where the vault is, will lead us to another office close to the manager's, but smaller. It is occupied by the branch's Loans Officer.

Time to circle back again, to the cluster of desks behind the open counter. Here we find the desk of the Head Savings Teller, the Demand Deposit desk, the Liability desk, the Branch Administration Officer, a Trainee desk and the desk of the Proofing Officer. If you go and stand at the counter looking helpless, one of the occupants of these desks will arise and ask if they can help you and, quite often, they can.

It will aid us to understand what all these people are doing if we bear in mind that we are looking at a store, but one that buys as well as sells — think of a pawn shop, or a second-hand store — except that what is bought and sold is money. Everything we see is designed to make us part with money cheerfully; whether we are buying or selling, the bank will take a markup, and whatever services have to be performed will be charged for, one way or another. It will also help us to keep in mind that this branch is part of a huge organization, with 36,928 employees. As part of a mammoth organization, they are governed by bureaucratic rules that are very little different from those that govern the civil servants with whom this branch has so many dealings. Their working lives are ruled by a catalogue of looseleaf books, with black covers, each containing complex and complete instructions on exactly how to handle every aspect of banking from cashing a cheque to dealing with attacks on the bank. One thick volume, recently updated, is called Extortion, Robbery and Bomb Threats. Work is structured exactly as if these books contained army regulations or Treasury Board instructions. If it's in the book, it can be done according to regulations; if it isn't, forget it.

A Paint-by-Numbers Business

"It looks pretty complicated when you peek in the door," says a man who has worked for the Royal for nearly three decades, "but it isn't. You look it up, follow the rules, or you won't last long. This is strictly a paint-by-numbers business."

The main function of this branch is to service federal bureaucrats and the employees of nearby businesses. There are 4,000 salary accounts on the books (essentially, accounts for the depositing and cashing of salary cheques, which the bank handles on a fee-for-service basis with the employers) along with 4,339 savings accounts (with an average of $5 million in total in them at any one time), 130 current accounts, from which businesses are run, 730 loan accounts (set up to service the notes out to various borrowers) and 1,700 chequing accounts. This is not impressive in the Royal Bank network, which has $33 billion[3] on deposit in five million accounts, but it all adds up.

The heart of the branch is the length of counter where the tellers work, taking in deposits, cashing cheques, paying bills. These women – they are all women in this particular branch – are not sitting on a stack of bills worth $5 million, of course. Cash in the till doesn't earn anything, so the actual money on hand is kept as low as possible, and the surplus is shipped out each night in a large, locked, canvas bag (extra money is brought in as required the same way, whenever there is a government payday). The surplus is put to work elsewhere in the system. Each teller has a cash desk in front of her, with two drawers divided into sections for various bills and other notes. To one side is a transaction sheet, on which business is recorded for later verification. At the start of the day, each teller draws a float of money from her own section of the vault – which can be opened only with her key and the Branch Administration Officer's key. If she needs more cash, she goes to the Head Savings Teller, as she accumulates money, she moves it – as soon as she has $2,000 on hand – from the cash drawer to a locked compartment below it. This compartment has a two-minute timer on it; if a holdup man appears with a note and a gun, he will have to wait two minutes before he can get anything more than the cash float. From here, money is transferred periodically to the vault. The vault-lock has a five-minute delay. The theory is that no bandit will stand around waiting with the cops on the way – there are alarms at each teller's station and another in the manager's office – but will be content to take the floats and run. The maximum take for a robber at this bank should be $16,000 – $2,000 from each teller's drawer. Most banks are now moving to a system under which only one teller has any money, and all the others will go to this Paying Teller to acquire and deposit cash. This will give the banks tighter control and make life less rewarding for bank robbers, but it will inevitably mean longer delays for customers. At the Royal Bank branch here under discussion, there are eight women to handle cash rather than one.

If we open an account with one of these women, by passing $100 across the counter, it will go into the cash drawer, and we will go onto the bank's books with a few strokes of the keys in the computer behind the teller. To activate this computer, she has an access code, and the number of letters in the code regulate the degree of access. A four-digit code – "Fish," say – will allow access to the first level of the computer operation. Other codes, changed each day and posted behind the teller area, allow the teller to talk to the bank's main computer in Montreal. A friend of mine working in a bank whose manager came from Portugal reasoned that the boss, entitled to an eight-digit code, probably used "Portugal," tapped that into the computer and Presto! was into the main computer at the manager's level. The banks talk as if their computer systems were sophisticated; they are not.

Computers have certainly revolutionized banking, but a quick look around this branch will show us that the real gainers are the banks, not the customers. For the bank, the new system means that a cheque cashed here drawn on the Bank of Commerce in Heart's Content, Newfoundland can be traced back to its home account at once – kiting cheques because they take several days to move through the clearing system can still be done, but you have to work at it. The bank is also able to shift money from branch to branch and region to region in a flicker of time, and one function of main branch banks is to trade in money, buying and selling huge amounts as prices change by fractions of a penny. But this won't help us. What is supposed to help us is the fact that the bank is now part of a multi-branch service — in most chartered banks, and soon, in all of them, you can enter any branch and use it as your own, depositing money, cashing cheques, paying bills. There is an advantage in this for customers, but it is marginal. Another alleged advantage is the Daily Interest Savings account; without computers to do all the calculating, we are told, such accounts were impossible. In fact, British banks have been paying daily interest since the turn of the century, long before the invention of computers.

On the other hand, the computers have two real disadvantages for the present, as well as many potential drawbacks for the future. The first is that the damn things are always breaking down, and since the banks have now become locked onto them, a breakdown brings much of the bank's service to a standstill. When I mentioned this to branch manager Pat Cobus, she laughed a merry laugh. "That's greatly exaggerated," she said, "we never have any problems with the computers."

However, in my first five hours in the bank, the computers went down four times. Each time, they grabbed onto whatever passbooks were in the system and wouldn't let go. Red-faced tellers then had to tell customers, "I'm sorry, but the computer is down, so I can't enter your deposit." "Fine," the depositor would say, "then just give me back my bankbook." Another blush. "Sorry, the computer won't let go." When they don't break down entirely, the computers are apt to skip several lines occasionally. One bankbook that passed through my hands showed a balance of $687.56, a deposit of $200.00, a withdrawal of $56.47, a bunch of skipped lines, and then a balance of $61.23. It turned out that this account actually had about $3,000 in it, although that didn't become clear until the next day, when a proofing teller spotted the discrepancy in a print-out and went back to the computer. Alix Granger, in her excellent consumers' guide to the Canadian banking system, Don't Bank on It, mentions a case in which a customer went to get money out of her bank for a holiday, couldn't because the computer was down, and had to borrow money -- for which interest was charged, naturally -- because of the malfunction.

The second real disadvantage of the computers, from the customer's point of view, is that they cost so much. These costs are shifted to the banks' customers although the advantages go mainly to the banks. This was not the way it was supposed to be. When computers were first under discussion, the banks said that because money cleared through the system so much faster, they wouldn't have to maintain so large a float, and that would reduce costs. Then the greater efficiency of the computer over hand-written bankbooks would cut costs further. It hasn't worked out that way; virtually every service charge in banking has gone up. The banks, when they hiked the cost for cashing cheques from sixteen cents to eighteen cents in 1978, said they were doing it because they hadn't increased charges for several years.[4] Well, why should they, if the computers were reducing costs? Heaven knows, their profits kept climbing, so it wasn't a matter of need; it can only have reflected an increase in expenditure brought on by the marvellous new computer programs that were supposed to cut costs. Now every service, including writing cheques and depositing money, costs from forty to seventy cents a crack[5] or more. So much for cost-cutting.

Here's something else to think about while we stand in line waiting for the computer to release our bankbook. The money in our chequing account pays 3% interest per annum. That's what it paid in May 1973; that's what it still pays in every chartered bank in the country. But if we borrow money from the bank and if we are able to get it at the prime rate, it will cost us somewhere around 17%. That cost will remain constant, no matter which bank we go to; it is the rock-bottom charge. Suppose you were to go into a car-dealership and discover that the most sought-after model of every make of car in the country cost exactly the same; and suppose you knew that while the price was going up every year, a major cost of building the cars remained exactly the same. Wouldn't that make you wonder about the car business?

What I am suggesting is that the inefficiencies of the banks, and some measure of the power of their oligopoly, are evident to anyone who cares to look carefully inside a branch.

If we peer around while we're standing here, we may be able to work out what else is going on behind the counter. Back in the corner where all the machines are buzzing, a woman sits at a proofing machine, feeding figures in and checking them against a tape. She is balancing the bank's transactions, so that they come out to zero. Beside her are the piles of transaction slips from each teller's cage – cheques, deposit slips, bills paid, etc. – and she is verifying each one. When the teller gives you $200, and marks on the back 10/20, she indicates that she gave you ten 20s. That makes up a transaction that shows a debit of $200 – the cash paid out – balanced by a credit of $200 – your cheque or withdrawal slip. The two must balance to zero, and if they don't, something is wrong. The proofing room should catch it. At the far end of the line of desks behind the open counter there is a woman sitting at a desk with what is obviously the print-out from a computer spread out in front of her. She is sliding a metal ruler down this, a line at a time. She is a proofing-teller, and the print-out came from the bank's dispatch office this morning. It contains a record of every transaction from yesterday's operations, and she is going over them, one by one, to make sure nothing has gone amiss. The woman in the proofing room is verifying the bank's internal books from transactions as they occur. The proofing teller is checking what has gone into the computer in Montreal against what shows on the bank's books. Together, these two form the nub of the bank's auditing system.

Four desks along from the proofing teller's operation sits the Branch Administration Officer – sometimes. Most of the time, she is moving around the office, initialling cheques – tellers, even senior ones, can't hand out more than $500 without a senior officer's initial – consulting with the manager, drawing up work-lists, handling the thousand-and-one jobs that make up the administration of a bank. If this branch had a point on one end and became a ship, Pat Cobus would be the captain and Rowena Evoy, the Branch Administration Officer, would be its executive officer. In the past, this job was called "Accountant," although the holder of that title seldom was an accountant; he, or she, was an administrator and assistant manager, so the title was changed. Evoy doesn't have hiring and firing powers – those reside with the manager, in conjunction with the bank's personnel office – but she is responsible for the day-to-day operation of the bank.

The structure of this system, a talk with Evoy soon reveals, is quite rigid. The tellers report to the head teller, the head teller reports to Evoy, Evoy reports to Cobus, Cobus reports to the Ottawa Regional Office, which reports to the Ontario Region, which reports to head office in Montreal. "And at the top," says a long-time employee of the Toronto-Dominion Bank, "sits the Chief Executive Officer. Picture a field marshal, and you get the idea." Behind Evoy's desk are the black books that breathe life into the bank, the books of regulations. One of these sets out pay scales of bank officers, which are not unlike those of civil servants. The nation is divided into areas, reflecting differing costs of living between, say, Toronto, Ontario and Charlottetown, PEI. Then the areas are divided into pay zones, reflecting the fact that it costs more to live in a city than a small town. Then the jobs are parcelled out, by grades. Administrative officers are classified differently than janitors or messengers, obviously. The lowest rung on the ladder, a junior teller trainee, starts at $10,500 annually, in the Ottawa region, then rises slowly through the ranks of AS 1, 2, 3, 4, 5 ("AS" stands for Administrative Staff). The size of the bank also affects pay levels, especially at the upper end. The assistant manager of a large bank will carry more responsibility, and get more pay, than the manager of a small branch. I counted sixty-three grades of bank employees, ranging from a low of $10,500 to a top of $54,500 in the Ottawa region – above $54,500, the figures are classified. Every bank employee knows his or her grade – just as every civil servant does – and what the minimum and maximum for that grade are (they depend on length of service and performance). Banks do not pay well, a fact that should make them ripe for unionization, but they have managed to fight off that process, with some exceptions (there are currently seventy-two branches in the entire nation covered by union contracts), by methods that have sometimes combined the cunning with the reprehensible.

One woman, who worked for the Bank of Commerce in Ottawa, describes what happened when a union showed some interest in organizing her branch. "I was approached by an older employee, who told me that unions were communist, and that if I wanted to get anywhere in the bank, I would be foolish to join the union. If you do, they find some reason to fire you. Besides, she told me, there is no need to join. As soon as a few union cards show up, we get a raise."

Another Commerce employee, who eventually quit, has bitter memories of working in a bank – especially working as a woman in a bank. "There used to be contests. The staff would be divided up into teams to try to get new accounts out of the customers. A guy would come in to cash his cheque and you would say, 'Do you have a Gold Account?' and if he didn't you gave him a lot of shit about what a great deal it was, and then that would be another account to your credit. They marked them all up on a board in the basement, in the staff room, and some of the girls really took them seriously. We were divided into teams – we were the Beavers – and your team got points for every new account. Our team's ahead. Whoopee.

"Tellers are masochists. They're beaten. You get a girl who was a good little girl for her father and she's a good little girl for the bank manager and a good little girl for her husband. 'Did you have a good day, dear? Yes, dear.' Yuk.

"Over-achievers are not welcome, not if they're women. You get a woman in a bank, perhaps an assistant accountant, and some guy comes along. She spends her time telling him the system, showing him how the books work, correcting his mistakes, setting him right – the kind of training no girl gets. Then after about six weeks he goes off to be a manager somewhere or on his way up the ladder, and she stays to teach the next one."

I asked Pat Cobus about women in banking and she replied, "Well, the policy is that men and women are equal, but if there is a man going for a job and a woman going for the same job, and they are equally qualified, the man will get the job. That's a fact of life."

The Royal Bank is sensitive on this subject. When then-Chairman Earle McLaughlin explained that the Royal had no women bank directors because of a shortage of acceptable candidates, a storm of protest burst over the bank.[6] It has since managed to find two – of forty-eight – directors who are women. So I put it to a senior officer – a woman — in the Royal's head office in Montreal that there was some improvement under way, at least. "I think that's right," she said. That didn't sound very positive, so I rephrased the question: "Would you say that women are now treated equally with men at the Royal?" She replied, "Ho, ho."

A Woman's Place

Women, once a rarity in the banking business, are now in the majority,[7] but they don't seem to be the kind of women who want to organize into unions. Or, if they are, the banks won't let them. The Canada Labour Relations Board found that the Bank of Commerce had interfered with the rights of employees to organize.[8] In one case, two workers were fired out of hand after becoming involved in an organization drive; in others, wages were frozen at branches where a union had been certified or applied for certification. The bank's president was ordered to send a letter out to the branches, explaining that his bank had violated the law. That was in December 1979. In May 1980, the bank was back at the old stand, locking out employees of two Quebec branches when they walked off the job for two days to protest the fact that the bank had withheld a scheduled wage increase after the branches became unionized.[9]

In another case, a Vancouver woman who worked for the Bank of Montreal was fired, on June 5, 1981, after she handed out union leaflets near her bank branch. She filed a grievance with the Labour Relations Board and went to work with Toronto-Dominion. She was fired there four days after her name appeared on union leaflets distributed outside her branch.[10] She grieved that firing, too. The Bank of Montreal re-hired her in settlement of her grievance with them, and the Toronto-Dominion paid her a month's salary after the Labour Board set a day for hearing her grievance against them. By going aggressively to law, this woman was able to win a moral victory, but she does not appear headed up the executive ladder of any bank.

If your teller doesn't flash you the friendly smile promised in the commercials, it may be because she is pretty cheesed off with her employer, and afraid to say so.

Keeping up the morale of tellers is the Bank Administrative Officer's job. It is not an easy one. She is also responsible for the bank's general ledger, the account of all its financial operations.

Next door to the Branch Administrative Officer's desk is the Liability desk, where loans are monitored. This branch can lend up to $10,000 on the manager's signature. "I can lend you that much just because I like the colour of your eyes," Pat Cobus explains, "but of course, if you don't pay it back, I have some explaining to do." Over that amount, the loan must go downtown for processing. This branch doesn't do much mortgage work, and, while it handles investments, doesn't give investment advice. Nor can it by law act as a trustee for estates — that work is reserved for the trust companies. So its loan business is pretty straight-forward. It is handled, by and large, by the Loans Officer, who makes recommendations to Pat Cobus. Then, when the loan is issued, an account is set up for repayment, and it is the job of the Liability desk to see that these payments are made, or to know the reason why not. In the next chapter, we will learn what happens when the process comes unstuck.

The Liability desk, and the desk of the Head Savings Teller, nestled at the end of the line of tellers, are the two places where the boom is likely to be lowered on a slow-paying customer. If a cheque bounces, it will wind up in one of these two places — depending on whether it is a savings matter, a loan, or a current account. The constant checking of transactions soon shows up a pattern of slow-paying. A business account which has a lot of money going through it may often fall temporarily in arrears and its cheques will be honoured, anyway, on the initials of the Loans Officer. A private individual who has ₃kated a few cheques by in the past will be abruptly pulled up, a cheque bounced and a $5 charge levied against the account.

In these decisions, the customer is at the mercy of the bank. It has the right to move money from any account held by any of its customers to any other account of that same customer, without consultation, to cover a shortage of funds (even if, as sometimes happens, that shortage occurs because the bank simply made an error). That being the case, you would think the banks would set up a system by which customers could leave most of their money in savings accounts, which pay interest, for automatic transfer out to chequing accounts, which don't, to cover cheques. Fat chance; the banks say it is too complicated. Like much of what they say, this sounds right, but isn't. In the United States, the law requires banks to provide exactly this service. In Canada, they can switch the funds, if they choose to, or bounce the cheque, if they choose to do that.

Your Money is Safe from Everyone but the Bank

Individual customers in Canada can make such a deal with a bank manager, but the service is never advertised, and depends entirely on the manager's whim. The banks would rather sell you something like the Commerce's "Sufficient Funds" contract, which provides an automatic over-draft, but at the bank's going rate for loans.

Two examples of what the bank's power to shift funds means may help to clarify the unequal balance between customer and bank.

1. In Montreal, Mrs. Lena Kierans had two accounts at the Toronto-Dominion Bank, one current, the other savings. On November 6, 1979, an investment certificate she held with the bank was redeemed, and the proceeds, $14,391.14, paid into her current account. She later moved the money out of that account into savings. In January 1980, the bank suddenly decided that it had given her too much money the previous November by error, so, without any sort of notice, the bank extracted $390.30 from the elderly woman's savings account.[11] Then it sent her a note that said simply "Redemption error on pre-encashment of certificate," which meant nothing to her, so she took it to her son, Eric Kierans, a former cabinet minister in the federal and Quebec governments, and a tough nut. He raised hell with everyone he could, from the president of the Toronto-Dominion Bank to the Inspector General of Banks. He argued that in cashing the certificate, the bank had made a deal with his mother; now it wanted to change the terms of that deal, and was able to do so without explanation, let or hindrance. He got nowhere. The Inspector General, William Kennett, explained, "Banks cannot arbitrarily seize funds in depositors' accounts but where money is owed to them by depositors, they do have the

right to offset balances in accounts against each other."[12] And who decides when "money is owed to them"? The banks, of course. Or, to put it another way, the banks *can* arbitrarily seize funds.

2. In Toronto, Ellen Roseman, consumer columnist for the Globe and Mail,[13] reported, a woman who separated from her husband obtained a court settlement under which he was ordered to pay $4,015 outstanding on a credit card which had been held in her name. He simply refused to do so. The bank closed the card out, and notified the woman that she would have to pay the balance due. She told them what had happened, and wrote to her husband, to try to get him to honour his commitment. A week later, the bank seized $4,145.02 (it had to have interest, of course) from the woman's account. Had the bank been required to sue her in order to collect, she might have counter-sued her husband, but as it was, she was beaten before she started.

The customer and the bank are not on anything like an equal footing. The Bank of Nova Scotia bounced a cheque of mine to the Receiver-General of Canada, a cheque aimed at paying my taxes and keeping me out of jail. There was more than enough money in the account to cover the cheque, and when I asked why the bank had not honoured it, the only explanation I got was that a mistake had been made. Graciously, the over-draft charge was returned. If I had made a mistake, and owed the bank, it could seize money from anywhere I had it stashed on the premises to right the wrong I had done it.

In a Canadian bank, money is safe from the depradations of everyone but the bank itself.

Why are the banks so hard-nosed? That's simple enough. Each branch operates as a profit centre, and the performance of each member of the branch is monitored with that in mind. If the friendly Loans Officer who smiles so winningly across the desk at you can work another buck out of a deal, it helps the branch, and helps him or her. When you negotiate a loan – with the manager, or the Loans Officer – you will be told what the interest charge is going to be, and if you are like most Canadians, you accept the figure quoted to you as the will of God. It isn't, although it's the next thing to it, the will of Bank. Actually, there is a good deal of room to negotiate; if you refuse the first interest-rate laid before you, you will quickly learn that another, and lower, rate will be offered (unless, as sometimes happens, the bank doesn't particularly want to lend money right now, in which case you can forget it). The bank is in exactly the same position as the pawn-broker trying to shove up the cost of his second-hand rings; the more you pay, the better. The only difference is that you expect to be stiffed by a pawn-broker, but you assume the bank is — in the words of one bank's slogan — "On your side." It is to laugh.

An elderly widow in Ottawa discovered, in the spring of 1981, that a Guaranteed Investment Certificate worth $30,000 had come due four months earlier, and the money plus interest had been transferred into a chequing account, where it paid 3% instead of the 15% it had been paying. When she complained that she had not been well-served by the bank, it was explained to her, correctly, that if she had wanted the money put into a savings account, or re-invested in a Guaranteed Investment Certificate, all she had to do was say so. But of course, she didn't know to say so. The bank made the difference, 12% on $30,000 for four months — $1,200 — but the widow is checking her accounts much more carefully now.

In another instance, a Toronto man of Ukrainian extraction, who speaks little English, went into his friendly neighbourhood bank with $15,000 to place on deposit. He was directed to a chequing account, again at 3%, and left the money there for six months before a relative discovered it. By that time, the bank was up about $825. Banks are not required to give you the best deal possible; it is up to you to work that out for yourself — caveat depositor — but they spend millions of dollars in advertising every year to persuade us that we can trust them to look after our interests. Like every other business, they look after their own interests.

The notion that things are otherwise is all part of the merry old flim-flam that makes up banking, and all kept under the watchful eye of the Liability desk, or the Demand Deposit desk, where chequing accounts are monitored, next door.

There is more to a bank than this tour suggests, but we know enough now to understand that the banks are not exactly what they seem. The smiling, laughing-eyed Mary of the television commercials is a figment of the imagination, and the smooth efficiency of banking mythology is part of the same pipe-dream. These are businesses like the rest, no worse, no better, but with infinitely more power than other industries. They are also much more concentrated than most other industries, and aimed at a simple goal – to get as much out of you as possible and to provide as little service in return as possible, consonant with the public image of the institution as a demon of efficiency hidden in the bosom of a cuddly huggy-bear.

5
The
Collectors

*"We had a kind of a saying there, 'Break a phone
and you'll get a raise.'"*

Ian Kerr, *Collector*

The telephone rang just after 8 a.m. in my Ottawa apartment, and when I answered it, a deep voice asked me if I was Walter Stewart. Guilty as charged. "Then you owe the Royal Bank $202.39," said the voice, which identified itself as belonging to an Ottawa collection agency. Nope, I said, you must have the wrong customer. He wanted to know if I had ever lived in Winnipeg. Nope. He wanted to know if I worked for a news agency. I did (FP News Service, now, alas, defunct). Then, he said, "I have information that you are the Walter Stewart who owes this money."

"Then you have the wrong information," I said, and hung up. My wife was giving me one of those *Now what?* looks, so I explained the contretemps to her, with many a merry quip. She didn't see anything merry about it. If a bank has put the collectors on your tail, she said, they are going to pass the word on to the local credit bureau, and your credit rating is going to be down among the dregs and spirits. So I sat down and wrote a rough letter to Rowland Frazee, Chairman of the Royal Bank of Canada, at the bank's head office in Montreal. I asked him the following questions:

"Since I have never had a bank account with the Royal Bank, nor borrowed any money, nor become indebted to it in any way, how did my name get onto your list of deadbeats?

"When and how and why did the Royal Bank turn the file

on me — or, presumably, some one of the many other Walter Stewarts — over to a collection agency?

"Is it the practice of the Royal Bank, when it has detected a deadbeat on its books, to put out damaging information about every person of that name, or do you narrow it down a little before the libelling starts?"

There was more, all good, ripe stuff, aimed at getting the hit-man off my tail. About the time I started typing, Ian Kerr, the collection agent who had telephoned me, reported to his manager at Financial Collection Agencies' Ottawa office. "I think we've got the wrong guy," he said. "This guy says he never lived in Winnipeg, and he sounded as if he meant it." Kerr's boss was not impressed. Deadbeats always take the innocent line, he said. Roust him again.

My letter to Rowland Frazee was dated January 25, 1981. I got a reply from him on February 14 (dated February 4) which said that he "appreciated" my writing to him (I'll bet), and that the matter would be investigated, and I would hear from him again. But I didn't. However, I did hear again, that very afternoon, from Ian Kerr, the collector. He called me at work, told me that I still owed the Royal Bank $202.39, and demanded that I pay up. I told him again that he had the wrong party, and he asked me if I worked for "EP News Service."

I said, "No, FP."

"They Usually Sound Scared"

He said, "Whatever," and went on to repeat the accusation that I had walked away from a debt in Winnipeg. I bellowed a denial. "I guess we're going to have to settle this in front of a judge," he said. I said that would suit me down to the ground. In fact, if he didn't sue me, I was going to sue him, for libel and harassment. I slammed down the phone, and wrote two more letters, one to Kerr and another one to Rowland Frazee. I figured, why should he miss all the fun? Once more, about the time I was writing, Ian Kerr was wondering out loud if maybe he didn't have the wrong guy. He told me later, "You didn't sound scared, just mad. They usually sound scared."

I also contacted a lawyer, to ask him what rights I had in a case like this. He told me that if I thought I was being libelled, I could sue, but he didn't recommend it. I said this wasn't a question of libel, just mistaken identity; why couldn't it be resolved by letter? The lawyer said he wouldn't count on that doing much good. He was right.

Two weeks later, when nothing had happened, I strolled over to the Ottawa Credit Bureau to find out if someone had put a black mark beside my name. There are credit bureaus in every major Canadian city, many of them owned by Equifax Inc. of Atlanta, Georgia (although not the one in Ottawa) and all of them tied into a computer network. They are financed by the credit-granting institutions and by businesses large and small who spend much of their time chasing bad debts. They come under provincial jurisdiction, and the amount of information any member of the public can glean from his local bureau varies from province to province; so does the amount of protection he has from the passing-on of wrong information about him; it depends on the disclosure laws of each province, some of them not very good. In Ontario, any member of the public who thinks he may be the victim of a bum rap has the right to be told what is in his file, although not the right to see the file itself. So I filled out the proper form (under Reason for Interview, I put "Threatening phone call from collection agency"), and was told that the last entry against my name was my application for an American Express card, back in 1972. "Credit-wise," the interviewing officer told me, "You're flawless."

Bucked by this indication that the Royal Bank didn't have any hard evidence to hang on me, I phoned the bank's Public Affairs office in Montreal, and after a good deal of to and fro, got passed to Press Officer Robert Racine. I told him I wanted to know how the bank's collection system worked, how it got me confused with somebody else and how – most important – other Canadians are going to be protected from mixups as we move deeper and deeper into the web of computer-stored credit data. "I'm not a shy person," I told Racine. He said he gathered that. But what happens to a shy person when the bank turns him over to one of these guys? Racine said he would get right back to me with answers to all my questions.

But he didn't. It turned out later that I had been passed to the wrong press officer. Racine was in the Quebec office. I wanted the national office. Six days later, when nothing had happened, I phoned Racine again. He told me he had passed on my request to the appropriate office, and that I should be hearing from them any time now. I said not to worry; I was coming to Montreal on business on March 28, and would call around at the Royal Bank. Could he arrange to have someone brief me? He said he would get right back to me on that.

But he didn't.

On March 19, nearly two months after the original phone call, I walked into the office of Financial Collection Agencies on Metcalf Street in downtown Ottawa, demanded to see Ian Kerr, the collector. He was on the telephone, a nondescript man in his twenties; when a secretary put a note in front of him with my name on it, he looked up, startled. Later, he told me, "When I saw you standing at the desk, looking sore, I said to myself 'I knew we had the wrong guy.' I mean, hell, if you really owe the money, you don't come barging in to the collection agency."

While I was waiting for Kerr to get off the phone, I stood at the desk making notes on the telephone conversations taking place in the long, rectangular office. There were five men at desks, obviously all talking to people whom the agency had been told were deadbeats. "What's the matter, Mister," one man was hollering into the phone, "you on welfare?" Another man, pursuing the soft approach, was saying, "Well, how much can you pay? Uh-huh. Well, get that in to me today, and we'll see if the court case can be stopped." A third was bellowing, "Well, just because they're grinding on you, don't try to grind on me."

"It is a rather distasteful business," Kerr said to me later. He added that sometimes, "You use equivocation."

When he got off the phone, he went into the manager's office – he was trying, in vain, to get the manager to come out and deal with me – then came to the counter. I told him I wanted to see whatever information the Royal Bank had passed on to him about me, and I wanted a letter acknowledging the fact that he had made a mistake. Kerr went back to his desk and shuffled some papers, then reported that he couldn't find the information on me. It seemed to have disappeared. He was willing to acknowledge, however, that the affair was "a mixup." A man with a name similar to mine had gotten onto the Royal Bank's books in Winnipeg, through neglecting to pay a bank overdraft. When the bank's collection department phoned about the overdraft, the man had apparently moved. So the bank had turned the case over to Financial Collection Agencies, who would receive a percentage of whatever they could get out of me. Because the Royal does so much business with FCA, the fee is set on a job-lot basis, at fifteen per cent of the amount owing. FCA was going to collect $30.35 if I coughed up the whole $202.39. They couldn't afford to be very thorough in trying to determine if they had the right man.

Kerr said he was sorry if he had sounded rough on the telephone, and sorry for the mistake. There were "a lot of coincidences" that pointed to me being the man they were after, he said, but he wouldn't explain what the coincidences were. After my letter to him offering to meet in court, he had written to the loans officer of the Royal Bank in Winnipeg, and in a subsequent telephone conversation, that gent had told him it "wasn't worth it" to keep hounding me for such a small amount.

I asked, "Then you mean they still think I'm a deadbeat?" Kerr couldn't say.

"If the money involved had been larger, would you still be after me?"

"Draw your own conclusions."

However, he realized I might be in the clear, because I didn't have the same Social Insurance Number as the one on file in Winnipeg. I said I thought SIN numbers were not supposed to be used for credit checks, and Kerr replied, "Would you rather have me still hassling you, or using the SIN number?"

In short, because the bank had blundered, I was harassed, but because the amount involved wasn't worth chasing, I was off the hook. I wanted to know, "If the bank was still pushing wouldn't my credit be tied up for years while this went through the courts?"

Kerr said he realized "The way the system works isn't fair." After some more stalling, he gave me the name of the Loans Officer at the Winnipeg bank, and I left.

Then I telephoned Don Ledwos, the Loans Officer, who told me, "I have a big file on you, right here on my desk." He said that a man named Walter Stewart had overdrawn his account in Winnipeg and then skipped town, and I became involved through "a strange set of circumstances.

"This fellow was a consultant in Ottawa, and was writing for newspapers from time to time." I was not a consultant, had only recently moved to Ottawa, and wrote for a news service. Ledwos said he thought that was probably close enough. He said the bank had not made any mistake, but perhaps the collection agency had done so. I said that it was the Royal Bank that had started the action, and I wanted to know what he proposed to do to end it.

Ledwos said "Nothing." He said he had had a letter from Kerr in Ottawa, in which Kerr had said that my letter to Rowland Frazee had been "neither fair nor accurate," and that he hoped the bank wasn't sore at him because I had "over-reacted in unfounded anger." After looking at that letter and the file, he, Ledwos, had decided there was little point in trying to collect the debt: "For $200, it wasn't worth the hassle to pursue you any further."

I said it was worth it for me, and I wanted to know if he still had a file that said I was a cheat. He said, "Yes . . . I can't prove that you are the right Walter Stewart, but I have no proof that you aren't, either."

"Find out," I suggested, but he said that there was an amazing resemblance between me and this doppelganger who goes around stiffing banks. I asked for details. Well, he said, we had the same name. No we didn't, I said. I was Walter D. Stewart; who was the other guy? Walter P., he said. Well, then there was the fact that we both wrote. I said the woods were full of people named Walter Stewart, and full of people who wrote. What else did he have? Well, nothing. A man who once lived in Winnipeg (I never had) with a different SIN number than mine, and a similar name, decamped on the Royal Bank. Then my byline popped up in an Ottawa paper. "Anyone could assume it was the same person," Ledwos said. I said that anyone could find out if a mistake had been made by doing a little preliminary checking before calling in the collectors, and when Ledwos said again that it "wasn't worth it," I retorted testily, "Well, if my name was Rowland Frazee, would it be worth it?" Well, yes, Ledwos thought that might be a different matter.

But he didn't think the bank had done anything wrong; it had simply turned a bum account over to a collection agency; what happened after that was between me and the collection agency. He was willing to admit that "It's very definitely a crude way of doing it."

When I finished talking to Ledwos, I tried the Royal Bank's head office in Montreal again, and got through to Roy Howard, another, and national, press officer. He said that, much as the bank would like to explain everything to me, no one was going to be available on March 28, when I would be in Montreal. He offered to work out another time. I said I would get back to him.

Then I sat down and wrote a story for the member newspapers of the FP News Service, and they all ran it in large, angry type. The Winnipeg Free Press ran it on Page One, with a nice picture of the bank and of Ledwos. Guess what? It then transpired that the Royal had time to talk to me after all, and when I went to Montreal on March 28, Rowland Frazee personally apologized for the mixup. "I have been in battles with American Express," he said, "and I know how frustrating these things can be."

In due course, Financial Collection Agencies came through with an apology, too, and I wrote a follow-up piece explaining, as the bank explained to me, that when it received my first strong objection, and that worked its way through the system, the bank had told the agency not to hassle me any more until they knew they had the right man, but somehow, even that message didn't get through.

When it was all over, I was left with a feeling of profound unease. What had helped me was my own non-shy nature and the clout I was able to exercise through the newspapers. On my own, I would still be sitting on the Royal Bank's books as a deadbeat. What happens to people who don't have a way to hit back? Well, in most cases, they pay up and shut up. Soon after my article on the collection business appeared, I received a number of letters outlining cases similar to my own, but which hadn't worked out so well. In one case, a man who had borrowed $2,000 from a bank branch in Ottawa went overseas, and sent back cheques to the bank manager — a personal friend — to cover the note. When he returned to Canada, it turned out that the bank manager had been defrauding the bank and, among other things, cashing this man's cheques for himself. As far as the bank's records showed, he hadn't paid a nickel on his loan. Soon, a collection agency was on his tail. The man consulted a lawyer, who told him that he might as well pay up. Otherwise, he would face at least two years in which his credit rating would be nil. He paid up.

Another case involved a **Winnipeg** man who bought Olympic coins by mail, billing them to his Chargex card. The coins cost $39.95 each, and there were sixteen in the set. After receiving eight, the man cancelled, because he didn't find the goods satisfactory. But the monthly bills kept rolling in. He refused to pay, pointing out to the bank that he had paid for what he received, and then stopped the service. The bank turned him over to a collection agency. He wouldn't pay the agency, either, and because the amount was small – $216 in his case – he, too, was dropped from the collection agency's rolls in due course. However, when he subsequently moved to Edmonton, the agency reported to the Edmonton Credit Bureau, which duly changed the man's rating from R-1, the best, to R-9, the worst. When he found out about this, the man started legal action. That brought an apology from the bank, but he is still pursuing the case and who knows, any year now he may be back where he started.

There were other cases, some of them heart-rending, some just plain silly, but the common thread of the complaints was always the same – the banks are not very careful in turning cases over to collection agencies, and not very concerned about the ordeal this puts some of their customers through. Sometimes, they are sloppy, cheap and callous, and, most of the time, they assume that the customer is wrong until he can prove himself right.

Eventually, I heard again from Ian Kerr, the collector who had been set on my trail by the Royal. He was no longer with Financial Collection Agencies – the parting had not been amicable – and he wanted me to know that "There was a lot more to your case than they ever told you at the time." Kerr hinted that the information he was given about me when he began on the case was studiously misleading. There were a lot of things in the file on me, he said, that just weren't true. "It really looked as if you must be this other guy, from the information in there."

I said I was sure Canadian banks were very careful in releasing information about their customers to outsiders. There is a confidential relationship there, I said, established by law. Kerr thought I must be kidding.

"Some of them don't really care what they release to creditors. It isn't at all unusual to get information from a bank, just by asking, from how much money you have to who you owe money to... You just phone them up and identify yourself on the phone. Most banks will release anything to anyone."

"Nobody Cares"

I said the Royal Bank had told me that credit information is a closely guarded secret. Kerr snorted. "It's up to the discretion of the individual bank manager. Some of them are lenient, some of them are careful. Not many of them are careful. You could do it yourself, call up a bank and say you were with a collection agency and ask about anybody. Chances are the girl who answers the phone will go and look it up and give it to you. Nobody cares. Take this thing about SIN numbers. They aren't supposed to be used, but as soon as you call up, the first question is, 'What's his SIN number?' That's the basic check."

Kerr also told me that some bank employees are not above using the collection agencies to pressure their customers. "I can remember one case where this guy in the civil service got into some money problems. He had a relatively decent job, made maybe $40,000 a year, but he was a slow payer. He had a debt with a bank out in Alta Vista (an Ottawa suburb) for maybe $35,000, but only half of it was secured. Then he got into a jam, because he owed American Express $2,000, so the loans officer at the bank found out about it and phoned me. He said, 'Why don't you threaten to sue this guy unless he comes to me and gets a mortgage on his cottage – put the guy up against the wall.'" That way, the bank would have all its money secured. Kerr claims that instead, he sent the man to a credit union, where he got a better deal. "No way was I going to sue him for the bank's benefit."

Kerr also explained that there is not enough money in collecting to worry about the niceties, such as whether or not the right party is being hounded. "In most cases, you have to work on a high volume. The bank will be paying maybe twenty-five per cent, maybe as low as fifteen per cent of the amount collected, it depends on how hard it is to get the money, and where the guy is. You don't really have time for much checking. You phone up and you really talk to the guy. In your case, when I said I thought we had the wrong guy, one of my bosses said, 'He's pulling your leg.' He said, 'Blast him . . . see if you can shake the money out of him.'"

I said I had an impression that any debt under $200 would go uncollected. "Not always," Kerr replied. "Sometimes they will want to make an example of somebody, and go after him even if it isn't going to pay off. But as a general rule, you're right; under $200, they tend to forget about it after a couple of phone calls."

Banks have collection departments of their own, whose job it is to trace slow and non-payers. The bank will sometimes, just as the ads say, work with a client who is in trouble to help him or her meet payments. They will even re-work the original financing, on occasion. Re-scheduling, it's called; as in, "There has been a slight delay in bringing around the tumbrel, m'Lord. You're not for the chopper until tomorrow." Moreover, if you manage to get into the bank's ribs for a really substantial amount, you are not going to be turned over to the telephone-shouters. Lawyers, certainly, and bailiffs, maybe, and all the lads with the foreclosure papers, but not the lowly collectors. Their specialty is scaring the bejabbers out of the low-born. The banks wash their hands of this rough stuff, as not consonant with the image they spend so much money promoting. But they are not fussy about what is done on their behalf by the collection agencies. Kerr says, "They don't care who pays it. I know of people paying accounts they don't even owe, just to get rid of the collectors."

The collectors are not the invention of Canada's chartered banks. They work for loan companies, department stores and other firms. In the banks' box of tricks, they are just one of the ways in which these prestigious institutions go about their business. Banks certainly don't condone lying, bullying or collecting money that is not owing – neither do the head offices of the collection agencies.

It's just the way things work out, sometimes.

6
Nearer
My Bank To
Thee

*"Well, no, tricycle going up against a steamroller, I
don't call that competition."*

James Sayers, Secretary,
Trust Companies Association of Canada

When the current Bank Act was being discussed in the
Senate Banking Committee, which is the font of all wisdom
and most power on such matters, an interesting exchange
took place between William Kennett, Inspector General of
Banks, and Senator John Connolly. Kennett said:

> "Banks are not all that different from various aspects of
> the operations of trust companies, loan companies,
> credit unions, caisses populaires, and so on."[1]

And Connolly replied:

> "They are different because they operate out of cathe-
> drals."

The notion that the essential difference between, say, the
Royal Bank and your neighbourhood credit union, is that
the Royal works out of more impressive quarters, is
quaint. There are no other institutions in this nation
capable of competing seriously with the banks; the so-
called "near-banks" listed by Kennett are not really very
near. However, the major differences are not always visible
to the naked eye, and because I will be arguing that for
many Canadians the sensible course is to use the near-
banks in combination with the real banks, it will be worth
while to visit some of these near-banks, to see how they

work, and how they differ from the giants who bestride our economy. What follows is a brief survey of our major "deposit-taking" institutions. These consist of:

Banks
Trust and mortgage loan companies
Credit unions and caisses populaires
Government savings offices[2]

There are other financial institutions, of course. There are life insurance firms, personal finance companies, mutual funds, brokerage firms and investment houses — which fill some banking and credit functions. There are wholesale banks, which lend money in large blocks to businesses, and there are leasing and factoring firms. Leasing companies buy large, expensive items, like jet aircraft, and rent them out. Factoring companies buy accounts receivable at a discount and collect them for profit — the banks have done this work through subsidiaries, but under the new Bank Act will be able to do it directly. A lot of these institutions take customers, of course, but they don't take deposits; they are not "near banks."

One way to get an idea of the overwhelming importance of the banks is to consider them in simple terms of size, and in Table 4 in the Appendix, you will find such a comparison. In brief, the banks have more than three times the assets of all their rivals put together; they hold seventy-one per cent of all assets in the system, and their dominance grows with every passing year.

The major functions of the deposit-takers are:

(1) to provide deposit accounts, where Canadians can place money, or have it placed by an employer, for purposes of paying it out later, usually by cheque;
(2) to provide savings accounts and certificates, in which money can be held to earn interest while awaiting use;
(3) to provide loans; and
(4) to finance mortgages.

The banks provide all these services, and their activities are many and manifest. They handle chequing, current and savings accounts, term deposits, business and personal loans, mortgages, the purchase and sale of securities, treasury bills, foreign exchange, Canada Savings

Bonds, and such tax-deferment schemes as Registered Retirement Savings Plans and Registered Home Owner-ship Savings Plans. They also provide safekeeping and safety deposit boxes, and will accept payment of such bills as hydro and telephone for a fee. And they run the nation's most aggressive money-creating scheme, the bank-card system, through Visa and MasterCard. They own their own realty companies, leasing companies, mortgage compa-nies, personal finance companies, and holding companies. If it has a dollar-sign attached to it, chances are a bank can do it, a major exception being that they are not allowed to act as "fiduciary agents" – estate trustees – a function that is left to the trust companies. Banks are the only institutions allowed to call themselves banks. They are federally incorporated, which gives them the notion that they are not required to abide by provincial law. That would be laughable if it didn't turn out to be true.

The nearest of the near-banks, the trust and mortgage loan companies, are provincially incorporated, and much more regionally based, with some exceptions, than the banks. They range from the modest to the monumental. If you wander into the office of Morgan Trust in downtown Toronto, you will not know you are in a deposit-taking institution. The office is on the twenty-seventh floor of the Toronto-Dominion Centre, and it looks like any other business office. At the reception desk, a woman will ask your business; when you tell her you want to buy a Guaranteed Investment Certificate (on which Morgan Trust pays a substantially higher rate of interest than any bank), you will soon be joined by a middle-aged woman of pleasant manner in a room that looks like an old-fashioned dining-room, with patterned upholstery on the ladder-back chairs. Sitting on one of these, you will fill out a form on what looks like a dining-room table. You have just made a deposit.

If you choose to do the same thing with Canada Trust or Canada Permanent – where, again, you will get a better rate than the banks offer – you will perform the ritual in one of the plastic, chrome and glass mausoleums that appear to differ in no important respect from a bank.

Between the tiny Morgan Trust and giant Canada Trust are ninety-three other trust and mortgage loan companies, with such names as The Effort Trust Company, Evangeline

Savings & Mortgage, Mennonite Trust Limited and the Regional Trust Company, as well as the more familiar Royal Trust, National Trust and Victoria and Grey. There is, in fact, a difference between the mortgage loan companies and the trust companies, although they are so close in their general line of work that they are lumped together by the Bank of Canada Review and in statistical summaries.

Trust companies act as executors, trustees and administrators, as well as performing such bank-like functions as handling savings accounts, cashing cheques and selling Registered Retirement Savings Plans. They cannot engage in business financing, the major portion of a bank's activity, but they can and do make both mortgage and personal loans.

Mortgage loan companies specialize in mortgages. They raise money by selling debentures and accepting deposits, as trust companies and banks do, but they invest the money mainly in mortgages rather than general business and personal loans, as banks and trust companies do. However, their functions overlap those of trust companies and banks so much that they are often lumped into one of the other categories. Canada Permanent Mortgage Corporation, for example, is a subsidiary of Canada Permanent Trust Company; for the customer who comes in off the street, the two are indistinguishable. Every bank has its own mortgage company, sometimes using a similar name, like RoyMor Mortgage, the Royal Bank subsidiary, sometimes using quite a different name, like Kinross Mortgage, a subsidiary of the Canadian Imperial Bank of Commerce. These bank subsidiaries represent a substantial share of what is assumed to be a rival operation. Taken together, the ninety-five[3] trust and mortgage loan companies hold total assets of $61.88 billion, which is less than the $62.37 billion held by our second-largest bank, the Commerce, alone.

And, of that $61.88 billion, the mortgage loan subsidiaries of the banks hold $12.20 billion,[4] leaving only $49.68 billion for all the other non-bank-affiliated trust and mortgage companies. Thus, the banks' main rivals, the trust and mortgage loan companies, in total are smaller than either of the two largest banks; and what is more, about one-fifth of their assets belong to subsidiary companies owned by the banks. Finally, just to complete the circle, some of the banks are major partners in trust companies, too. The Toronto-Dominion Bank and the Bank of Montreal each own about ten per cent of Royal Trustco, the nation's largest trust company. They are its largest stockholders. The Royal Bank is a major stockholder in Montreal Trust.[5]

Essentially, trust companies were established to handle the administration of estates, and the accounts of people who felt uncomfortable about investing their own money. Of late, they are getting rather picky, for an industry that claims it is in trouble; they don't want to handle estates with a value of less than $100,000. They also handle individual management contracts and agency agreements. Again, no paupers need apply – the usual minimum is $500,000.[6]

They maintain seventy-five per cent of their "eligible assets" as defined by law in first mortgages on residential property; in short, they are heavily dependent on household mortgages. Restrictions on the way they can invest money have historically forced them to operate at a spread between what they pay for money and what they can get for it which is about one-half that of the banks.[7] They are at a severe disadvantage.

In partial compensation, they are not required to maintain reserves, as the banks are, and when the 1980 Bank Act amendments lowered the reserve requirements for banks, the trust companies complained, in a brief to Parliament, that "These measures will enable the banks to obtain money more cheaply than before and encourage them to move strongly into mortgage lending, leasing and other business." The banks, which have the gall of an army mule, retorted that they thought the trust companies should have to maintain reserves too, since they were in the deposit-taking business.

The trust companies, unlike the banks, have been having a hard time making a profit, which is too bad for them, but presents some advantages for us. One is that, while they offer most of the deposit and chequing services of the banks, and while they have the same automatic deposit insurance, they pay more for our deposits, on the whole, and often charge less for loans.

In the Appendices, you will find Table 5, comparing the rates paid by the Big Five banks and five of the largest trust companies on savings accounts as of October 28, 1981. In almost every case, the trust companies pay more. While the banks were offering a uniform 3% on chequing accounts, the trust companies were paying 3¼%, 6%, and even 7%. When the Toronto-Dominion Bank was paying 15¼% on a non-chequing daily interest account, Guardian Trust was paying 19½%.

The trust companies don't do this because they love us, but because they have to; unlike the banks, they face competition, which they meet by competing in price, something the banks seldom stoop to.

The trust companies also normally offer a slightly better deal on term deposits and RRSPs. The best way to shop for either of these is to look up the tables most newspapers carry at regular intervals in their business pages, and then check with the institution – usually a trust company – that seems to be offering the best deal. I say "seems to be" because my experience over two years of phone calls is that what appears in the newspaper may be a guide, but it is not necessarily what you're going to get.

By and large, when you are looking for a bank, pick the closest one to you; the differences between the large institutions are minimal – the Bank of Montreal has a more sophisticated computer set-up, and therefore longer line-ups; Nova Scotia has dumber contests, but it seems to give more attention to the role of women in management positions. I'm not saying that there is no difference among the banks, but that from the consumer's point of view, the differences are too small to matter.

At the same time, there are real advantages in using a trust company either instead of a bank or as well as a bank. Here's one:

Canadians have become increasing addicts of the credit card. The banks, and trust companies too, for that matter, have been shoving them down our throats for a decade now, all the while complaining that Canadians can't control themselves, and that we must cut back on inflation and spending. The credit cards are seductive, because they are so convenient. They are also expensive, with interest rates running now as high as 24% annually on bank cards and even higher on department-store cards. The contracts behind bank cards allow the issuing institution to swoop down on your account and clean it out to cover a debt on the card – even if the debt is a blunder.

Suppose, for example, you bought a coat for $200, and the store, either wilfully or by error, billed you for $500 – or the bank misread the amount. Or, suppose you didn't like the coat, took it back for a refund, and the store refused to give you one. In either case, the bank (or trust company, come to that) would pay over the money and bill you. After that, it would be up to you to straighten out your battle with the store. And if you didn't pay up, the bank would start charging you interest, and then it could grab any money you had in any account to discharge that interest – without giving you notice of what it was doing.

In fact, the law is so asinine that, if a bank makes an error on your account and you don't catch the mistake and rectify it within fifteen days – even though you may not have received the notice, because of a postal strike or other act of God or bureaucrat – you owe the money, and it can be taken out of your account.[8]

Elementary prudence suggests that the way out of the stranglehold the law-makers and bank lobbyists have given the financial institutions is to split your accounts. Put the credit card under one bank's umbrella and your other accounts either in another bank or, better yet, in a trust company. This will not restore equity to the battle between consumers and financiers, but it will shorten the odds in your favour. (There is another possibility, of course: cut up your credit cards. But few of us are prepared to be that smart.)

The Credit Unions

The credit unions, and in Quebec, the caisses populaires, grew out of what a couple of researchers for the Economic Council of Canada, where they are not known for snappy turn of phrase, called, "the legislative inability and social myopia of other financial institutions in meeting the financial requirements of households."[9] The social myopia of the banks consisted in sitting on their well-padded butts and refusing to help to finance homes or personal spending. About the turn of the twentieth century, small groups of people all over the country began to organize themselves into local financial co-operatives – just as building societies were formed – to take on the job the banks spurned.

At first, credit unions were joined by a common bond — members of a union, employees of a company, or co-congregationalists in a church — and many such credit unions remain. They were, and are, co-operatives, but with money instead of groceries on the shelves. Members buy at least one share in the union — the usual price is $5 per share — and deposit funds for loans for themselves or others. Traditionally, credit unions have provided lower-cost loans than the banks — as well as being less snooty about the loan-granting process — and the members stood to gain two ways; first because they received better terms than they would get from a bank and secondly because their shares paid dividends as the credit union made money.

In the province of Quebec the caisses populaires filled the same role as the credit unions, while another type of institution, the caisse d'entreaide — mutual aid fund — also sprang up, modelled on the same lines but specializing in small business finance, which, again, the banks had traditionally neglected.[10]

In theory, the credit unions and the caisses are a marvel to behold. In fact, they have run into some problems. Management was not always first class. Having the money is one thing, knowing what to do with it is another, and there have been some collapses in the credit union movement, and other cases where collapse was only prevented by the intervention of a credit union central — a grouping of local credit unions — or a government.

Both credit unions and caisses have turned in uneven performances, especially since interest rates began to soar, and many of them were caught with long-term notes at lower rates while they had to raise new money at higher rates. Like the trust companies, they carry a heavy proportion of mortgages, and many of these were long-term and low-rate — which led to a classic mismatch of funds when they had to go into the market, again like trust companies, to buy money at a high rate. The well-run credit unions and caisses have continued to thrive, but some others have not done so well. One caisse in St. Bruno, Quebec, paid a 19% dividend on shares, which are a combination of ownership and deposit, in 1981, while another, in Brossard, paid 5½%.[11] In mid-1981, the Federation des Caisses d'Entreaide Economique du Quebec was shaken when one of its seventy-seven locals went under, and a run began on the caisse central in Alma, Quebec.[12] (The caisse funds are not covered by deposit insurance.) The federation underwent some reorganization and survives, but some of the bad publicity reflected on the Caisses populaires Desjardins, the organization of caisses in the province, which hold about $12 billion in assets.

It is both the strength and weakness of the credit unions and caisses that they are based in the community. Whereas banks will not appoint a manager to serve in his own hometown, on the ground that he may have locally developed prejudices, the credit unions insist on local managers, on the ground that they know the community. They are more compassionate and less conservative than the banks and trust companies; they are also, often, slower to act. You can get a loan from your local bank within a matter of hours; in some credit unions, you will have to wait for the next meeting of the board of directors. Then, as the union grows and succeeds, it becomes more and more like the other financial institutions. A friend of mine who belongs to Canada's largest credit union,[13] Vancouver City Savings, complains, "Hell, I can't tell it from any other bank. I keep expecting Mary, the friendly teller, to come leaping across the counter at me."

Despite its problems, the credit union movement has grown steadily, in part because many Canadians are looking for an alternative to the banks; between 1975 and 1980, membership grew thirty per cent, from about 7.5 million to 9.7 million[14] – that's more than forty per cent of the total Canadian population. The bulk of these are in Quebec – 5.1 million – with nearly 2 million more in Ontario and just under a million in British Columbia.

Credit unions can't perform some of the sophisticated money-market services of the chartered banks, but for ordinary customers, they offer a much better deal than the banks. Like trust companies, they aren't required to keep reserves – and, again, the bank lobby wants that changed. Again like trust companies, they have until recently been dependent on the cheque-clearing services of the Canadian Bankers' Association. Beginning in early 1982, they and the trust companies became, with all cheque-issuing institutions, eligible to join the Canadian Payments Association.

The credit unions are growing up. They don't provide a complete banking service yet, and some are still not well-organized, but they do represent a real alternative to the banks, if they continue to grow.

Snuffing out the Regional Banks

Minor players on the banking scene, the Province of Ontario Savings Offices and the Alberta Treasury Branches are the last remnants of a series of attempts to establish regionally oriented banks. Government-owned banks existed as early as the 1830s, when Newfoundland and Nova Scotia both established savings banks.[15] All government banks became federal at the time of Confederation, and were funnelled into the Post Office Savings Bank, which was dissolved in 1968. Attempts in Manitoba, Saskatchewan and British Columbia to establish provincially oriented banks were snuffed out by the central banks.[16]

In 1920, Ontario and Manitoba had another try at establishing their own banks,[17] and while the Manitoba version only lasted a decade, the Ontario Savings Offices are still in existence. They provide only one service – savings accounts – and turn the proceeds over to the Ontario Treasurer to use as he sees fit.[18] Despite their limits, they pay higher rates than the chartered banks, and are well worth investigating for anyone who lives near a branch.

In 1938, Alberta launched its Treasury Branches, which have grown into full-service banks in 195[19] communities across the province. If I were an Albertan, that's where I would do my banking, confident that I would be getting at least as good a break as I would get at a chartered bank, and that the proceeds would be used to benefit Alberta, not Toronto or Montreal.

Discontent with the centralized control of banks resulted in other, more recent, attempts to found regional banks. In 1964,[20] the province of British Columbia announced that it would set up a bank, twenty per cent owned by the province, with a federal charter, to provide competition for the giants of the industry, but that didn't last long. The federal Senate Banking Committee – which at that time had a heavy proportion of bankers as active members – derailed British Columbia with a recommendation that a charter be refused until after the next revision of the Bank Act, which didn't take place until 1967 and which included a limitation of ten per cent on provincial ownership of any bank.[21] The Bank of British Columbia, which rose from the ashes of the 1964 attempt, is a privately owned, regionally oriented bank, indistinguishable, except in its comparative smallness, from the rest of the chartered banks.

The Bank of Western Canada, uniting the talents and haughty spirits of James Coyne, former Governor of the Bank of Canada, and Sinclair Stevens, who was later to become, briefly, President of the Treasury Board in the Clark government, set off bravely into battle in 1967 but came unstuck, with financial and organizational problems, and never did open its doors.

There is one other near-bank in Canada, the Montreal City and District Savings Bank, which doesn't fit into any of the categories above. It was founded in 1841 and chartered provincially under the Quebec Savings Bank Act in 1871. It is in effect the provincial version of a federally chartered bank, and operates in much the same way.

How the Banks Dominate

These near-banks have varying capacities to compete with the banks in line with the four major functions the deposit-takers perform.

(1) Chequing accounts

At the end of 1980, Canadians had $24.3 billion in demand deposits,[23] reachable by the simple signing of a cheque; seventy-seven per cent of this was held by the banks, and seventy per cent of it by the Big Five. Credit unions had eighteen per cent and the trust companies a meagre six per cent. The banks have lost a little ground in this area – in 1967, they had eighty-seven per cent of the business – while the credit unions have increased their share from five per cent to eighteen per cent.

(2) Savings accounts

Canadians had $166 billion[23] in savings accounts at the end of 1980, and the banks' share of this was $109 billion, or more than sixty-five per cent. Two out of every three savings dollars sit in a bank, and five out of every six of these sits in one of the Big Five banks.

(3) Consumer loans

Before 1967, the banks were not the major force in personal loans that they have become in recent years. That is because, by law, they could not charge more than

6% interest, and the way Robert MacIntosh, President of the Canadian Bankers' Association, tells it, Canadians were suffering. "The ordinary guy was in the power of the finance company," MacIntosh told me. "He took a screwing." The banks did work a couple of wrinkles to get around the law. The Bank of Commerce discounted loans in advance, for example, thus jacking up the effective interest rate. You paid 6% interest on the full $100 you borrowed, but you only got $90 in your hand – the other $10 (the "discount") stayed with the bank. Other banks lumped in service charges to raise the take. But the main job of financing vacations, cars and appliances was left to the finance companies.

The 1967 Bank Act, sub-titled Blueprint for Competition, changed all that. Ostensibly, the Act was to provide competition for the banks, but instead it turned the banks loose on the finance firms, by removing the ceiling on interest rates the banks could charge. Killer whales were put into the barracuda tank, and it was no contest. The banks can get their money easily and cheaply through their far-flung branches; the finance companies get theirs either by borrowing from the banks or by going out into the money market on their own, to sell shares or debentures or other financial instruments. However they do it, they pay more than the banks. The result was that the banks could under-price the loan companies, but still charge enough to make a fat profit that got fatter as rates moved inevitably up. They took over the market.

Between 1967, when the banks first got into the personal loan business in a major way, and 1981, the consumer credit market multiplied five times, from $8.6 billion[24] to $42 billion. The banks had a little more than thirty-four per cent of the 1967 total, or just under $3 billion;[25] now they have more than seventy-seven per cent, or $33 billion, in consumer loans.[26] Credit went up five-fold, the banks' share went up eleven-fold. And guess what? The Canadians who were suffering because of the exactions of loan companies charging as much as 12% interest are now privileged to be able to pay their friendly chartered bank 21% instead. Thank God the banks stepped in to rescue us from the friendly finance companies.

The loan companies were bludgeoned to their knees; from thirty-one per cent of the market in 1963, they plummeted to less than three per cent in 1981; they actually handled fewer dollars in 1980 ($2.7 billion) than they had a decade earlier ($2.8 billion).[27] One finance company, IAC Limited, turned itself into Continental Bank, but I don't know whether that was its way of trying to get revenge or giving up.

Credit unions have done well in the consumer loan field, too, although not in the same league with the banks. The credit unions handled $1.5 billion in consumer loans in 1970, and $6.4 billion in 1980.[28] Their share of the market, however, has not changed much; they were just under fifteen per cent a decade ago and they are just under sixteen per cent now.

(4) Mortgages

Again, the banks played a small role until the 1967 Bank Act change. With some minor exceptions – serving National Housing Act mortgages – they were barred from the residential mortgage market until 1967, and in that year held about thirteen per cent[29] of the mortgage market. Then the wraps came off, at least in part, and they were allowed to invest up to ten per cent of their demand deposits in mortgages. They even got around the ten per cent limit by establishing their own mortgage companies, as well. Just as with consumer loans, they enjoyed the twin advantages of a well-established and far-flung branch system and cheap money. They cleaned up. Between 1967 and 1973, the value of the banks' mortgage holdings increased by 1,170 per cent; the insurance companies and the mortgage loan companies (though not the trust companies) were dust beneath their chariot wheels. The insurance companies held forty-nine per cent of all residential mortgages in 1963 and seventeen per cent a decade later; the mortgage loan companies went down from twenty per cent of the market to sixteen per cent in the same period. By 1981, the insurance firms were effectively out of the mortgage market, which now broke down this way: Trust and mortgage loan companies, 55.6%, banks 22.3%, and credit unions, 20.8%.[30]

The banks, as well as owning their own mortgage companies, are allied to trust companies and the trust companies to mortgage loan companies and in some cases they are all tied together in realty companies, making for a cosy arrangement all around.

It is part of the bankers' line that ordinary Canadians have benefited from the way they have moved into the mortgage market, but I'm damned if I can see it. The bank argument holds that, without their presence, mortgage rates would be even higher than they are today, but if you want to call that pigeon poop, I won't object — crude, but true, I'll say. Mortgages have been tremendously profitable of late — the mismatch of funds in 1980 caught some institutions with long-term mortgages out at low rates while they had to bring in new money at high rates. So the banks have been jumping in and out of the market to suit themselves. In most cities, for example, most banks won't give you a mortgage on a townhouse — they just don't like them. At the same time, they have disrupted the normal market. The end result is that Canadians are paying more than twice what they did for mortgage money before the banks got into the act.

The Death-Grip of the Big Five

Many of the near-banks do a job that is as effective as, or more effective than, the banks, but none is a competitor, in the real sense, with any of the Big Five. I would rather borrow money from a credit union than from a bank, rather buy an RRSP from a trust company than from a bank, and it would help us all if the competitive position of the near-banks was strengthened. The death-grip the Big Five have on the nation's financial system suggests this is not likely, at least in the short run, but some obvious reforms are waiting in the wings.

In the meantime, it will pay us to look more closely at how the network of chartered banks operates to protect the nation from the rude shock of competition in our economy.

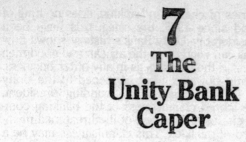

7
The
Unity Bank
Caper

*"Why don't you just get on a plane and go down to
the Cayman Islands? That's where the story is."*

William Noble, *director of legal services
for the Bank of Montreal, 1975*

I was standing in front of the land titles office in Georgetown, Grand Cayman, when it occurred to me to ask
myself, What in the name of God am I doing here? The sun
was smiling down on sand and sea, tourists were frolick-
ing along the beaches, and even the birds were giving
work a miss and curling up on their respective branches
for a midday nap. But here I stood, in my three-piece suit,
trying to look respectable, but only managing to look hot,
dithering around in front of a land titles office whose files
– if I could ever get at them – might or might not tell me
what a small group of people in Canada were so excited
about. If I didn't find what I was looking for – and I didn't
know what I was looking for – I was going to have a hell of
a time explaining my expenses to the Managing Editor. If I
did, I was probably going to be sued right down to my
socks. Well, enough moaning and theorizing, it was time to
get on with it. I picked up my battered briefcase – which
was to turn out to be crucial – and pushed open the door.

I was on the track of a story about Unity Bank of Canada,
a Canadian institution that no longer exists, but whose
bold beginning, spectacular ascent and sullen decline give
the lie to all the stories about stability in the Canadian
banking system. The Unity Bank story suggests that the
chartering process, which was supposed to protect us

from the vagaries of chance in banking, does nothing of the sort — and since 1975, the safeguards have been slackened considerably. Unity Bank's history shows how good intentions can wind up in the ashcan and good men on the sidelines, in the banking, as in any other, business. Most importantly, however, what happened to the Unity Bank and to Richard Higgins, its founding president, underlines the inbred clannishness of the banking community, which circles around one of its threatened members like a herd of musk-ox. This clannishness may be a tribute to the loyalties of bankers, but it is a threat to the public purpose.

My involvement began with a telephone call to my office at Maclean's Magazine in the late spring of 1975. The caller was a man named Bobby Bonnell, whom I had met years earlier in New Brunswick, when he was an aide to Charlie Van Horne, leader of the Progressive Conservative Party of New Brunswick, at a time when it looked as if Van Horne was about to become New Brunswick's premier. I had written a story about Van Horne that contained a lot of information he would have preferred to keep to himself, and the story helped contribute to his defeat. Bonnell remembered that, and thought I was probably the right person to do a story about what he called "the scandalous things going on at Unity Bank." As it happened, I had been thinking about doing a story on the bank. Glowing reports about Unity had appeared at regular intervals on the pages of the Globe and Mail's Report on Business when the bank was first launched, but in recent months there had been only sketchy paragraphs hinting at problems. Obviously something was going wrong, and Bonnell was hinting that he knew what. He asked me to meet him at the Hyatt Hotel on Avenue Road in Toronto, after work. He would buy the drinks, he said.

At the Hyatt, I went to a room rented in the name of Dennis Dwyer of Montreal, and occupied by Bonnell and Dwyer. Dwyer was a middle-sized, middle-aged, excitable man with a balding head and sweaty hands. He is now a clergyman in a small Quebec city — which shows the power of redemption — but at that time was working for a small Montreal financial house which had acted as adviser to Unity Bank in the formative stages. He was, he told me, a shareholder in Unity Bank, and one who felt badly because its original purposes had been betrayed. Bobby Bonnell was a smaller man, rather cherubic – in appearance only – and he described himself as the president of an international sporting goods firm. He, too, was a Unity Bank shareholder but, more to the point, he had been executive assistant to Leonard Walker, when Walker was president of the Bank of Montreal. In that capacity, he said, he had come to know a good deal about Richard Higgins, the president of Unity Bank, because Higgins had been a senior executive at the Bank of Montreal before he took on the Unity job, and Bonnell thought that someone – me – should tell the public about what Higgins had done and was doing. Why? I asked. What had he done, and what was he doing?

What he had done, Bonnell said, was something very tricky indeed, something the public had a right to know. I wanted to know why I was being brought into this thing now, three years after Unity was launched. There was a short, embarrassed pause. Then Dwyer explained that he and Bonnell had been hoping that the mess at Unity would be straightened out behind the scenes, but that was not happening, and not likely to happen. I said that what they meant was that their own shares had declined in value. Right, said Bonnell. Then, I said, what they were hoping was that if Maclean's carried a story about the bank, that would bring pressure on the board of directors to do something drastic. Right, said Bonnell. And then, I went on, their shares would go up again. Well, said Dwyer, that wasn't why they had called me. The public had a right to know these things. But in the end, yes, he would admit that they had something to gain.

I asked if they could tell me what it was that Higgins had done. Well, no, they couldn't. Bonnell knew it had something to do with real estate in the West Indies, and he knew that Walker, his boss at the Bank of Montreal, had regarded it as pretty shady. One day when the two of them were getting on an elevator and Higgins, who was still at the bank, went by in the corridor, Walker had said to Bonnell that Higgins was not "our kind of people." That was pretty tough stuff, from a banker. They suggested that I might want to call Bill Noble, who was legal adviser to the Bank of Montreal in the Montreal headquarters. He might be willing to say something about it. There was a great deal more, about the internal power struggles then going on at Unity Bank, about the way its original concept had been abandoned, about its record of bad loans and the declining value of its stock, but in essence, these two were a couple of disgruntled shareholders complaining to the press, and hoping to get some action out of it. They made me profoundly uneasy.

However, the next day, I went to the public library and looked up the files on Unity. They were extensive, particularly in the bank's early days, and most of the ink was given over to Richard Higgins, who seemed, in all the accounts I read, to be a combination of Superman, Horatio Alger and the Man from Glad. Handsome, smart, charming, a man of whom other bankers had nothing but good to say. A whiz kid when he started, then a rising rocket and now, a superstar. The bank was getting into trouble – that was clear, reading between the lines of the more recent stories – but Higgins? No. Stainless steel. I went home and put in a person-to-person call to William Noble at the Bank of Montreal. He was not helpful.

"A Fine Fellow"

He said he was not in a position to talk about Richard Higgins or Unity Bank, although he knew a great deal about both. "I am the manager of the legal and tax departments here," he said. "I had a considerable amount to do with Richard Higgins. My views about what happened are personal views." I told him I thought something had gone wrong and he knew it. I said he and his bank had a duty, if that was the case, to inform the public. Noble replied that "It would certainly be improper for me to discuss this without consulting my own masters." I asked if he knew anything about Bobby Bonnell, and Noble replied that he was "a fine fellow." More than that, he would not say.

When I put down the telephone I knew that, if I hadn't hit the jackpot, I certainly had the lemons spinning. Something had gone wrong, and at least one senior officer of the Bank of Montreal knew it. Whether I would ever be able to prove it was something else, but it was obvious that Noble was going to talk to someone higher up in the bank, and might very well provide the information I needed.

I went down to the Maclean's office and proposed a story on Unity Bank. I pointed out that Canadians have always believed their banks to be sacrosanct, above suspicion, and solid as the Rock of Gibraltar. But here was a bank in trouble, and here was the stuff of scandal. I was told to go ahead, and spent the next few days shuttling between libraries and interviews, on the trail of the story of Unity Bank's rise and decline. I quickly found myself fascinated, and I discovered that this was the story of two men, Richard Higgins and Benjamin Levinter. They could not have been more different.

Benjamin V. Levinter was short and dark and round. He talked rapidly, with vast gestures. Enthusiasm bubbled out of him, an uncapped well. Everybody called him "Bunny," and not everybody took him seriously. "Oh, Bunny," his friends would say, and laugh. Or else, "Have you met Bunny yet? He's a character." Bunny went to Upper Canada College and married the granddaughter of an early editor of the Toronto Globe and Mail. His father, Isadore Levinter, was a prominent Toronto lawyer, and the dominant force in Bunny's life. Everything Bunny did – law school, joining Dad's legal firm, working for the right causes – he did to win Isadore's approval. Bunny bought a farm, just across the road from Dad's, near Maple, Ontario, twenty-five miles north of Toronto, as a proper place to raise his family. Maple, as the name suggests, is a town festooned with Canada's loveliest trees; Bunny was content to settle down in their shadow, and that of his father, until he got this terrific idea of starting a bank. That's how he got to meet Richard Higgins.

Richard Higgins was tall and blond and slender, a handsome man who could have made a living posing for Arrow shirt ads. He was a great talker, too, but his talk was more measured than Bunny's. He always sounded as if he framed his sentences on internal cue-cards, flashed them across some mental screen, edited them, and then allowed them to exit through the mouth. No bubbler. Until the Unity fiasco, he was always taken seriously. Some people called him "Rich," but mostly it was "Mr. Higgins." He was known as a "smart cookie," a "tough egg," a "real comer." He didn't live in anybody's shadow. His father cut shingles in a sawmill in Vancouver, and Rich made it on his own, with good marks, and impressive athletic prowess, at the

University of British Columbia. After graduation, he took a job at the Bank of Nova Scotia, where he had worked part-time during university, and instantly began to clamber upward. Eventually, his clambering brought him into the ken of Bunny Levinter, and, for a time, they were yoked together, like a badger and a gazelle, in Unity Bank. It was not a happy union, but the bank was a noble idea.

Unity was born at Bunny Levinter's farmhouse, one night during the fall of 1970. It came out of a speech by former finance minister Walter Gordon, which Levinter had never even heard. His wife Marion had been there, at a dinner meeting addressed by Gordon, and she came home vibrating with the ideas Gordon had presented. He had said that it was regrettable that Jews were cut off from the mainstream of Canadian finance, which flowed through the chartered banks. As a result, many brilliant ideas never came to fruition, because the banks were the preserve of Wasps, and Wasps were notoriously hidebound and conservative. Marion Levinter thought Gordon was right, and so did Bunny. In fact, he was aflame with the idea. Why not, he said, start a bank of our own? A bank that would serve the special needs, not only of the Jewish community, but of the Chinese, Ukrainians, Poles, Germans and other minorities who so often find the vault-door slammed in their faces. An ethnic bank. It would be good for the minorities, and good for Canada. Not only that, if he launched his own bank, Bunny would be someone in his own right. Dad had done many things in his time, but he had never launched a bank. Bunny would prove, once and for all, that he was his own man.

Bunny was an enthusiast but he also knew how the country is run. Launching a bank was not a matter of finance; it was a matter of politics. Fortunately, his political connections were solid. They began right in his father's own office, with Gordon Dryden, former treasurer of the Liberal Party of Canada, a partner in the Levinter law firm, and a man with a lot of friends in Ottawa. Dryden embraced the idea of an ethnic bank, and became general counsel to the fledgling bank. He was the key figure in steering it through the chartering process.

That process had always worked the same way. A group of backers discovered the need for a new bank. They pledged $1 million in capital (this figure has now been raised to $2.5 million[1]) and they turned over half this amount in cash to the government of Canada, to prove that they were not triflers. Then they got a friendly MP to introduce a bill chartering the bank; they were vetted by the Inspector General of Banks, by the Senate Committee on Banking, Trade and Commerce, by the House of Commons Standing Committee on Finance, Trade and Commerce and by the Bank of Canada.

There was no provision in the law for a detailed, public probe into the men behind the bank. All the frisking took place in a cloakroom, away from the rude gaze of the many-headed. Too bad, because such a probe might have raised some questions about Unity. Just the same, the process sounds so cumbersome, and appears to have so many built-in safeguards, that it has always been considered failsafe. One word in the right ear that the sponsors are not top drawer, m'dear, and the brakes went on.

If they survived all this examination, the bill was duly passed and the bank came into being. By that time, they had raised enough money from the public to go into business. The stock sale provided the bank's kitty; the original $1 million pledged by the founders was just a refundable bond.[2]

The system of parliamentary charter was held to be so safe as to stifle competition, and the Bank Act revisions that came into law in December 1980, provide for a new form of chartering, by way of letters patent. Instead of having to shepherd a bill through two houses, the bank's sponsors put up their money and then petition the Minister of Finance for a charter. He, after a suitable examination by the bureaucrats, makes a recommendation to cabinet, which issues a charter.[3] That is how foreign banks have been setting up in Canada recently, and forty-seven of them came away clutching their charters in the first twelve months,[4] while one Canadian bank was working through the parliamentary process. The letters-patent route provides even less public information than the parliamentary process, which does, after all, have two public hearings, in the committees, and the opportunity for a public debate. Now, it's all done behind the scenes, and the chartering is turned over almost entirely to the ministrations of the Inspector General of Banks and other bureaucrats. That strikes me as a very bad idea, especially when you consider that the old way, where there was at least the opportunity to air legitimate concerns, proved so inadequate in the Unity case.

What happened in that case was that friendly Liberal MPs rallied around, and friendly senators rallied around, and the charter was pushed through Parliament in six months, although it had taken more than two years for the Bank of Western Canada to obtain a charter (which it was never able to exercise because internal divisions brought the bank down before it could open its doors). But the Bank of Western Canada was essentially a Tory creature, backed by Sinclair Stevens, later the Conservatives' President of the Treasury Board, and by James Coyne, sometime Governor of the Bank of Canada. They were no friends of a Liberal government. Unity Bank had Judy LaMarsh, former Minister of Health, on its board of directors, and Gordon Dryden as general counsel. Stanley Haidasz, later a Liberal cabinet member, and James Jerome, later a Liberal Speaker and Robert Kaplan, now Solicitor General, and then Chairman of the House of Commons Standing Committee on Finance, threw their weight behind the venture, and it was a considerable weight. In fact, it was Kaplan who gave the bank its name. Bunny wanted to call it United Bank, but the United Trust objected, so Kaplan proposed a minor change to Unity Bank and Bunny agreed.

Not only did the bank have political allies, it had no natural enemies. That was because the concept was so obviously good. Once, when Dennis Dwyer was speaking to the Senate Banking Committee, he began to be hectored by a senator who knew a good deal about banking, and reckoned that Dwyer did not. Another, friendly, senator mouthed the word "motherhood" to Dwyer across the committee table, and he launched a speech about the virtues of the Unity idea. The heckling stopped. That is hardly surprising; what Unity proposed to do — and I set this down because the ideas were never used, if anybody else wants to take them up — rested on four strong pillars:

First, the bank would involve Canadians "of many ethnic origins in every facet of its affairs." The bank was to represent Canada as it exists, not merely the Wasp upper crust.

Secondly, no individual or group would be allowed to dominate the bank. No shareholder could vote more than two-and-one-half per cent of the stock, even if he owned more.

Thirdly, there was to be a "strong social commitment" to develop under-privileged areas of the country and "a certain percentage of the deposits in an area (would) be set aside for that area's development." No more raiding the piggy-banks of the Maritimes to build Ontario factories.

Fourthly, "mini-boards" in each region of the country would guide the bank's activities, and ensure that proper attention was paid to each area.[5]

These were the promises the bank made when it was going through the chartering process, but it is doubtful if more than a handful of people believed in them, although no one raised that point at any time during the public hearings. Richard Higgins would tell me later, "The concept the charter was obtained under was an ethnic bank. I think they believed it. It helped get the charter." Then he added, "That was his (Bunny's) idea, not mine."

Sweetness and Light

No one knew, when the bank was being put forward, that its raison d'etre would be abandoned almost at once. There is no provision in the Bank Act, or anywhere else, to ensure that a bank, once launched, performs the way it said it would when it was coming before Parliament as a humble petitioner. It certainly became clear to the original sponsors that their broad-minded notions were not being received with the same acclaim in the financial community as they were in Parliament. When Dennis Dwyer was describing the bank to the president of one of the nation's top financial houses at a luncheon, that worthy snorted, "When you cut away all the crap, you've got a bank headed by a Jew. It'll never fly." Another financial wizard, more circumspect in his language, told Dwyer, "Your bank seems a joke in dubious taste." Not a whisper of these concerns – or bigotry – was allowed to seep into the public arena. There, all was sweetness and light, and the chartering process went through without a hitch.

In part, that was because Parliament was told that the president-to-be of the new bank was a man of sterling qualities, although they were not given his name. That man was Richard Higgins. After joining the Bank of Nova

Scotia in 1961, Higgins had moved swiftly through the ranks and onto the executive ladder. In 1965, he went to the West Indies as an assistant branch manager in Trinidad; a year later, he got his own branch to manage in St. Lucia and in 1968, he came back to Canada, as deputy manager of the bank's international banking division, stationed in Toronto. Robert MacIntosh, President of the Canadian Banking Association, says that he knew Higgins when both were in the Bank of Nova Scotia, and knew "there was something wrong there," but there was no hint of that when Higgins suddenly jumped to the Bank of Montreal in 1969, and resumed his upward climb. He was sent back to the West Indies to look after that bank's developing subsidiaries, and was Managing Director of the Bank of Montreal, Bahamas and Caribbean when in June 1971, he met Richard Bain, a Toronto lawyer in Nassau on holiday, and they got to talking about a new bank being launched in Canada by Bain's friend, Bunny Levinter. Higgins liked the sound of it, and Bain liked Higgins, so, as soon as he returned to Toronto, Bain called Bunny and suggested that this might be the man they were looking for to fill the president's job at Unity. Levinter flew down to Nassau, interviewed Higgins, liked him, and, soon after, offered him a five-year contract as Unity's president. At that time, Higgins had been in the banking business nine years. In an industry that clocks its executives by the decade, and generally picks its presidents from thirty-year men, he was almost a novice.

No public announcement could be made about Higgins before the bank got its charter (suppose something went wrong? His bosses at the Bank of Montreal might not be too pleased that their bright new recruit was thinking of jumping ship). Just the same, it was obvious that the quality of the bank's president was a matter of some interest to the parliamentarians. Bunny described the Nameless One before the Senate Banking Committee as "a senior Canadian banker." Later, before the House of Commons Standing Committee on Finance, Bunny promoted his protoge to "a very, very senior official in the Canadian banking scene."[6] W. A. Scott, then the Inspector General of Banks, was asked before the Senate committee whether the president-to-be was "a man of banking experience and integrity." He replied, "I have no reason to doubt that."[7]

Nor did he. No one told him anything unworthy about Higgins, and he certainly didn't do much investigating of his own. He interviewed Higgins, once.[8] In Canada, we believe Those In Authority must know what they're doing and Those In Banking must be All Right. A three-minute phone call, to or from the Bank of Montreal, might have altered matters, but apparently it never occurred to anyone, at any level, to insist on finding out something about the key figure in the new bank before Parliament gave its blessing.

That blessing was bestowed in mid-1972. Unity had a charter and a president and a board of directors, now it needed some money. To get money you must have money, that is banking's creed. If you don't happen to have a barrel of the stuff in your basement, and none of Unity's founders did, it is customary to go to the stock market, issuing shares which the public will buy, in return for a piece of the action. This sounds simple, but isn't. It depends on an underwriting. The underwriter's role is crucial; it is he who places the shares on the market, through brokers. The fledgling corporation and the underwriter agree on a fair value for the shares, and the underwriter promises to turn over a cheque covering the value of the shares to the corporation on a given date, in return for a fee. It is thus "underwriting" the issue in a direct way. Then the underwriter sends the shares to stockbrokers, who sell them to a waiting and anxious public. That's the theory. But what if the public is not waiting and anxious?

A Scheme is Born

Underwriters tend to be a twitchy lot, given to gloom and conservatism. They were not enthusiastic about Bunny's ethnic bank. It was different, for one thing – who knew if it would work? Then, there were all its worthy qualities, which sounded fine in a parliamentary committee room, but naive and dumb to the business community which, frankly, doesn't give a damn if one region of the country is screwing another, provided the process returns a profit. It soon became clear that the normal underwriting process wouldn't work; no underwriter was prepared to put up the $25 million it would take to launch the bank. That was where Dennis Dwyer came in. When the Unity concept crossed his desk, he decided it was for him. He knew many of the insiders, and shared their enthusiasm; he became the chief financial strategist for Unity, working through a small firm in which he was a partner. If the big financial houses wouldn't underwrite the bank, and the little ones couldn't, Dwyer reasoned, then the solution would be to turn the normal process on its head. Unity should mount a public relations campaign.[9] Customers would then pour into the brokers demanding stock in the new venture, the brokers would pass the word to underwriters, and the issue would be launched.

So senior officials of the bank-to-be were soon criss-crossing the country in what one of them described as "our dog and pony show," making speeches about regional control and ethnic openness, and soon the customers were banging on the shutters of the brokers' firms, crying out for Unity shares. Before long, underwriters who had collapsed in hysterics when first approached were negotiating with the bank. In all, offers from four underwriting companies were received, and, as usual in large transactions of this sort, the job, and risk, were parcelled out among them. The leading firm was to be Gairdner & Company of Toronto. It would be backed by the prestigious Wood Gundy Limited, with a clump of lesser firms taking smaller portions of the offering. This group undertook to distribute three million shares of Unity stock at $9.25 each. That would bring in $27,750,000. For their role, the group would receive sixty-two cents a share, or $1,860,000, and turn over the residue, $25,890,000, to Unity Bank on October 10, 1972.[10]

Bunny and his friends were going to have the money to launch their bank. They were also going to make a potful for themselves. As we have already seen, the Bank Act required the founders to put up at least one million dollars, half of which had to be raised in cash and deposited with the Minister of Finance for later refunding. However, this was a minimum, not a maximum, and more shares could be bought from the corporation's treasury by the founders as part of the original equity. What is more, these shares could be "subscribed" — that is, ordered but not paid for — for as little as ten per cent down (in the new Act, they must be paid for in full). In Unity's case, the founders undertook to purchase $3,310,105 worth of shares for themselves, and they put up $570,000 in cash.[11] And much of this money was borrowed from the Toronto-Dominion Bank. Once again, we see the magic and the hokum of banking. A $27 million bank was going to be launched, with all the might and majesty of a parliamentary charter behind it, on the basis of investments by a dozen men of $50,000 each, less than a substantial mortgage, much of that borrowed. But that wasn't where the profit came in. The subscribed shares were to be distributed, like the original shares, directly from the company treasury rather than through the underwriters. Their price was to be $8.62 each, which was the issuing price of $9.25 less the underwriters' commission. The bank's founders, however, were able to order these for as little as eighty-six cents each, under the ten per cent down rule. In other words, for eighty-six cents of investment, an insider could get shares valued at $9.25, and if these increased in value the way everyone expected them to, the founders were going to be rich. One of the directors kept saying at board meetings, "All I want is a quick $100,000."

Richard Higgins, to take a pertinent example, subscribed for $500,000 worth of stock — 54,054 shares — and put up the ten per cent minimum of $50,000.[12] Gairdner & Company in its underwriting letter to tout the stock, valued it at $11.10. If that estimate proved correct, Higgins' 54,054 shares would be worth $600,000 within a few weeks; he would make $100,000 profit on the basis of a $50,000 investment. If all went well, he would triple his money.

But all did not go well.

The Unity share offering hit the market in the fall of 1972, when the economic climate was uncertain, and a number of other share offerings were out competing for investment dollars. Then a Japanese firm that had been angling for a large chunk of the stock got around to reading the fine print, realized that it would not be able to vote more than two-and-one-half per cent, and withdrew its offer. That rattled the market. The stock opened at $9.25, as advertised, but soon plummeted past nine dollars on its way to eight, then seven.

The underwriters were left with what the trade calls, beguilingly, "a large rump," which is to say, shares for which it had to turn over money to Unity but which it had not been able to sell. The public was not told about these unsold shares, almost fifteen per cent of the total, word of whose existence would have driven down the price even more. On December 5, 1972, Gairdner sent out a research letter that purported to prove that Unity shares were worth $11.10. The company did not point out its own role in Unity's launching, nor did it mention the large rump still unsold; the letter looked like sound advice for any investor from an unbiassed source – just part of the general funning that makes the financial world such an interesting place for widows and orphans. The letter didn't work; most of the rump remained in the hands of the underwriters, who, bravely biting their lips, turned over the required $25,890,000 to Unity.

The bank was in business, but it was not, alas, the business it said it was going to be in. Richard Higgins didn't care much for the ethnic angle on which Unity was based, nor for its claimed regional emphasis, nor its "mini-boards" to advise the main board, so these notions were simply dumped. They had served their purpose, in getting the bank its charter. Nor did he care for the rule limiting any shareholder to voting two-and-a-half per cent of the stock – too restrictive. When Unicorp, a company controlled by George Mann, then president of United Trust, offered to buy the bulk of the rump of unsold shares for $7.50 each, the voting rule was changed from two-and-a-half per cent to five per cent, and Mann became the dominant shareholder.[13] Finally, Higgins was not keen on the slow, gradual and regionally balanced growth pattern laid down for the bank in Bunny's original plan. That wasn't his style. He was aggressive, a hunch-player, a risk-taker, all the things a banker is not supposed to be. The plan called for Unity to establish five branches in 1973; instead, it opened sixteen, most of them in Ontario.[14] Overhead soared.

The market reacted by dropping the stock-price even further – at one point in late 1974, after release of the bank's annual report, it got as low as $2.75. Now the share-purchase arrangement that looked so profitable when the founders got into it had become a trap. They were committed to paying $8.63 a share for stock that wasn't worth anything like that amount in the market. If they fulfilled their subscription commitments, they would lose a great deal of money. So many of them didn't. Only two of the original subscribers paid up in full and at once — Gordon Dryden, the general counsel, and BDM Fund, a company controlled by Chartec, Dennis Dwyer's firm. Other stockholders found out about the arrangements favouring the insiders, and began to grumble about the "free ride" granted to the founders. Maxwell Rotstein, a lawyer and Unity stockholder, told me, "If ordinary stockholders had known about this deal, they would not have bought the stock." By "this deal," Rotstein was not complaining about anything crooked, rather that ordinary shareholders could not get their stock for ten per cent down, the way the founders did. The way to make the delinquents pay up was to have the board of directors pass a motion requiring them to do so. But the directors were, in many cases, the very people who had not paid up. Nothing happened. Richard Higgins told me that "If you were to call it (the subscription obligation), I couldn't pay it." There was no time limit on when the subscribed shares had to be fully paid for.

By mid-1975, the bank was in serious trouble. Instead of a projected 1974 profit, there had been a loss of $562,351. Part of this was due to the bank's rapid expansion, and part due to bad debts. In 1974, Unity had to set aside $4.5[15] million to meet debts that were not ever likely to be collected. Bad debts are a part of every bank's experience, but Unity had more than its share. Some of these resulted from hiring incompetent or inexperienced branch managers — one of them was described to me as "an out-and-out drunk." There were management problems at head office, too. Eaton Luck, the original general manager, quit and went to work for the Department of Finance in Ottawa. He wouldn't say why he left, only that he wanted to stay out of "that mess." The assistant general manager, marketing, also left, and so did a number of others, one of whom told me, "All I can say is that from an organization that presumably was supposed to be employing professionals, they acted very mysteriously and in defiance of the rules of banking." Many of the complaints had to do with what were considered to be the "high-handed" methods of Richard Higgins. A new general manager was hired. He was David Mathews, a solid, pleasant man who really was experienced in banking, and under his guidance, the bank began to make a come-back.

But Bunny Levinter, the man with a dream, had been dumped. He was eased out of the chairmanship just before Unity's 1974 annual meeting. Higgins told me that he and Bunny had quarrelled over such matters as the appointment of a public relations man (Higgins fired Bunny's choice), the role of Bunny's father on the board (Higgins didn't want him there) and whether it was appropriate for Bunny to print business cards calling himself "Founding Chairman" of Unity and to go out seeking business with them (Higgins thought it was not). Higgins won all these disputes, but at some cost to the air of cheerful camaraderie both men adopted for public occasions. Bunny told the shareholders that he was stepping aside because his task was finished, and the bank was well launched, but not many believed him. He was replaced by Dr. Gerald LaSalle of Sherbrooke, Quebec, a founding subscriber who had put up $55,000 to buy shares valued at $325,000. LaSalle had no illusions as to why he was taking over Bunny's chair; it was because Bunny couldn't get along with Higgins, and Higgins was the chief executive officer, the man who ran the bank.

By the time I received Bobby Bonnell's telephone call in mid-1975, there were a lot of unhappy shareholders at Unity, the stock was hovering around $4, and a general sense of unease pervaded the organization, but there was no suggestion that Higgins was anything but a prudent, upright man. The first real suggestion of where to look for evidence on that account came in my second telephone conversation with Bill Noble, the Bank of Montreal legal adviser. I received a message that he wanted to talk to me again, and called him from a pay-phone in the Yonge-Eglinton subway station in Toronto. My notes of that call show that he repeated virtually everything he had said in the first conversation, including the line about talking to his masters, and then suddenly suggested that I should go down to the Cayman Islands. When I wanted to know why, he would only say that it would be worth my while.

It was.

I knew from my research that Higgins' last job in the West Indies had been to set up a subsidiary of the Bank of Montreal in Georgetown, Grand Cayman, so I presented myself in the office of Cliff Harris, manager of that subsidiary, and asked him what he could tell me about Richard Higgins. A great deal, it turned out, and all of it favourable. Harris had worked for Higgins in Nassau, liked and admired him, and knew nothing that would reflect on his reputation whatsoever. That was that, then. I thanked Harris, put away my notebook, and got up to leave. Just as I was going out the door, I asked him if he knew the lot number of the building we were in. He called in his secretary, and she looked it up. Then I went over to the land titles office, just around the corner, to see if there was something about the real estate itself that would tell me why Noble thought I should be down here.

When I went into the land titles office, a clerk asked me what I wanted, and I asked for the file on the lot number Harris had given me. "Are you a solicitor?" she asked. I didn't say a word, but lifted up my battered old briefcase and put it on the counter — lawyers are notorious for carrying around briefcases alleged to reflect their onerous work. The clerk handed across the file. Fifteen minutes later, I burst into Cliff Harris' office in the Bank of Montreal and demanded that he come with me. He was startled, but he came along. I took him to the land titles office, handed him the file on his bank, and asked him what he thought it meant. "Oh, dear," he said. What the file showed was that the bank had owned the land it was built on, but sold it, then leased back from a Nassau-based company, at a generous rate, then bought it back again. "This is not the way to do business," Harris said.

It took another two weeks to work out the details of the transaction, scattered in files between Georgetown, Nassau and Montreal. In brief, the story went like this:

In April 1971, while he was still managing director of the Bank of Montreal, Bahamas and Caribbean, Richard Higgins made a deal with a colourful Australian entrepreneur named Richard Kenny, whom he had met at a cocktail party in Nassau. Kenny was to build a branch of the bank in Grand Cayman, the British crown colony and tax haven 180 miles northwest of Jamaica. Through interlocking companies, Kenny was to buy land and erect a building. The bank would put up the money for the deal, then lease one floor from Kenny's company. Between April and August 1971, the bank advanced $500,000 to Kenny, who said Thank you very much, and disappeared, never to be seen again.

Kenny didn't get away with the entire $500,000. The bank got the land he had assembled in Grand Cayman and a house he owned in Nassau. Higgins moved into the Nassau house, and began to structure a new deal much like the old one.

On April 5, 1972 — when he knew he would be leaving the Bank of Montreal to become president of Unity — Higgins signed three documents constituting a contract with Robert Wharton, a developer from Mississauga, Ontario, a close personal friend, and one of the founding subscribers of Unity Bank (he signed up for $150,000 in stock, for which he paid $50,000 down). Higgins sold the land Kenny had assembled for the bank to First Realty Limited, a company registered by Wharton in Grand Cayman, for a fair market price of $330,000. Then, the bank took a mortgage debenture from First Realty under which First Realty could draw up to $750,000 from the bank, for the purpose of constructing a building. Finally, the bank agreed to lease 7,000 square feet on the first floor of that building, plus some parking space, at a rate of $16 per square foot per annum for fifteen years. In short, the bank would provide the land and the money for a building that would then belong to Wharton, and rent back one floor of that building for $112,000 a year, or $1,628,000 over the term of the lease. If he could keep his construction costs below $750,000, Wharton would not have to put up his own money, the lease would pay off his loan from the bank, and the rest of the three-storey building's rent would be gravy. And he would own a nice piece of property.

The day after he signed this deal, Higgins resigned from the Bank of Montreal, which knew nothing of the transactions entered into in its name, although it did suspect that there was something amiss. Carlos Garin, secretary of the Bank of Montreal in the Bahamas, and Richard Pearse, an assistant manager, had been abruptly transferred back to Montreal at Higgins' request. They mentioned something of the deal to officials in the mother bank, but nothing was done until Higgins' sudden resignation. That brought Garin and William Noble down to the island, and what they found — essentially, what I found — sent them scurrying to Peter Shaddick, then executive vice-president of international banking.

Shaddick called the developer, Wharton, to Montreal, and killed the deal. On November 29, 1972, the bank bought its land back from Wharton for $500,000 – a profit of $170,000 for Wharton – and built its own bank, with Wharton's role reduced to a small contract to oversee construction.

When I had pieced the story together, I went to see Higgins in his office at Unity Bank in Toronto. We talked about the bank's problems, and I then invited him to tell me what he could about the construction of the bank building in Grand Cayman. He was not willing to divulge any details, but would only say that he had made "the best deal I could get at the time." After Kenny vanished with the bank's money, he had turned to Wharton because he knew Wharton had had experience building in the Caribbean and was a man who could be trusted. He saw no significance in the fact that the contracts with Wharton were signed the day before he left the bank, but admitted "in retrospect" that it might have been better not to commit the bank to a contract running for fifteen years one day, and resign the next.

As soon as I left Higgins' office, I telephoned Wharton to ask for an interview, which he refused. He did admit that he had not, in fact, done any building in the Caribbean, and said of the deal, "As far as I'm concerned, there were no unusual circumstances to it, although there were circumstances."

When I got home, there was a message waiting for me to call Richard Higgins, and when I called, he asked if we could have another interview, to "clarify certain matters." At our second interview, six days after the first, he said he had been talking to Wharton and learned that he had not, in fact, done any building in the West Indies, so he thought I should know that. He had also remembered that the deal he had left behind for the bank was not perhaps the best he could have gotten after all. He had intended to improve it, he said, but his resignation was accepted by the Bank of Montreal so suddenly – the day it was tendered – that he had not had a chance to do that. He said that he wasn't a developer or builder, so it was natural to call in an outsider for such a job, and that if the Bank of Montreal was now critical of what he had done, well, that was a matter for them, not him. He thought the bank had "too much bureaucracy; it's got to go nit-picking."

When I had my research done, I went to Montreal to talk to Bill Noble and, with him, to Fred McNeil, then the executive vice-president of the Bank of Montreal. I told both of them that I couldn't understand why, if the Bank of Montreal thought the Grand Cayman deal reflected a lack of prudence, or something stronger, on Higgins' part, word was not passed to the Inspector General of Banks before the Unity charter was granted. The Bank of Montreal's position was that this was not its concern. I said I thought I had been turned loose by the bank — which pointed me to the Cayman Islands knowing what I would find there — because it was unwilling to take a public position. I said that I expected to be sued when the story came out, and expected the Bank of Montreal to provide evidence to help my case when I was sued. McNeil said the bank would always do its duty when called upon to help the courts determine facts that came under its purview.

So I wrote the story, leaving the Bank of Montreal almost entirely out of it. But I never did get sued. Instead, Richard Higgins' resignation from Unity Bank was announced in mid-November, 1975, a month after my article appeared. The press release announcing this gave as a reason "Indications that profit expectations, committed to by Mr. Higgins, were not being achieved." The bank lost $607,000 in the fiscal year ending October 31, 1975.[16] Higgins went back to British Columbia, and his post was taken over by T. L. Avison, a former vice-president of the Canadian Imperial Bank of Commerce, who was brought out of retirement[17] in a forlorn attempt to save the faltering Unity Bank.

Although Higgins was gone, over the next eighteen months timebombs set during his presidency continued to explode. The bank had given out a number of dubious loans, including one to Clairborne Industries Limited of Toronto of more than $7 million.[18] The chairman of that company was later charged with defrauding his own firm. Then the board learned that low-interest loans to bank employees had soared to over $2 million. In addition, a number of lawsuits broke out, including a complex one in which the bank and Dennis Dwyer were suing each other at the same time.[19] When the bank attempted, at long last, to collect on the shares subscribed for, but not paid up,[20] only about twenty-five per cent of the money was forthcoming, and Bunny and Isadore Levinter managed to get an injunction[21] to keep the bank from declaring their shares forfeited because they were not fully paid for – they would have had to pay $8.63 for shares that had by this time – in early 1977 – sagged to $2.70 a share.

There was a rumour of a run on the bank after the Metropolitan Toronto school board decided to withdraw a $2 million deposit in February, 1977.[22] A few days later, a Unity Bank manager in Mississauga, Ontario, was sentenced to fifteen months in reformatory on four charges of falsifying bank documents.

William Kennett, then Assistant Inspector General of Banks, was asked about an amalgamation proposal under which Unity would be folded into the Provincial Bank. He told the press that there was "Some evidence that (Unity Bank) was beginning to suffer the loss of confidence of its depositors," but no pressure was being put on the bank. "No initiative was taken on our part in this amalgamation."

Before that amalgamation could be completed, there was another dramatic development – Richard Higgins was charged[24] in Victoria, B.C. with accepting benefits of $110,000 in return for "showing favour" to William Alfred Eastgate, a Saanich, B.C. businessman who obtained a loan from Unity with Higgins' help. Both men were also charged with conspiring to obstruct justice by destroying documentary evidence of their deal. They were convicted in March 1978, and sentenced to one year in jail each. When the arrests took place on May 7, 1977, it appeared that the amalgamation of Unity Bank with the Provincial Bank might be threatened, but after another check of Unity's loan portfolio, Provincial took over the troubled bank in June 1977; today, it is part of the National Bank of Canada, formed from the merging of the Provincial Bank and the Bank Canadian National on November 1, 1979. By that time, Higgins was back at school. After serving three months of his sentence, he was paroled, and he got a job as a labourer, earned enough money to go back to school, and began the study of psychology. He was working on a master's degree when he died, quite quickly, of cancer.

Bunny Levinter went back to practising law, Dennis Dwyer got religion, and Bobby Bonnell went back into business.

Looking back, it seems astounding that Unity could

8
The Club Of The Worthy

Mr. Frazee: My understanding is that all corporations are extremely careful — and certainly the Royal Bank is extremely careful — on this subject to ensure that there is no suggestion and no possibility of any conflict of interest issues arising.

The Chairman: Mr. Frazee, I can remember, looking away back, in connection with some of my earlier activities, that when it was felt that there might be a conflict of interest, the persons who might offend were asked to leave.

Mr. Frazee: That is still the case.

Testimony before the Senate Banking Committee,
November 29, 1978

The exchange recorded above says volumes about how our banking system is run, if we care to set it in context. The exchange came about in the first place because a draft of the Bank Act then working its torturous way through Parliament had had the temerity to suggest that bank officers ought not to be allowed to be directors of other firms. The concern was that these worthies might be led into a conflict of interest between what was best for the bank and what was best for the outside corporation. A far clearer worry is the potential for conflict when bank directors, who are also corporation directors, come to consider matters affecting competitors who apply to the bank for a loan. No one had the courage to suggest that banks should drop outside directors, but the first step was under way — limiting the outside directorships of the bank officers. The exchange at the opening of this chapter began with an invitation to Rowland Frazee, Chairman and Chief Executive Officer of the Royal Bank of Canada, from Sen. Hartland Molson, who happens to be a former vice-president and director of the Bank of Montreal, to comment on this sensitive subject. Frazee responded that there was nothing to worry about. Then Salter Hayden, Chairman of the Banking Committee, waded in to say that directors always avoided even the possibility of a conflict. The Sen. Hayden who said this was, and still is, an "honorary" director of the Bank of Nova Scotia. "Honorary" means he doesn't receive a fee, nor attend board meetings. But why the long-time chairman of the most powerful government body that deals with banking would allow himself to be directly linked to a bank remains a mystery. Hayden is also a partner in McCarthy and McCarthy, the Toronto law firm that acts, on occasion, for the Toronto-Dominion Bank.

So you have a former-bank-director-senator and an honorary-bank-director-senator and the chairman of Canada's largest bank in solid agreement that there is no need to worry about conflicts of interest by bankers, or bank directors.

How the System Works

Some examples of the operations of bank boards in real life suggest how these high hopes translate into practice. We can drop in to a meeting of the board of directors of a major Canadian bank, where a brisk discussion is under way about the paint business in the Province of Quebec. The president of an independent paint company has an application before the board for an extension of his considerable loan. The board turns for expert opinion to the one man among its members who happens to know a lot about paint. He is the vice-president of one of the nation's largest paint firms. He says that paint companies in Quebec are facing hard times; competition is stiff, and the market crowded. The bank decides to call its loan and the company goes bankrupt, which certainly makes the vice-president a good guesser.

Again, we might be lucky enough to attend the meeting of another bank's board of directors considering the request of a western Canadian lumber company for a multi-million-dollar loan. The board turns to its expert in the lumber business, the president of one of the largest firms in that industry in Canada. He suggests that this is not a good time for the petitioning firm to expand, and the loan is turned down. This time, the company does not go bust; the owners are able to persuade an American bank to ride to the rescue and the company is doing very well, thank you. The guess was not so good.

Now, we drop in on a 1980 conclave of top officers of the Toronto-Dominion Bank while the boys talk about what to do about Royal Trustco, Canada's largest trust company. The company, which is nine per cent owned by the Bank of Montreal, is the object of a takeover bid by Campeau Corporation of Ottawa, whose chairman, Robert Campeau, is not one of our kind of people. Brash, he is, and there is concern that he will use the trust company to expand his real estate holdings. Campeau has approached William Mulholland, President of the Bank of Montreal, about a loan to finance the takeover. Mulholland has refused. The Bank of Nova Scotia will loan the money, though. If somebody doesn't act, soon, a crude outsider will take control of Royal Trustco. What should the T-D do? What it does is to buy about ten per cent of Royal Trustco at about $20 a share – although shares had been selling earlier in the year at between $12 and $16.[1] Campeau is beaten. The Canadian Imperial Bank of Commerce buys some shares, too. The Toronto-Dominion Bank explains that it acted to help keep the shares of the trust company from being concentrated in one pocket (namely, Campeau's). Queried about this, a bank spokesman insists that "It was a straight-forward business transaction." Buying shares for $20 that you wouldn't touch with a bargepole at $12 is straightforward business? "The circumstances had changed," he replies. The net result is that a man considered unworthy of admission to the club is blackballed from high finance in Canada, and two banks end up with a substantial proportion of a major competitor.

Finally, we pay a call on a 1981 board meeting of the Canadian Imperial Bank of Commerce, when it has to consider what to do about Massey-Ferguson, the troubled farm implement maker. Massey has been losing money, and if it doesn't get help, it will go bankrupt.[2] It is heavily in debt to, among others, the Commerce, Toronto-Dominion and the Royal Bank of Canada. Two Massey officers have been on the boards of each of these three banks throughout the period of the troubles, and the vice-president of the Commerce, Charles Laidley, is now on Massey's board. The Commerce decides to go along with Massey, buys $150 million in convertible preferred shares, and helps put together a $715 million infusion of new capital to the company, as well as forgiving loan interest. Whether Massey will survive is still uncertain; the only two certainties are that the Commerce — and other banks — didn't guess very well on Massey and that that company was treated rather differently from either the paint maker or the lumber dealer.

In theory, our senior bankers are prudent, impersonal, hard-boiled gentlemen who consider only the "bottom line." In fact, they are an exclusive club, who know the difference between the general run of customers and the group of worthies at the top of the financial heap, who are linked together in so many ways that conflicts of interest are not merely possible but inevitable. A small paint company in trouble gets the back of a bank's hand; Massey-Ferguson, in much greater trouble, gets repeated loans and then, when the banks become over-extended, a massive infusion of capital. A small lumber manufacturer gets the bum's rush; the management of a trust company partly owned by another bank gets a helping hand. The key to these decisions has nothing to do with prudence, the public interest or normal banking practice — it is not at all normal for Canadian banks to buy large blocks of stock. It has to do with a social and political question: Are they, or are they not, our kind of people? The bankers aren't prudent, they're particular.

Their world is divided into the Deserving and the Undeserving, the Acceptable and the Rest Of You Bums, and the decision as to who is which is a matter for a close-knit group at the top of the banking community. The close links between banks and businessmen would not be so disturbing if real competition existed in Canadian finance, but it does not. When a Canadian is turned down by one bank, he cannot simply cross the street to another, because the rules will be exactly the same over there. If you are a bum to the Bank of Montreal, you are a bum to

Toronto-Dominion, and the criteria for determining your bummishness have less to do with your financial background than with your connections.

In the Appendices at the back of this book you will find three tables that contain a great deal of information about the links between banks and other corporations. Table 6, headed "Bank Directors on Corporate Boards," is a table of some major Canadian corporations which have bank directors on their own boards of directors. It will give you some idea, not only of how pervasive the influence of the banks is, but of the cross-pollination that must take place at board meetings. Abitibi-Price, the paper-making giant, has men on its board who also represent five different bank boards – the Royal, Canadian Imperial, Toronto-Dominion, National and Continental. Argus Corporation has five bank directors on its board, Bell Canada has twelve, and Canadian Pacific eleven. Richard M. Thomson, Chairman of the Toronto-Dominion Bank, is on the board of Eaton's, along with Conrad Black and Doug Bassett, who are on the board of Canadian Imperial, and David Kinnear of the Bank of Montreal. Do they ever talk banking? Kenneth Thomson, Chairman of the giant Thomson empire, is on the Toronto-Dominion board, and also on the board of the Hudson's Bay Company, which competes with Eaton's. There, he shares table-space at board meetings with four directors of the Royal. Two other Royal directors are on the board of Simpsons, which is part of the Thomson empire. How do these people keep their loyalties straight?

We are not discussing idle theory here, but the way business decisions are taken, in a world where the role of the banks is increasingly obtrusive. Consider, for a moment, the troubled case of the attempted takeover of F.W. Woolworth in the United States by Brascan Limited of Toronto, in 1979.[3] Woolworth's largest single banker, worldwide, at that time, was the Commerce, which agreed to finance the takeover for Brascan, to the tune of $700 million. Three Brascan directors were board members of the Commerce, and the bank's former chairman was on the board of Woolworth in Canada. In a nasty corporate battle, Woolworth's Chief Executive Officer, Edward Gibbons, charged that the bank became involved on the basis of information obtained about Woolworth through its banking operations. The bank's reply was righteous. "CIBC has advised Brascan that while some officers of CIBC may receive information about Woolworth's Canadian subsidiary from time to time, it has a long-standing bank policy that all information received from borrowers about their business and financial condition must be treated with confidence and may not, under any circumstances ... be imparted to any third party."[4] The bank officers who gave the initial approval of the loan had no prior participation in any banking transaction involving Woolworth, and had not received any confidential information, the bank said. It is a fact that the terms of the bank loan, taken by themselves, were advantageous to the Commerce, which suggests that there was no need to use inside information. However, it is no reflection on the integrity of bank officers to worry about conflicts of interest in situations like this. The Brascan bid was beaten back, and the questions raised were never settled. They remain unsettled, but there must be some more satisfactory standard than a pious belief in the probity of bank officials to govern business conduct, especially considering the range and nature of bank directorships.

Directors are a Prolific Breed

The banks are strong on directors: they like to have lots of them around. They make no bones about the reason — they help to bring in, and hold, business. You get paid for being on the board of directors of a bank, and the pay isn't bad at all. In 1980, the thirty-four directors of the Bank of Nova Scotia received an average of $14,067 each, plus expenses; Toronto-Dominion's forty-three directors received $12,428 on the average, and the other members of the Big Five ran down from there to an average of $9,241 for the fifty-three directors of the Bank of Montreal. Not a fortune for the kind of people who get these appointments, but better than a kick with a frozen boot, especially when you add it to other directorships. John H. Coleman, former deputy chairman of the Royal Bank, is still on that bank's board of directors, at the age of seventy. He works, as a consultant, out of an office in Royal's golden tower in downtown Toronto.[5] He can have lunch, at subsidized rates, in the company dining room one floor up, and he gets his shoes shined, free every morning by the man in the blue jacket with "Royal Bank" emblazoned on the pocket, who comes around to polish up the nobs. Helping the Royal Bank's board is only a tiny part of Coleman's job. He is the president or chairman of five companies outside the bank, and sits on twenty-four boards, for which he receives retainers ranging from $5,000 to $30,000 each annually, to attend ten meetings, plus $500 each for four or five committee meetings, plus, of course, travel and entertainment expenses. Let us say, being conservative, he receives $300,000 a year.

Coleman provides good value for the money, by all accounts, but doesn't the setup make you just the least bit nervous? For one thing, how much sympathy do people who hold these kinds of jobs and make this kind of money have for the lot of us lesser mortals, whose lives can be unplugged by a doubling of the interest rate? Bank directors get their loans at special rates. At the 1982 Canadian Imperial Bank of Commerce's annual meeting, it was revealed that both the Chairman and Vice-Chairman had substantial loans from the bank at about 6% interest, or about one-third of the prime rate.[6] When interest rates go up, so do profits; if you were in a job where increasing the price of your product added to profits, and you didn't have to pay the increase, which would you favour, higher interest rates or some other technique to attack inflation?

For another thing, doesn't all this mixing and matching get confusing? John Coleman is on the board of Thomson Newspapers, whose chairman is on the board of Toronto-Dominion. Should he be trying to switch Thomson business to the Royal Bank? Well, no, that would be a conflict of interest, and no one has suggested that Coleman has ever been caught in such a bind. I would be, though, every time. I wouldn't know what the hell to do. Bank directors have no such problems. They are another breed.

They are also a prolific breed. The Bank of Montreal doesn't need fifty-three directors to oversee its operations; it has them for two reasons, which were explained to me (frankly, but off the record) by a senior official of the bank:

"Well, the first reason is obvious. These guys are smart. You want to know about meat-packing, you put the president of a meat-packing company on your board. You are rounding up expertise, in other words. The second reason is just as obvious, to bring in, or hold onto, business. You have the head of Joe's Screw and Nut Company on your board because he does a lot of business with you. If he stops doing business with you, he won't last long on the board, that's for sure. Why should you pay him for something he isn't doing?" Sen. Salter Hayden, Chairman of the Senate Banking Committee, put this same point another way: "Having ceased to be a customer, his chances of becoming a director are somewhat lessened."[7] A bank with fifty-three directors has a line into all those companies, and the directors' fees are small potatoes compared to the business those people represent. This leads me to a naive question: If a company has a president on the board of a bank – call it Bank B – and he discovers that his company can do better by dealing with another bank – Bank C – isn't he going to be in a hell of a pickle? Should he yank the company business away from Bank B, and give it to Bank C? But if he does, will he lose his directorship at Bank B and the money that goes with it? If he doesn't, isn't he betraying the trust of his shareholders, on whose behalf he must make the best deal possible? This is what is known as a conflict of interest, and how all those directors avoid it is a mystery to me.

The dilemma represented by the case I put is multiplied on paper by the thousands, as a glance at Table 6 will show, and it is a mere sample of the interlockings of banks and corporations in this country. In all, the eleven chartered banks have 351 directors on their boards, and those 351 men and women (nearly all men) hold 2,294 directorships among them. That represents a web of interests that spans the nation and the economy; it is the Club of the Worthy. When these people ask for loans, extensions, special consideration, they are not in the position of some poor, dumb hog-farmer in eastern Ontario who got into the bank's ribs when interest rates were 12%, and went under when they hit 25%. He is just a customer. The boy on the bank board is a Customer – something quite different. He is the one who gets the Prime Rate, he is the one who belongs to the same clubs, shares the same views, works in the same charitable organizations as the other boys in the bank.

Table 7 in the appendix, Bank Executives on Corporate Boards, looks at the same phenomenon from the other direction. It shows the officers of the banks who are directors in outside corporations. These are the ones Rowland Frazee was assuring us at the beginning of this chapter could never be caught in a conflict of interest. Incidentally, not a single one of them is a woman, for the very good reason that, while banks are beginning to countenance women in executive positions, they have not quite reached the stage of letting them out of the office and onto the boards of other corporations. In all, the eleven chartered banks have sixty-three executives holding down 228 outside directorships, and if you will run your eye down the list you will wonder with me how they manage to do it without ever getting into a conflict of interest.

The Chairman of the Canadian Imperial Bank of Commerce, Russell Harrison, is on the board of three insurance companies, and his president and vice-chairman is on a fourth. Do they ever talk about insurance, or what is going on among the competing companies whose boards they grace? Of course not. Suppose Richard Thomson, Chairman of the Toronto-Dominion, who is on the board of Prudential, got to chatting with his president, who is on the board of both Aetna Casualty and Excelsior Life, or with his vice-president, who is on Acadia Life and Phoenix Assurance boards? Wouldn't it be putting something of a strain on them? I'm sure these gentlemen are above reproach, but if I were on one of these interlocking boards, I would assume that the whole purpose of my being there was to bring back information that might be useful to the bank. To avoid telling one company — especially if I were on two similar boards, as well as that of the bank — what was going on at another would require me to erect a kind of internal mental blockade. I can't do it, but I am not a banker, and the bankers insist there is nothing to worry about.

If there isn't — I don't wish to be rude about this, but the question keeps nagging at me — then what is the fuss about? Why don't they just give up their outside boards?

The bankers' reply, when I put this to them, comes in two ways. The first is an offer — from the more aggressive kind of banker — to punch me in the snoot, for reflecting on the integrity of the breed. When this subject was before the Senate Banking Committee — with its generous sprinkling of former bankers — the honourable senators made it clear that any suggestion that steps should be taken to avoid conflicts of interest was insulting to the fine men who run our banks. No, it isn't. It is no insult to say that the law should be written in such a way as to prevent such conflicts, not invite them; that is common sense. The second way to reply to my insulting suggestion is the soft answer that turneth away wrath: "We can quite see the point that some people might make," the official spokesman for one bank told me, "but it is quite misplaced. The reason bank officers appear on the boards of outside corporations is so that those corporations can benefit from their expertise and experience and, in turn, so that our officers can acquire useful information about the subjects under discussion. If your bank has several million dollars out in loans to a large farm implement dealer, to take a case in point, it is a good idea to have someone over there to learn about the business. And, not incidentally, to keep an eye on things on behalf of the bank."

One of the many troubles with this explanation is it isn't necessary for bankers to hold positions on the boards of their customers to provide them with information and expertise. There is, after all, the telephone. Another problem with the explanation is that, in the most spectacular case involving a loan to a farm implement dealer I can think of – the Massey case – having interlocking directors didn't prevent the company getting in over its head, and probably encouraged the process. In fact, the Massey case underlines one of the disturbing new trends in Canadian banking. The bankers are no longer bankers; they are up to their hips in the businesses they are supposed to be dealing with at arm's length. The decline of the stock markets and bond markets – traditional places to raise capital for corporations – has left the banks in the role of funding much of the nation's capital requirements. They say they have been forced into this role, but they show every sign of relishing it; although it adds to their risk – the "exposure," as the bankers like to call it, on a corporation like Massey is both high and dangerous – but it can pay handsome dividends.

If we are moving into a world where the banks play a greater and greater role in capital formation – not merely lending money, but overseeing its use – then the dangers of conflict of interest and insider knowledge are multiplied many times over. In this situation, it is simple nonsense for the banks to keep murmuring, as they do, "Trust me." Even if there was nothing to worry about in years past, there is plenty to worry about now.

There is no need whatever for outside directorships for bank officers, just as there is no need for the huge, cumbersome and highly paid boards each bank has assembled. These arrangements exist for the benefit of the interlocked directors, while the risks belong to the financial world as a whole, especially the small business operators who have been denied entry to the club.

Table 8, which looks at directorships, carries all the positions held by all of the board members and other senior officers of the Bank of Nova Scotia. There are sixty-one names here, thirty-four of them directors and the rest officers. Among them, they hold 301 directorships, thirty-four within the bank and 267 outside. This list not only sets out the interlocking nature of business in this country, but suggests the range of interests of the bankers. It is an astonishingly narrow list, despite its length. The bankers are into some activities outside the world of business and finance – charities, university boards, good works – but very few. There are no ballet buffs here, no one heading the Lily Society or high up in UNICEF. No one from the consumer groups, co-ops, farm bodies, tenant associations, small business associations, student groups, arts bodies – those who represent the people who have been bearing the brunt of bank policies over the past decade. There isn't a recognizable nationalist here, either, nor anyone in a position to explain the regional rage in western Canada to the thinkers at head office. No boats are rocked. Then, just run your eye down the outside of the list, where the names stand out: two lords, one baronet, one woman, and one name, Martinez, that sounds faintly foreign. Overwhelmingly, these people, the overlords of finance, are male, Anglo-Saxon – with a small sprinkling of French Canadians for flavour. They live in Toronto or Montreal, with some exceptions, and they resemble a cross-section of Canada about as much as Mackenzie King resembled King Kong. I chose this bank to list because it is typical; all the others look the same.

Banks are not parliaments, and it is unreasonable to expect them to load up with women, consumers, and representatives of other ethnic groups than the two mainstreams of Canada's past. However, it is not unreasonable to expect the people who hold our financial destiny in their hands to make some attempt to listen to other voices. Again, when I put this to a bank director, he replied, after some embarrassed shuffling of papers, that while the banks do not represent all Canadians, by any means, they are open to a wide variety of views. "We listen," he said. The fact that there is no one named Olesewisc on the board doesn't mean that Ukrainians are treated as second-class citizens. "They don't have to be on the board to talk to the bank." If that is so, then the whole rationale for massive, inbred bank boards falls to the ground.

In fact, it is not so. Directors are chosen to serve the needs and pursue the interests of that narrow band of brothers, the boys in the bank.

9
The
Boys In The
Bank

The Chairman: And you want to be in on that — the consumer?

Sen. Salter Hayden, *February 7, 1979*

You can't blame Sen. Hayden for being upset. Helen Anderson, Co-chairman of the Economic Policy Committee of the Consumers' Association of Canada, had been giving a presentation before the Senate Banking Committee, as it worked its way through a new Bank Act, and she had the nerve, the immortal rind, to suggest not merely that there be some consumers on the boards of Canadian banks, but that they have something to do with the operation of the clearing-house system, through which banks and other deposit-taking institutions exchange cheques and balance their books. Senator Hayden, the white-haired, full-jowled, tough-minded dean of the banking committee, did not slap Mrs. Anderson across the chops, because that is not the way senators behave, but he and the other senators, including former bank director Hartland Molson, managed to bludgeon her arguments to the ground in a series of exchanges highlighted by Sen. Louis P. Beaubien harrumphing, "I never heard such nonsense."

Right on. To have the consumers in on bank business is a monstrous notion, like letting the sheep join the wolf-pack, or rounding up sardines to man a fishing-fleet. Bankers are bankers, and customers are customers, and never the twain shall mingle. (Sen. Molson: "Have the banks' customers asked you to present a brief in their behalf?") Everybody knows what a banker looks like, and it isn't in the least like a consumer. He is of medium height and middle age, sports a three-piece, dark suit, carries an umbrella and wears rubbers, even when the sun is shining, drinks moderately and doesn't fool around. According to Peter Newman, who chums with the breed more than I do, bankers have cottages instead of mistresses. Let us meet some of them. (Bankers, not mistresses.)

William Mulholland is Chairman and Chief Executive Officer of the Bank of Montreal. He is an American citizen — born in Albany, New York, in 1926 — and proud of it. He is white-haired, thick-set, charming and voluble. A reporter who went to interview him for fifteen minutes once stayed two-and-a-half hours and came away captivated. He is a colourful talker. When he took over the bank in 1974, it was in the doldrums, and he turned it into one of the nation's most profitable institutions; he attributes this success to convincing his underlings that "they really weren't Clark Kents, they were Supermen." He also likes to quote a Cossack saying, "Throw your heart over the wall and your horse will follow."[1] The Globe and Mail reporter from whom I borrowed these two quotes described Mulholland in print as "unassuming." He is about as unassuming as Mount St. Helen. A woman who worked with him recalls his reaction when she was putting on a slide presentation and the projector kept jamming — "He threw an apple at me." Not your average banker.

In Montreal, he works out of the bank's cathedral-like premises on St. James St. When he is in Toronto, he works out of the sixty-eighth floor of First Canadian Place, that marble slab on King Street, behind layers of guards who operate the electronic security doors. He is surrounded by quality paintings and objets d'art and served by a valet who brings the coffee in a silver pot. His recreations are "fishing, shooting, riding, and fox hunting."[2] Just one of the boys.

Mulholland came out of the Brinco deal that tapped the power of Churchill Falls in Labrador, in the late 1960s. He was then a partner in Morgan Stanley, the New York financial house, which he joined after a career as a soldier — in World War II — and policeman — working his way through Harvard Business School at the same time. The Brinco deal shows how a bank can get around. The Bank of Montreal, in this instance, acted for, first the Province of

Newfoundland; second, the crown corporation working for the Province of Newfoundland; third, the Province of Quebec; fourth, Quebec-Hydro, which was working the deal with Newfoundland; fifth, Brinco, the private corporation that handled the project; and sixth, then-Premier Joseph Smallwood of Newfoundland, who borrowed money from the bank to buy shares in Brinco. Mulholland played a crucial role in putting together the money package that made the deal work, and required the signature of, among others, the Iron Ore Company of Canada, which was going to buy power.[3] At one point, the Iron Ore Company of Canada was showing no signs of wanting to commit itself to a purchase agreement, necessary to reassure other partners. So Mulholland ordered a printer to produce a final agreement on heavy paper as bait. The Iron Ore Company would see the agreement, note the heavy paper, assume the deal was concluded, and have to decide whether to take it or leave it. While waiting for the printer to produce this document, Mulholland challenged the Iron Ore Company lawyer at billiards in the recreation room of the print shop – he shoots a mean set of billiards. Mulholland won. When the printed document was produced, the Iron Ore Company was convinced this was the last chance to get in on the action, and the deal was concluded.

Mulholland became Brinco President and Chairman of Churchill Falls Corporation in 1969, and, once that project was well-launched, jumped to the Bank of Montreal, with whom he had had so many dealings. He started one rung from the top, as President, but worked his way up to Chairman in 1981. His reign has been marked by controversy and success. Many managers were sacked, many changes were made. Montreal took to computers faster and more thoroughly than the other banks, and is still a leader in this field. From modest earnings in 1974, Mulholland brought the bank to the highest return on equity – the proper measure of banking profits, and the one banks use when boasting, but never when talking about excess profits – of 19.65% at the end of October 1980.[4] A considerable achievement, it put Montreal, at least temporarily, ahead of every other bank in the nation in this measure of profitability. (It was not enough for Mulholland though; he thinks complaints about high bank

profits are nonsense; they aren't high enough to suit him.)
Despite, or perhaps because of, his success, Mulholland is
not popular with his fellow bankers. It's nothing they can
put their finger on; it's just that he's so brash. Being an
American is all right – the banks have never shown the
slightest sympathy for Canadian nationalism – but does
he have to be so American?

I don't know what he earns at the bank, because Canadian
bankers don't have to tell, not even their shareholders –
although American bankers do – but the average of the
top five officers in the bank is $360,083 per annum,[5]
highest in any Canadian bank, so it is safe to assume
Mulholland's pay is somewhere over $400,000 a year.

Mulholland is an interesting man. Which is to say that
he is not a typical Canadian banker. A far better example of
that species is Rowland Frazee.

Frazee, Chairman and Chief Executive Officer of the
Royal Bank, has never worked anywhere but at the Royal.
He is sixty-one years old. He is a man of medium height
and regular features, with a high forehead unencumbered
by hair. He wears glasses with dark, heavy plastic frames,
and, much of the time, a winning smile. The New York
Times once described him as "outspoken," but they must
have had a microphone hidden in one of his two executive
washrooms (one in Montreal, one in Toronto), because
his steady, pleasant voice produces an almost unending
stream of unexceptional prose and unexceptional ideas.
He is against inflation, untidy dress, nonconformity and
government interference; he is for team play. He says
things like "Everything in economic history suggests that
inflation is as great a threat to the social and economic
health of a country as a war," a statement that suggests he
hasn't read much history, economic or military. I guess the
real upset in Japan was the way the yen went crazy after
they dropped that bomb. Frazee radiates decency, durability,
and dullness – not bad things for a banker – and he is
regarded by those who work with him as "a fine man." I
asked one man who had been at the Royal for more than
two decades, But What Is He Really Like? "I haven't the
foggiest," he said. He thought awhile and then added, "He
has always been friendly to me." He thought some more
and said, "I've never seen him with his tie undone." With
this kind of piercing stuff on hand, it was only natural that

I should ask Frazee about the dress of bankers. He said that it was "stuff and nonsense" to imply that all bankers wore dark, three-piece suits — but they certainly should wear suits. And he allowed that he would be "pretty upset" if he walked into a Royal branch and found a man there not wearing a tie.

Rowland Frazee was born in St. Stephen, New Brunswick, where his father was a bank manager for the Royal. So was his uncle. He was a good student, and played hockey (defence) for a local team, which is where he says he learned about team-work. The lesson certainly sank in; when I asked him the qualities required to be a successful banker, he put "ability to work with others" and "willingness to follow rules" and "fitting in" at the top of the list, followed by "liking people." How about being smart? Well, yes, he said, that was nice, too, although he made it clear that a man can be too smart for his own good.

In 1939, when he was eighteen,[6] Frazee joined the hometown branch of the Royal Bank, and worked there for two years, until he enlisted in the army, which increased his "appreciation that you can't do everything yourself." He saw active service in the infantry, and when the war was over, came home, took a commerce degree, and re-joined the Royal. He thought he would do well in business, but "I never really wanted to start an enterprise of my own."

"Some people," he says, "are never happy in a large corporation, where you have to go by the book. I was. There is red tape, certainly, and sometimes it can be pretty darn frustrating, but there is usually a reason for these things, and if you are not willing to go along, well, banking is not for you." Frazee always got along, and trudged steadily up the corporate ladder — 1955, Inspector, in Halifax; 1962, regional supervisor; 1972, Vice President; 1979, President; 1981, Chairman.[7]

His chief accomplishments as head of the bank have been to set up a number of committees to share responsibility — his predecessor, Earle McLaughlin tended towards the autocratic — and to push the bank into international operations. Now there is a ten-man management committee to oversee Royal's field operations, and a four-man strategic committee for long-term planning, on top of all the other regional and national and operational committees.[8] Frazee has offices in both Montreal — the Place Ville Marie — and Toronto — a downtown tower with gold-leaf in the windows — and he has a complete set of duplicate files in each office. He also travels widely, as do all of the top Canadian bankers, visiting the far-flung empire, which spanned forty-five nations at last count. But his visits are supervisory and symbolic; he doesn't go chasing around the world making deals and scratching down the details on the back of an envelope. After a Frazee trip to the southern United States, where the bank is expanding rapidly, a puzzled Canadian posted down there reported, "Frankly, I don't know what he was here for. Just passing by, I think. It was sort of like a Royal Visit, except there was no kid with a bouquet."

Another banker, who has been with Royal only a few years less than Frazee, says, "What you have to remember is that Canadian banks are run by guys who came out of Brantford, Ontario and St. Stephen, New Brunswick, and Medicine Hat, Alberta, and got to the top, not by doing anything right, but by never doing anything wrong. They took the boys out of the smalltowns, but not the smalltowns out of the boys."

I put it to Frazee that we were moving into a new world of banking, and that a new kind of banker was emerging — smart, highly educated, skilled in disciplines other than banking, such as economics and computer-science, the kind of mover who might work for Canada Packers one year, and the Royal the next and the Bank of Nova Scotia after that. I had been reading the Financial Post, which is always finding new breeds of executive. Frazee thought I was daffy, although he was too polite to say so. "It is true we are hiring more specialists, computer experts, people like that, but mostly to work as specialists. I imagine that the qualities that help to produce top bankers will continue to be the same." Loyalty, in a word.

Loyalty, which is another way of putting all the stuff about team-work and getting along ("conformity" is yet another way to put it, but Frazee prefers loyalty), is the key. Bankers actually say things like "Here on the T-D team," and "It's a privilege to work for the Bank of Nova Scotia." They guide their conduct by the notion that, like Frazee, they expect to spend their entire lives working for the same corporation. Japan, with its corporate paternalism, is the Canadian banking system writ large. The banker who flirts with another bank is not merely frowned upon – he may be turned out. The loyalty tends to be one-way. John M. McIntyre worked for the Royal Bank for twenty-five years, and wound up as a regional representative in Houston, Texas, where his desk was graced by a pen-set inscribed, "Galt, 1966-69," marking three years of service as an assistant manager there. In 1980, the Royal proposed to post him to San Francisco, without a word of consultation. He didn't want to go. "House prices were crazy in San Francisco, I had kids in school – I asked the bank to reconsider." He also went out looking for another job, and landed one, a better job, with Barclay's Bank, also in Houston. "When I sent in my resignation, I got a phone call that said, 'Fine.' That was it. Nobody called me up to Montreal to find out why I was leaving. Two other senior people took jobs outside at the same time. Nobody called them, either. You could be one of Rollie Frazee's moulded boys or you could get out. They didn't want any back-chat ... I had been working for the same people for twenty-five years, and they didn't give a shit when I left. After twenty-five years, they should give a shit."

McIntyre doesn't agree with Frazee that bankers will be bankers forever. He thinks the loyalty-bond will weaken as time goes by, and that moving to other banks will be a normal occurrence during a banker's career, and not a mortal sin. When I put this to Frazee, he was not impressed.

A Social Asset

Frazee knows, and accepts, that women are playing an increasingly important role in banking, but when I asked him about the subject, he assumed I must be talking about bankers' wives, not female bankers. "She plays a very important role," he said. "There is no doubt the job involves social activity, and the wife can be a very important part of that activity. I have no doubt my own wife has been a tremendous asset to me in a business sense."

Actually, a certain amount of sexual liberation has begun to peek in at the door of banking, in practice, if not in theory. The banks have advanced to about where the real world was in 1955. A banker today can have a divorce – which was unheard of a few years ago. Bankers no

longer have to go to the manager for permission to marry
— as Frazee did — and there is even some room for a
certain amount of kinkiness, as long as the word doesn't
get out. In this line, my favourite story concerns a
middle-executive with one of the major banks who appeared to have all the attributes of a banker until the
unhappy day when his wife came home and found him
dressed in her clothes. She ratted on him to the bank,
which worried and fussed and then solved the whole issue
by making him into a consultant. He is performing essentially the same job he had before, but if he ever gets
publicly nailed as a transvestite, well, he's not one of ours,
is he? Very civilized.

There can be few people in the nation with a better
opportunity to influence the direction of economic policy
than the head of the country's largest bank, but no one
could accuse Frazee of exploiting his position. His major
economic speeches consist of repetitions of exactly the
same nostrums that issue from the mouths of all the other
boys in the bank. He wants lower spending by governments, lower taxes, and a tight lid on the money-supply.
His loyalty to the status-quo is almost as strong as his
loyalty to the Royal, and if you say that it is easy to want
things to stay the way they are when you have $400,000 a
year, two offices and a chauffeur, you do him an injustice.
Frazee is sincere. He is not, however, deep. I asked him
whether he supported the policy the Bank of Canada has
been following, in curbing the money supply and using
high interest rates to combat inflation. He certainly did;
his only regret was that the Bank of Canada's program was
not pursued more vigorously, and that government spending was not being curbed more rigorously. When I asked
him why, he looked a little startled — dumb question —
and then replied, carefully, "In these matters, Mr. Stewart, I
tend to support the conventional wisdom. I believe there
is a trade-off between unemployment and inflation, and
that we must control inflation, even if it means increasing
unemployment, although it is regrettable that those at the
bottom end of the ladder are the ones who suffer."

I said, "Yes, but we've been following the same policy for
six years, and it hasn't done a damn bit of good. Inflation is
higher than ever." He looked even more startled, and
thought a bit while I got the old pen down to the notebook.

Here, I thought, comes the real goods, Canada's top banker on the nation's top economic problem.

"Yes," he said after a minute. "Funny, isn't it?" He was able to expand on that a little – "You are certainly well-advised to avoid increasing the money supply. But the amazing thing is that we don't seem to be solving inflation. I wonder if we are not looking these days to some new dimension in economic thinking."

Well, there it is, folks. You may have just lost your house or your cattle or your job to a giant jump in interest rates, but it doesn't follow that the giant jump is going to do any good. It's a sort of rain-dance. "All I can go along with, I have to admit, is the conventional wisdom that you've got to suffer a bit if you're going to control inflation."

Suffering is Good

Suffering is good. They used to chuck a virgin over a cliff on these occasions, when they could find one; it was more popular with the spectators than with the virgins, but it gave the priests something to do. Frazee is one of our priests – none higher. He is in the happy position that the treatment he prescribes, high interest rates, brings in more and more and more profits to the bank. But I believe he is perfectly sincere. He isn't going to suffer, but he does believe in suffering. In fact, by a happy coincidence, none of the boys in the bank is going to suffer. It's just the way things work out; for every bum chucked out onto the street, another filet mignon for the high-priests. This isn't economics, it's theology.

Between Montreal's Mulholland and Royal's Frazee stand the Chairmen of the other three top banks – Cedric Ritchie of the Nova Scotia, Russell Harrison of the Commerce and Richard Thomson of Toronto-Dominion. But really they don't stand between Mulholland and Frazee, they are solidly grouped down at the Frazee end of the room. They are remarkably alike.

Cedric Ritchie was born in Upper Kent, New Brunswick, in 1927, graduated from Bath, New Brunswick, High School in 1945, and joined the Bank of Nova Scotia that same year.[9] He was eighteen. After serving in a number of Maritime branches, he joined the Inspection staff (like Frazee) and began his upward climb: Assistant Inspector,

1954; Accountant, 1956; Inspector, Credit Department, 1959; Assistant Manager, 1959; Chief Accountant, 1960; Assistant General Manager, Administration, 1963; Joint General Manager, 1970; President, 1972; and finally, Chairman in 1974. A mere twenty-eight years after signing on at the bank, he was its top officer, earning something over $300,000 annually in salary. Directors' fees from thirteen outside posts are, of course, extra. He has been able to get a bank loan — at his salary, he is a good risk — and had as much as $670,265 outstanding during 1980, at an average interest rate of 14.33%.[10]

Russell Harrison was born at Grandview, Manitoba in 1921, and joined the Bank of Commerce in 1945, after serving in World War II with the First Canadian Parachute Battalion.[11] He, like Ritchie, Frazee and Thomson, has never worked anywhere but at the bank he now heads. Harrison started as a teller in Winnipeg, then was moved to Hamilton, Ontario, to begin the upward clamber: Assistant Manager, Inspector, Chief Inspector, Regional Superintendent, Assistant General Manager, Executive Vice President, Chief General Manager, President and Chairman. He attained the bank's top rung in 1976, thirty-one years after he began. He earns somewhere around $300,000 a year in salary, in addition to directors' fees from a dozen outside firms.

Then there is Richard Thomson, whose career does contain some variations from those of the rest of the bunch. For one thing, he was born in a city, Winnipeg, and for another, he has more than a high-school education. He took an engineering degree at the University of Toronto, an MBA at Harvard and the Fellows' Course in Banking at Queen's University. In consequence, he has virtually rocketed through the ranks to his present eminence. He was hired by the Toronto-Dominion (or, as his official biography puts it, "entered service of Toronto Dominion";[12] if you want to know the difference between being hired and entering service, I would put it at about $5 a week) a scant quarter-century ago, in 1957, when he was twenty-four. He went through the usual clutch of posts — Senior Assistant Manager, Assistant to the President, Assistant General Manager, Chief General Manager, Vice President, General Manager, President and finally, Chairman, in 1977, twenty years after joining the bank. A damned upstart, if you ask me. His pay, too, runs around $300,000 a year, and he had a loan of $353,320 outstanding at his bank in 1980, on which he·paid an average interest rate of 7.42%.[13]

Common Bonds

Among them, the five Chairmen of Canada's top banks have accumulated 146 years of service, even allowing for that whipper-snapper, Mulholland, who has put in a mere eight. Four of the five have never worked anywhere but at the bank they now head. Three of the five have no more than a high-school education. None has ever had to run a business on his own, or meet a payroll, or struggle with a farm mortgage. They are able to get loans at or below prime. At the Royal, such loans are interest-free for the first three years. (Frazee does not have any such loans outstanding, but other chief officers in his bank do.) But these men share more than chauffered limousines, free shoe-shines and the capacity to exhort the lower ranks to pull in their belts. They share a common outlook, born of their common experience in finance, their common bonds, their shared comradeship with like-minded men. Mulholland and Frazee are the Ying and Yang of Canadian banking. Their methods of operation, their personalities, their nationalities, even, are different. But there is not a single point of importance in the field of economics on which they differ. Both think the banks should be making more profits, both think controlling inflation is the nation's first order of business, both resent government interference, and are filled with scorn for government regulations and red tape – although not for the regulations and red-tape that govern their own empires. Both have an international outlook, in the double sense that they think foreign capital should be allowed to enter Canada free of interference and Canadian capital should be allowed to roam abroad free of interference. Both are strong and instinctive supporters of free-enterprise capitalism functioning under the umbrella of government protection, although neither of them would put it that way. Both believe in competition, and operate in an oligopoly. In short, despite their obvious differences in style – Mulholland brash and canny, Frazee quietly aggressive – there is not ten cents' worth of difference between the two men, or between them and the other chief executives of Canada's major banks, on the major policy matters of Canadian economics.

Because we are used to such sameness in our bankers, this remarkable situation has disappeared from our notice, like the Purloined Letter, hiding in plain sight. But if you think about it for a minute, it carries some implications for us. Publishers do not think alike; nor do doctors, poets, engineers, lawyers, musicians, pedlars, prostitutes, or bicycle repairmen. Economists are always shrieking at each other, and politicians do it for a living. Teachers are fractious and divided, street-car conductors go off in as many directions as their trolleys, and the man who can get ten journalists to agree on anything must be armed with a golden tongue or a loaded pistol, or both. But here, at the heart of the economy, squats a band of brothers, said to be at daggers drawn, who agree on virtually every matter of policy touching their own line of work. Remarkable. One of the few occasions on which any major bank took a stance that differed from any of the others was during the revision of the Bank Act, when the Toronto-Dominion bank, under Richard Thomson, refused to support a common stand in favour of forcing foreign banks operating in Canada to domesticate themselves, become Canadian banks, and hold reserves. "Our feeling," the bank said in its brief to the Senate Banking Committee, "is that it would be premature . . . to introduce into the bill positive legislation with respect to permitting access to a non-resident bank." Translation: Keep the bums out. T-D stuck to its heresy throughout the legislative process, but that is one of the rare occasions on which there has been any notable difference between the banks in matters of public policy.

Their forecasts differ, and minor policy squabbles break out, but in the main, whatever one major banker says on grave matters like the importance of curbing governments, the need to control inflation and the regrettable but absolute necessity of whacking up interest rates again could be inserted into the speech of any other major banker, and no questions asked.

The tight-knit circles represented by the boards of directors of the banks are both a reflection and a reinforcement of this phenomenon. Key elements of Canadian economic policy over the past four decades, from an inability to meet the problems of regional disparity, to a revulsion for economic nationalism, to a reluctance to finance Canadian ventures, can all be traced to the homogeneity of the banks. Send in the clones. Add to this startling sameness the wide reach of these crucial financial institutions, with their interlocked directorates, and Canada's dismal economic performance becomes, not a saddening aberration, but an inevitable conclusion.

And at the heart of this single-minded process, or if you prefer a stronger metaphor, at the centre of the web of the Canadian banking industry, sits the Big Daddy of the system, the Bank of Canada, Gerald Bouey, Prop.

10
Big
Daddy

"I had little aptitude for farming, being accident-prone with both horses and tractors. My very last attempt occurred ... when I volunteered to help my father-in-law on his farm near Moosomin, Saskatchewan and my first act on the tractor was to run him over with the harrows."

Gerald Bouey, *Brokenshell, Sask., 1980*

The Governor of the Bank of Canada, Gerald Bouey, is an austere, stern-looking man of medium build and plain features. At sixty-two, he looks his age; the straight hair is thinning on top and whitening along his modishly lengthy sideburns. Worry has etched lines down beside the mouth, and over the bushy eyebrows. He wears heavy, plastic-framed glasses, behind which lurk eyes that look mildly puzzled and mostly sad, the eyes of a man who has been responsible for Canadian monetary policy over the past nine years, a period in which it has been pretty badly screwed up. These sad eyes seem to ask: What went wrong? He is an intelligent man, a man of goodwill and excellent training; he is doing his best, following the rules of economics as they have been handed down, and his actions have had the sturdy support of those clever people over at the major banks. He is following the prescription dispensed by the United States Federal Reserve Board. But nothing seems to go right. His name, once whispered with hushed reverence in the Rideau Club (before it burned down), is bandied with scorn along the concession roads and in the living rooms of ordinary Canadians. Eugene Whelan, the Minister of Agriculture, mounts his soapbox to shout "Phooey on Bouey."[1] Despite his fine intentions, his hard work, his devotion to duty, he is not admired, outside banking circles.

That is because Gerald Bouey is still running people over with harrows, only now the teeth are being dragged by monetary policy rather than a tractor. In theory, final responsibility for that policy rests with the government of Canada, but as so often happens in this country, the theories of political science and the realities of power do not coincide. The government has been following the Bank's policy, whatever the textbooks say. A man who has worked in the Department of Finance for many years describes the relationship this way: "The Governor meets with the Minister of Finance, and tells him, respectably, what he should do. The Minister then agrees. The only time I ever saw a minister even bargain with the Governor was Jean Chretien, when he had the portfolio. The Governor would say, 'Mr. Minister, for the reasons outlined in my memorandum, I am proposing to raise interest rates by one per cent.' Chretien would say, 'Half a per cent.' The Governor would say, 'You will see from my memorandum that the required increase is a full per cent.' And Chretien would say, 'Half a per cent.' So it would go up half a per cent, but that was Chretien horse-trading. With every other minister, it was just, 'As you say, Governor.'"

What is a matter for judicious chevying in Ottawa assumes more significance away from the national capital, and the comfortable surroundings of the finance minister's office, or the green marble towers on Sparks Street that house the Bank of Canada. The rate at which money is bought and sold affects the price of everything else; it can spell prosperity or ruin. For a retired executive nestling atop a few hundred thousand dollars in Guaranteed Investment Certificates, the upward levering of rates brings nothing but blessings. A man with $100,000 in bank term deposits in September 1980, stood to make $10,250 on it; a year later, he made $18,000 on the same money, without stirring a finger. For a pork-producer who was persuaded by his bank manager to take out a larger loan to expand his operation, things worked out rather differently. In his case, borrowing on a demand note at one per cent above the prime interest rate, with the interest shifting every month as the prime changed, the $100,000 loan that cost him $13,250 in September 1980, was costing him $23,750 a year later. The sensible business decision of 1980 became the road to bankruptcy, through no fault of his own.

Both these men owe their fortune, good and ill, to the Bank of Canada, its Governor, Gerald Bouey, and to the untidy compromise that separates the Bank from political responsibility. To understand why, it is necessary to know something about the Bank of Canada, where it came from, and how it works.

The Bank of Canada is Born

It was clear, even at Confederation, that Canada, like every other nation, had to have some method of controlling the creation of money. Banks were able to issue notes; if there were no limit to the process, a lot of bad money would be fed into the system and, following Gresham's Law, drive out the good. Accordingly, the Dominion Notes Act of 1870 and the first Bank Act, in 1871, provided a control, of sorts.[2] The government was given the right to issue Dominion of Canada notes, in small denominations, backed, partially, by gold. That is, you could take a Dominion note to a bank and ask for its equivalent in gold, although if everyone did that, it would have been embarrassing, because there wasn't as much gold as there were notes. The banks could also issue notes, in larger denominations — over $5 — but were required to hold reserves against this issue, one-half of which was to be in Dominion notes. Up until this time, such control as existed was based on a requirement that the banks limit the creation of notes to a shifting proportion of paid-up capital. It didn't work. Under the new system, the supply of money would be regulated by the supply of gold. The amount of gold held by the government determined what it could create in the way of Dominion notes, the supply of Dominion notes determined the level of reserves, and the reserve-level determined how much money the banks could create. To enlarge its operations, a bank would buy gold, and give it to the government in return for Dominion notes, which could then support the expansion of its own deposits, several times over. While both Dominion and bank notes were legal tender, in practice the Dominion notes were not much used by the public; their role was to be held by the banks.

This method stayed in place until the beginning of

World War I, when it became apparent that, to fight the war, much more money was going to be required than could be justified by its backing with gold. This is one of the advantages of the mythology of money; a small adjustment in the myth permits a large adjustment in reality. The myth held that money was good because it could be traded for gold, which had real value. The Finance Act of 1914 knocked that one into the ashcan; notes were no longer convertible into gold specie, and the money continued to work just as well as ever.[3] Had this change not been made, there was reason to fear a run on the gold supply by people anxious to convert notes to specie because they were shrewd enough to know that with war comes inflation, and gold would be worth more than paper. To replace gold as the base of the money supply, the Minister of Finance was authorized to issue Dominion notes in return for "acceptable security" provided by the banks — bonds, for example, or government notes held by the bank. To issue more money, the bank had to turn over more securities, and the rest of the system worked as before. The trouble with this system was that the definition of what passed for "acceptable security" became wider and wider, and one study of the period notes that between 1914 and 1934 no bank "was ever denied Dominion notes on the posting of securities." This account continues, with guarded understatement, "The easy access to Dominion notes gave the monetary base unstable characteristics."[4] Which is like saying, "The banana peel on the sidewalk gave the fat gentleman unstable characteristics." The rapid multiplication of the money supply paved the way for the frenzy of the middle and late 1920s in Canada as elsewhere, and did its bit to contribute to the Great Crash of 1929 and the Great Depression.

A return to the gold standard on July 1, 1926 did not right matters, although in theory it should have. Canada was in one of its periodic balance of payments problems. We were spending more abroad than we were earning. Gold and foreign exchange reserves were required to balance our books internationally, and that led to a demand for gold. In theory, the banks should have had to cut back on the creation of money, because the gold supply was down. In fact, what they did was to borrow

Dominion notes from the government, convert them into gold and use that. They were able to meet the demand for gold, and for foreign exchange, and to continue increasing their deposit-base, by transferring the gold drain from themselves to the government. The obvious solution, to refuse advances to the banks, was not applied;[5] the Department of Finance did not want to spoil what was becoming everybody's party as spiralling bank loans financed the giddy whirl of stock-market advances.

By early 1929, the gold standard meant very little, and the government unofficially terminated the convertibility of Dominion notes to preserve its gold holdings. (This abandonment was made official in 1931.) When the Great Depression broke out in late 1929, the balance of payments problem grew worse; now gold and foreign exchange were being drained out of the banks and out of the country. However, money to replace these funds – not in gold, of course, but in paper – began to flow into the banks as Canadian firms facing harder times began to retire their bank loans; this put more cash into the bank vaults. The proper course now was for the banks to expand their lending to keep money circulating, but they did nothing of the sort. In response to then-current economic wisdom, they used the cash to reduce their advances from the Department of Finance, and the depression deepened.[6] Their action was not inspired by a wish to save interest charges, it was merely a reflex response based on the notion that debt was wicked and discharging debt good, no matter what was happening in the economy.

By 1932, a message was beginning to penetrate that there was a connection between the contraction of the money supply and the continuing depression, and the government forced the banks to borrow $35 million in Dominion notes. At the same time, the banks loaned the government another $35 million by purchasing an issue of Treasury bills, and used the bills to finance more Dominion notes. But, instead of loaning this money to individuals and businesses, the banks used it, once more, to pay off advances – it was the properly conservative thing to do – so the money simply circled out of one hole in the Treasury, fluttered around, and disappeared into another.

There had been some earlier agitation for the establishment of a central bank in Canada, which the banks were able to fight off. As the depression tightened its grip, this agitation returned, and a Royal Commission was appointed to investigate the issue. That commission reported, in November 1933, recommending the creation of a central bank with the sole right to issue money. It was to be privately owned, to act as the government's banker and to manage the public debt. Prime Minister R. B. Bennett had long since come to the conclusion that Canada needed a central bank, and the Royal Commission's recommendations were turned into law in what amounted to spectacular haste, for Canada. The bill incorporating the Bank of Canada was passed in 1934, and the Bank opened its doors on March 11, 1935. It was privately owned – and the initial share offering, of $5,000,000, was over-subscribed;[7] that is, there were more bids for the stock at the opening price than there were shares available. Despite this private ownership, the first board of directors was appointed directly by the government, not the shareholders. Creation of the Bank of Canada did not save the Bennett government from defeat by Mackenzie King's Liberals in the 1935 general election. The Liberals had argued, when the Bank of Canada Act was under debate, that the institution should be government-owned, and in 1938 the private shareholders were bought out, and the Bank became what it is today, a federally owned institution.

The Bank was given the usual powers and responsibilities of a central bank, and its major tasks are set down straightforwardly in the Bank of Canada Act. It is to "regulate credit and currency in the best interests of the economic life of the nation, to control and protect the external value of the national monetary unit and to mitigate by its influence fluctuations in the general level of production, trade, prices and employment, so far as may be possible within the scope of monetary action, and generally to promote the economic and financial welfare of the Dominion."

In short, the Bank of Canada was charged with controlling the nation's monetary policy, but was given no control over fiscal (tax) policy. It was also supposed to defend the dollar and smooth out bumps in the economy. It would issue bank notes, and over a fifteen-year period, its bank notes would become the sole legal tender – it took that long to retire all the notes in circulation that were issued by individual banks, which were simply replaced as they wore out, by Bank of Canada notes, signed by the Governor and Deputy Governor. The Bank would act as the government's banker, and manage the public debt. It would hold the reserves which the Bank Act required the chartered banks to deposit with it, monitor the level of those reserves, and protect Canada's foreign exchange. It would deal with other central banks. It would provide research and advice.

It has been performing all of these functions, except its primary one, controlling the money supply, with comparative smoothness and efficiency ever since it opened its doors. The Bank's two thousand employees operate through six major departments – Banking Operations, Public Debt, International, Financial Analysis, Research and Securities.[8]

The largest department, Banking Operations, contains 550 workers, and its main job is circulating and withdrawing currency. During 1980, the Bank issued 600 million bills, which were printed in large sheets by two private companies, British American Bank Note Company and Canadian Bank Note Company. The sheets are delivered in bulk to the Bank, where they are cut into individual bills and dispatched to the regional offices for distribution to the commercial banks, which can order them on a twenty-four-hour delivery basis. In return, used bills, 570 million of them in 1980, are sent back to the Bank as they are taken out of circulation. These bills are bundled, punched through, and, after careful counting, either shredded or burned in one of the Bank of Canada's incinerators. The burning of bills is an awesome process, and requires the presence of two senior officials, with dual keys to open the vaults where the incinerators are kept. The ashes are raked, repeatedly, to make sure nothing escapes the flames. The bank won't say what it does with shredded bills; in the United States, they are used for packing. The Banking Operations division is also responsible for distributing government bonds and Treasury bills to various banks and agencies.

Other Bank Divisions

The Public Debt Department is the second largest, with 400 employees, and its job is to serve as an agent for the federal government. About eight per cent of its effort goes to handling Canada Savings Bonds, and the rest is devoted to handling other government bonds and Treasury bills. These are the three instruments through which the government borrows money, as opposed to the Department of Revenue, where they collect the stuff by way of taxes. Keeping track of 1.6 million Canada Savings Bond applications, and discharging the bonds when they are cashed, keeps the department busy.

The Monetary and Financial Analysis Department has two major functions. One is to monitor the balance sheets of the banks and to prepare the weekly financial statistics on which much of the financial community depends for information. Another is to analyse and forecast financial developments, and to suggest alternative actions to offset the problems that turn up in the forecasts.

The Research Department controls the statistical model of the Canadian economy that the Bank and the government use as a basis for action. Blocks of information on everything from family formation to energy-use are fed into a computer, which produces a version of the economy which can be manipulated in an attempt to predict the future. Jack up oil prices, and what happens to housing? That's the sort of problem the thinkers in this department are always wrestling with – not very successfully – in between turning out official studies and papers on such subjects as productivity, wage rates and unemployment.

The International Department is the instrument through which the Bank protects the integrity (or otherwise) of the Canadian dollar. It runs our foreign exchange policy, although the substance of that policy is supposed to be laid down by the Department of Finance and the cabinet. I say "supposed to be," because foreign-exchange and money supply policies are inextricably woven together. There is a trading room in the Bank of Canada's Ottawa headquarters and another in the Toronto agency, both connected to the foreign exchange brokerage office run by the Canadian Bankers' Association. Here, Bank traders buy and sell foreign currencies to maintain, or attempt to maintain, control over the value of the Canadian dollar. "Orderly markets" is the watchword here; the Bank likes to see international financial arrangements run smoothly, so there is no scrambling around to defend a dying dollar. There are two ways in which the Bank can influence the value of our currency. If Canada is spending more abroad than it is taking in, then there will be more Canadian dollars on the international market. That is because when a Canadian manufacturer buys, say, a shipment of American television sets, he buys American dollars with Canadian ones to complete the transaction. If that is happening more often and in larger amounts than Americans are buying Canadian dollars to import our goods, there will be more Canadian dollars and fewer U.S. ones in the foreign exchange market. The value of those dollars will go down, in relation to the key U.S. currency. If the Bank intervenes by selling U.S. dollars from its reserve holdings, the Canadian dollar will rise, proportionately, because there are now more U.S. dollars on the market.

The same process works in reverse if the Canadian dollar begins to rise too quickly. By selling dollars from its reserve, the Bank increases the number of Canadian dollars in circulation in the foreign exchange market, and dampens the price.

The value of the dollar affects the level of prices inside Canada. The higher it is, the less imports cost Canadians – because it takes fewer Canadian dollars to buy them. But the greater the value of the Canadian dollar, the more our exports cost foreigners – because it takes more foreign dollars to buy them. Setting the value of the dollar is crucial, and the Bank's International Department keeps busy controlling the range of dollar trading. If the foreign exchange traders get it into their heads that the dollar is going to drop – or rise – their speculations are enough to bring the change about. That is why, on these occasions, our finance ministers step into the breach to announce that the dollar will be defended to the last drop of blood. Words are cheaper than dollars. If traders can be convinced that Canada has the money and the will to defend its currency, they will give up and go away to speculate on the Polish kopek, or the German mark.

Whenever one of these periodic spells comes over the market – when the Bank of Canada issues new figures, for example, showing an increase in the Canadian deficit with the United States – the politicians spring into action, and so does the Bank. On occasion, we have had to take out a line of credit with the International Monetary Fund, in U.S. dollars, to show that we mean business. We don't use the money, usually, we just brandish it to prove our determination.

The speculators in the foreign exchange markets include private individuals, corporations, governments and commercial banks. Money can be made on variations of fractions of a cent if large enough quantities are involved, even if the money is bought and sold again within a few hours. Since the banks are constantly buying and selling foreign funds to fulfill transactions both here and abroad, they all run trading departments for this purpose, and to make money on their trade. It is a nerve-wracking business, and the money traders are invariably young, with nerves of steel. They don't usually last long. Left to themselves, these traders might make a lot of money but leave the market in chaos; it is the interventions of the central banks of all the trading nations, buying and selling, that maintains the orderly market necessary to sustain commercial enterprise.

This is a crude, but direct, way to control the dollar. Another way is to manipulate interest rates, and that is the way we are using most often these days. It comes under the control of the Securities Department of the Bank.

This department conducts the open market operations of the Bank, selling and buying Treasury bills and bonds from its portfolio as required to influence their price, and through that price, interest rates in Canada.

The Bank wants to control interest rates because they rise and fall with foreign exchange rates. If Canadian interest rates are high, foreign money will be attracted here to take advantage of the high rates. Thus, an American investor, peering across the border, will see that he can make more money by buying Canadian bonds, for example, than American ones. He will instruct his broker accordingly, and the broker will make the purchase. To do that, U.S. dollars will be converted into Canadian ones. Now there are more American dollars on the market and fewer Canadian ones, and the value of the Canadian dollar will go up. If Canadian interest rates are lower than those in the United States, the money-flow will go back the other way, and the Canadian dollar will decline in value. That, in brief, is what all the fuss is about. To defend the value of the Canadian dollar, our interest rates must be held above those in the United States.

And why must we defend the value of the Canadian dollar? According to the Bank of Canada, because a lower Canadian dollar will contribute more to inflation than high interest rates. Bouey has been asked about this dozens of times, and it is worth reporting the full explanation he gave to the House of Commons Committee on Finance, Trade and Economic Affairs on October 25, 1979:

"Another question that frequently arises is how can a rise in interest rates help bring down the rate of inflation when the high rates themselves obviously add to the cost of doing business? The answer is that this effect is only part of the total effect on the rise in interest rates on costs and prices in Canada and by no means the most important factor. A rise in interest rates discourages borrowing and spending. This brake on spending causes markets for goods and services to be less buoyant and more competitive than they would otherwise be, with the result that businesses find it more difficult to raise their prices. The rise in interest rates thus increases the pressure on business to hold down other costs of production, including labour costs, as well as its profit margin and prices. These same influences should also operate in turn in the direction of causing employees to moderate their demands for higher money incomes. In addition, the rise in interest rates helps to maintain the foreign exchange value of the Canadian dollar, and therefore helps to protect business firms and others from the higher prices and costs of internationally traded goods that would result from a lower exchange rate."

Have you got all that? I certainly didn't, the first time through. What Bouey is saying is that even though higher interest rates add to the cost of Canadian goods and services, they bring down prices. That is because such rates will discourage investment, increase competition and (though he doesn't spell this out clearly) cause unemployment. Companies will then bring down their prices to retain their share of the market, and unions will abate their demands and inflation will disappear.

The only problem with this theory is that it doesn't work. The lion's share of the economy is managed, and has for years been managed, by groups that can protect themselves from the ravages of inflation. Governments needn't worry about rising prices, because they hold the perfect weapon – taxes – with which to meet them. What is more, a government can issue bonds, and use the proceeds to buy the higher-priced goods and services it requires. The printing press is all a government needs to keep the wolf at bay. In the private sector, dominant firms are able to control their own markets, because there are very few of them, and not much competition. When interest rates rise, these firms meet the problem by generating their own funds internally, borrowing from a foreign parent – in the case of the American subsidiaries who dominate Canadian manufacturing – or passing on the increased costs by raising their prices.

Unions, in turn, faced with higher prices and higher borrowing costs, demand higher wages with which to meet them. They get them, too. So the higher interest rates, instead of dampening inflation, have fuelled it. The Bank of Canada's solution works on the share of the economy where protection is scanty – small business, farms and non-unionized labour. The high cost of money increases unemployment. But, because it doesn't touch the managed sectors of the economy, the policy produces, simultaneously, inflation and unemployment. In theory, these two should not exist side by side; in fact, they do.

We are paying, through high interest costs, to protect the dollar as a means of controlling inflation; the technique has not worked, and has come under increasingly strong criticism.

My Dollar, Right or Wrong

University of Manitoba economist Ruben Bellan has calculated how much it has cost to support the dollar, working from the year 1975, when Canada officially adopted the Bouey approach. In 1980 we imported $80 billion worth of goods, buying U.S. dollars to pay for them at an average cost of $1.17 Canadian for each dollar in American funds. Had we been able to keep the dollar at the 1975 level – when it took, at one point, only ninety-nine cents to buy a U.S. dollar – our 1980 imports would have cost $67 billion instead of $80 billion. The decline in the dollar cost us $13 billion, which makes it look as if Bouey was right.[9] But hold on a minute. Bellan has also calculated what the rise in interest rates to defend the dollar has cost. Between 1975 and 1980, interest rates went up by 10%, adding $23 billion to mortgages and credit charges alone. The increase in interest rates did not succeed in holding the dollar at its 1975 level; that would have cost even more, but the saving on import costs would have been correspondingly higher. The principle remains the same − it costs almost twice as much, in inflationary terms, to support the dollar through pegging our interest rates to those in the United States as it would be to let the dollar find its own market value, and pay more for imports. "Bouey's remedy," Bellan says, "is doing more inflationary harm than the problem against which it is being applied."[10]

Not convinced? Let's take an example. In 1975, you, as President of Amalgamated Golfcarts, bought $80 worth of parts for golfcarts in the United States. You paid $6.33 in interest charges, at 8%, for the loan to support your purchase. The U.S. dollar at that time cost only ninety-nine cents, so your cost in current dollars for the transaction was $79.20 plus $6.33 interest or $85.53. In 1980, you bought another $80 worth of the same parts. You now paid $93.60 for the U.S. dollars; your total increase in price was $8.07 ($93.60 -85.53). You would be better off with the dollar back at its 1975 level. However, defending the dollar required a jump in interest rates, from 8% to 18%; you were now paying $16.84 in interest charges (18% of $93.60); the $80 worth of parts cost you $93.60 plus $16.84, or $110.44. Raising interest rates to defend the dollar cost you more than the decline in the dollar; with that $16.84 in hand, you could see the dollar go down a long way − a move that would help you sell more golfcarts abroad, incidentally − before that route would become more expensive than the high-interest solution. Of the two charges, the interest rate increase cost you nearly twice what the dollar decline cost. The dollar could have gone down to 75 cents or less without doing anything to your position except to make your foreign sales brighter because your product cost less in foreign funds.

Look at it another way. You are a consumer, with a $100,000 mortgage, and you buy $2,000 worth of imported products from the United States annually. The cost of defending the dollar, which necessitated a 10% increase in interest rates between 1975 and 1980, raised your mortgage interest from $8,000 to $18,000 annually – it cost you $10,000. The cost of an 18% drop in the Canadian dollar over the same period, on your imported goods, was 18% of $2,000 – $360. If interest rates were left to find their own level, and the dollar was allowed to slide even further – as low as, say, sixty cents– you would be paying as much as $800 because of the decline in the dollar's value; but you would still be better off.

The real world is more complex than these examples suggest, but the same rules apply. The argument that we have no choice but to ape American policies in order to defend the dollar is gravely flawed. And the cost of that flaw falls heaviest on those Canadians who don't work for banks or governments or giant corporations, and whose mortgages, businesses and jobs are being sacrificed on behalf of a monetarist crusade.

For that is what it is, a monetarist crusade. Monetarism is the belief that the money supply should be held more or less constant, in relation to productivity, as an economic regulator. Instead of spending more in recessionary times, and cutting back on the money supply in inflationary times, hold the throttle steady, and temporary cycles of inflation and depression will right themselves. The expectation of continued inflation, which is itself the most important contributor to inflation, will fade when consumers, workers and businessmen see that no new dollars will be created to fuel inflation. The monetarist theory came out of the so-called "Chicago school" founded by American economist Milton Friedman. Bouey was not an instant convert but, by 1975, was echoing Friedman. The American told the U.S. Senate Banking Committee in November 1975 that "The ultimate target should be a rate of growth (in the money supply) of roughly three per cent to five per cent a year. That would roughly match the rate of growth of our production potential." Bouey's version, a few weeks later in a speech at Saint John, New Brunswick, went, "If the ultimate goal – the restoration of a completely stable price level, that is, a zero rate of inflation – is to be achieved, this will eventually require the maintenance of an average rate of growth of the money supply no higher than the long-term average rate of growth of production of goods and services in Canada — that is, a rate of about five per cent a year."[11] Same thing.

There are other techniques available to control inflation than tying the Canadian interest rates to American ones. Breaking up the oligopolies that control the market might be worth trying. Replacing the strike with some less brutal instrument for managing labour contracts is a possibility. Wages and price controls, or profit curbs of some sort, get a mention from time to time. There are those who think the trick can be turned simply by curbing government expenditures (I am not among their number, but I'm willing to listen). However — and this is the crucial point — none of these comes under the care and control of the Bank of Canada. Its job, we have already seen, is to control monetary policy. If you own a hammer, nailing things is going to be high on your list of priorities, so it is hardly surprising that the Bank of Canada promotes monetarism.

The Bank's control over the money supply depends on two factors. The first is the moral suasion of the Bank, which is considerable. The Governor meets with the leading bankers, and talks to them on the telephone, and makes speeches which they read and heed. By happy coincidence, he is always saying what they want to hear, but, even if he weren't, they would be impressed, simply because he is the Governor. The second factor is the Bank's grip on the reserve system. The commercial banks are required to keep reserves. The central bank can force these up or down by the simple process of transferring money to and from the banks. They will expand or contract their activities accordingly. It can reinforce this by buying or selling government securities. If it buys such securities from the banks, it transfers money to their reserves, expanding them, and encouraging the banks to lend more. If it sells such securities to the banks, they must transfer the cash, lowering their reserves, and thus their ability to expand.

In addition, if the banks wish to borrow from the central bank, it can control the rate at which it will lend money; the more it costs the banks to borrow, the more they will have to charge — their interest rates go up. The less it costs them, the less they have to charge — their rates go down. Because the banks seldom have to borrow, in point of fact, this technique would not be effective except for the

Bank's moral suasion. The Bank indicates what it wants the commercial banks to do by indicating the rate which it would charge for such money in the event that such loans were made. The banks respond exactly as if they had to make such borrowings, raising or lowering their rates accordingly. This real response to symbolic action is of a piece with the rest of the mythology that governs money.

In the past, the Bank Rate, as this rate of borrowing-or-n ot-borrowing from the central bank came to be called, was allegedly determined by the Minister of Finance. In fact, it wasn't. It was determined by the Governor, who told the Minister what he wanted announced in the House of Commons, and the Minister complied. The forms of democratic action were in place.

However, making unpopular announcements in the House of Commons is not one of the things politicians like to do, and announcements raising interest rates, which seemed to be the invariable custom in recent years, were not popular. In March 1980, a new system was adopted, under which the government succeeded in turning responsibility for the Bank Rate – and thus, for much of Canadian economic policy – over to the Bank of Canada. Now, the Bank Rate is set automatically at one-quarter of one per cent above the average price established on 91-day Treasury bills each week. It works like this:

The government sells Treasury bills, which are interest-bearing IOU's that mature in varying terms, to raise money for its immediate cash requirements. You can buy such bills, if you wish, through a bank or stockbroker, in units of $1,000. They are a good buy – the interest is higher than that on a Guaranteed Investment Certificate. The Bank of Canada acts as the government's agent, and the bills are sold, in blocks of million-dollar amounts, at an auction that takes place in the East Tower of the Bank of Canada building every Thursday afternoon. There is no auctioneer, or banging gavel; instead, senior officials of the Bank feed bids, which have come in by telex, into a computer. If, for example, the Bank of Nova Scotia bid for $100 million worth of 91-day Treasury bills at a rate of 17%, and that was the highest bid, the Bank of Nova Scotia would get $100 million worth at 17%, which it would hold for three months and then cash. If the Bank of Montreal had bid 16.98% for $50 million, it would get the next $50 million, and so on, through all the bidders. At the auction on Thursday, January 14, 1982, the government offered $700 million in 91-day bills, $200' million in 182-day bills and $250 million in 364-day bills.[12] The highest bid for the 91-day bills was $96.513 for every $100, which would produce a return of $14.58% annuallized. The lowest bid was $96.493 − 14.49%. The average was 14.56%. There is nothing very mysterious about the bidding process; everyone knows what the bids were last week, and it is simply a matter of figuring out what they should be this week. To help things along, the Bank of Canada not only tells the banks where it thinks these bids should fall, it buys and sells on its own account to bring the average bid out to where it wants it to be. The banks bid both because the Treasury bills are a sound investment and because the Bank of Canada wishes them to do so. Then, when all the bids are in, the computer works out the average for the 91-day bills; it could just as easily use the 182-day variety, but settled on the shorter term. Then the Bank Rate is set, one-quarter of one per cent above that average, and announced by the Bank of Canada at 2:10 p.m. On the January 14, 1982 bills mentioned above, the average was 14.56%, so the bank rate became 14.81. It's as simple as that.

The Bank Rate − coming back to moral suasion − is the central bank's signal to the bankers as to where it wants all interest rates; if it is up, not only will the Prime Rate go up, so will mortgages, and everything else. If it goes down, then the other rates should go down, too. In fact, the banks tend to respond rather more swiftly when rates are going up than when they are coming down, and to make money on the difference. In Table 3 of the Appendices, the long table tracking interest rates, you will notice that when the bank rate fell consistently through the summer and fall of 1981, the banks held their interest rates steady, so that there was a widening gap between the bank rate and the prime rate. When the bank rate was going up earlier in the year, however, they matched it, week by week.

There is nothing that says the banks must move with the central bank, but any bank that refused to do so could find itself in difficulty − the other banks in the band would not be happy. Nor is there anything that says that all the banks must maintain the same Prime Rate − they do that because they please to, because it is the fair way to operate, or because there is no competition among them. Take your pick.

The Bank Rate controls the money supply indirectly, by making money more or less expensive. The Bank of Canada decides on how that should move by fixing its gaze on a single component of the money supply, called M1.

There are other Ms, and you will find them explained in the Glossary section of the Appendices. M1 is used as the bellwether; it represents cash in circulation outside the chartered banks, plus the money in demand deposits (pure chequing accounts, as opposed to savings-chequing or savings accounts). In November 1981, there was $24.8 million in M1, down from $25.7 billion in November 1980.[13] The Bank of Canada's program to control the money supply was working. At the same time, inflation in Canada was running at 12.2%, a new high, and unemployment was at 8.3%, on its way to a post-war high of 10.6% in April, 1982. More than one million Canadians were out of work, but, by golly, the Canadian dollar was holding on, at eighty-two cents U.S., and our interest rates remained comfortably above those in the United States.

As appalling statistics rolled out of Ottawa, month after month, a notion grew that the Bank of Canada's policies were wrong-headed, but Bouey kept saying "It's obvious interest rates will have to remain high."[14] If he had made any mistake, Bouey argued, it was in applying the monetary controls too gradually.[15] He also blamed the federal government − although he was discreet and elliptical in his references − because it had not controlled public spending with sufficient rigour.[16] Never mind, though; if we just held on to the current policy, inflation would at last begin to abate.[17] Tight money, embraced fiercely enough, will cause prices to decline. That is unquestionably true, just as it is undeniable that it is possible to stop a baby crying by tightening a thong around its neck and pulling. The question remains, Will some less damaging technique bring about the same stillness?

What we appear to have, as an instrument of national economic policy, is the equivalent of the practice of bleeding patients that enjoyed such a long run in medicine. Bleeding would cure a fever. It might kill the patient, but it cured the fever, dammit. Even if Bouey had the right approach, two points of interest remain. The first is, Why is the Governor of the Bank of Canada in charge of the economy? The second is, Why does that Governor fix his sights so firmly on one approach?

The answer to the first question is political and historical. The Bank of Canada is run by a board of directors, appointed by the government. They are fifteen in number: two insiders, the Governor and the Deputy Governor, and thirteen outside directors. The outsiders are appointed by regions, two each from Ontario and Quebec, one each from the other provinces.[18] At the moment, there is one vacancy – the Manitoba seat is not currently occupied. Of the twelve outside directors currently in place, six are businessmen, four are lawyers, one is a woman and one a labour official. That's a pretty heavy bias against ordinary folk, but never mind, the board can hardly run Bank policy, that is done by the managers, just as in most organizations, which is to say, the Governor and his deputies. What is more, in theory at least, government is ultimately responsible for Bank policy. In fact, however, as we have already seen, the government has transferred much of its control to the Bank, in the name of "independence."

This came about as a result of a battle between James Coyne, the Governor from 1955 until 1961, and the Diefenbaker government. Coyne, a strong believer in controlling the money supply, like Bouey, maintained a rigid posture of tight money throughout a severe recession. The result was to deepen the recession and raise interest rates. Prime Minister John Diefenbaker did nothing to meet a rising tide of criticism until 1961, when his advisors told him he was going to be in trouble at the next federal election. Diefenbaker then prepared to fire Coyne, in a messy affair that ended with Coyne's resignation, and damaged the government, but not the Bank, because it was seen as "political interference."[19] Louis Rasminsky, who succeeded Coyne, insisted on a statement to clarify responsibility for monetary policy, based on two linked ideas. The first was that in the ordinary course of events, the Bank would run monetary policy; the second was that if the government disapproved of what the Bank was doing, it could issue a directive compelling the Bank to change course. These principles were accepted, and encoded in an amendment to the Bank of Canada Act by the Pearson government in 1967.[20] They remain in force, although no government has ever told the Bank to change its policy. The Conservative government of Joe Clark contemplated doing so, in its brief tenure of power in late 1979 and early 1980, because Conservatives had, in opposition, constantly attacked the high-interest policy of Gerald Bouey. In power, however, the Tories suddenly decided that monetary policy, and the blame to be attached for mismanaging it, was the exclusive preserve of the Bank, and they didn't want to interfere. When Bouey's seven-year term expired in January 1980, he was reappointed for another seven years, and stuck to his high-interest approach. In March 1980, the successor Liberal government took the process a step further by tying the Bank Rate to the Treasury-bill rate, and washing its hands of the matter entirely.

There has been a lot of argument about whether Bouey applied his policies sternly enough, or in the right places. Some economists felt that every area of the money supply, not merely M1, should have been looked at. But there was general acceptance that, for good or ill, the Bank of Canada had the right to run the money supply independent of government. I have never been able to follow this logic, any more than I would accept that the Navy should be allowed to conduct its own foreign policy. In both cases, experts deal with complex matters requiring technical skill, but no one complains that "political interference" is brought into play when the Defence Minister is required to answer to cabinet for the navy. Another name for political interference is "democracy." It is the sloppy way in which we conduct important matters. The subject of the Bank of Canada's independence is seldom debated – it is simply taken for granted. That is too bad, because, as economist Scott Gordon wrote, "Nothing could be plainer than the fact that the functions of a modern central bank are functions of high economic policy."[21] Gordon went on to argue, "The Bank of Canada enjoys greater freedom from ministerial control than any branch of government, with the possible exception of the judiciary; yet it is endowed with responsibilities and powers for forming and implementing public policy that exceed those of any other public body, save the Department of Finance." The Department of Finance is headed by a cabinet minister responsible to the House of Commons; the Bank of

Canada is responsible, instead, to the banking community.

Gerald Bouey, the current Governor, illustrates the point. He was born in Axford, Saskatchewan, in 1920, and grew up partly on the farm, and partly in the community of Trossachs, where his father ran the grain elevator. In 1936, when he finished high school, the Depression had the area in its grip. As Bouey once explained to a reporter, "There wasn't much growing in those days," so he left the farm for the Royal Bank at Weyburn, where he got a job as ledger-keeper.[22] For five years, he worked in junior posts in a number of prairie towns. When the war broke out, he joined the air force and spent three years overseas. After the war, he married a girl from Moosomin, and went back to school on government grants, taking economics at Queen's University and winning the gold medal in his course. On graduation in 1948, he joined the Bank of Canada, and he has been there ever since. His career parallels with remarkable exactitude that of the commercial bank chairmen who are his colleagues, consultants and admirers. He is another smalltown boy who took one job in the heart of a large, bureaucratic organization and stuck with it until he rose to the top.

Bouey lives more modestly than the commercial bank chairmen do, on a quiet Ottawa street. His salary, at $104,500, is not much compared to theirs. There was a fuss in December 1981, when Bouey made a speech exhorting Canadians to tighten their belts to beat inflation, and then accepted a pay-raise of $9,500 to bring him to his current level. The timing might have been better. One day he was saying that if Canadians insisted on pay-raises of ten and twelve per cent, inflation would never be licked; the next, he was accepting a ten per cent pay raise, fattening his salary to $2,010 a week, compared to the $354 weekly earned by the industrial workers he was asking to hold back on pay demands.[23] Still, the Governor has not done exceedingly well — he started at $75,000 in 1973, and has only advanced thirty-nine per cent on that. He makes less than one-third of the income of a bank chairman at any of the Top Five, and less than some other civil servants — Michael Warren, head of the Post Office, earns $150,000 annually.

What the Governor of the Bank of Canada gets paid does not matter greatly to ordinary Canadians. How he conducts policy does. His background, training and the connections he has built up over thirty-five years of brushing elbows with the banking community incline him to a course of action which, as it happens, greatly profits them. There is a haunting inevitability about the use of interest rates to control inflation; the banks like it, Paul Volker, down at the Federal Reserve Board in Washington, advocates it, and it is, frankly, the only shot in Bouey's locker. He has been pushing it in every single one of his last six annual reports, while acknowledging in each one that it hasn't yet worked. The corrective that might be applied by exposing him to the experience of having to work in the economic climate he has created is not available. The corrective of control by politicians who must listen to the victims of the economic storm has been removed.

The Bank of Canada, founded to meet the problems of one depression, came perilously close, in 1981, to provoking another. It has become, with the best will in the world, the instrument of one sector of the community. The same, alas, can be said of the next institution we are going to meet, that other watchdog of the public purpose, the office of the Inspector General of Banks.

11

Watch Out
For The Watchdog:
He Bruises Easily

"Rafe Mair, British Columbia's consumer and corporate affairs minister, has complained repeatedly that the federally chartered banks are breaking various provincial statutes...(Inspector General of Banks William) Kennett said his office refers any complaints to senior officers of the bank involved 'to ensure it received a fair hearing in the bank.'"

Vancouver Sun, *April 13, 1978*

William Kennett, Canada's Inspector General of Banks, thought about the question for a moment, and stroked his chin, and looked at the ceiling, and fiddled with a paperclip, and finally said, "I think we'd better get Don in here." Then he got up and asked his secretary to call in Don Macpherson, the Assistant Inspector General. We were in Kennett's office, on the second floor of Place Bell Canada, on Sparks Street in Ottawa, a stone's throw down the street from the Bank of Canada. I is a spacious office, reflective of the authority and dignity of its occupant, with rich furnishings and wide windows overlooking the Sparks Street mall. On the walls are photographs, personally selected by the Inspector General, of Canada's major banks. In the course of a long interview about Canadian banking, I had asked Kennett, a blond and affable man who looks younger than his fifty years, about Rest Accounts. Every time I look at a bank's annual report, I told him, I see where the bank has transferred $100 million or $120 million, or some such impressive figure, to its Rest Account. I said that when I saw something like that, two words flashed into my mind;

the first was "tax" and the second was "dodge." Is that what a Rest Account means? That's when Kennett went for help. Don Macpherson, when he arrived in our midst, disposed of the question in a few sentences. No, a Rest Account is not a tax dodge. It represents a transfer of earnings from the bank's annual profits to, in effect, its capital base. Essentially, it is a way of ploughing money back into the business, money on which, incidentally, the tax has already been paid. Ah.

That left me more puzzled than ever. Why did we have to call in a technical whiz to sort that out? Could it be that the Inspector General of Banks didn't know what one of the major items on every bank's balance sheet means? Nonsense. Kennett is a career civil servant. He began working for the Department of Finance in 1957, when he came back to his native heath bearing a Master of Science degree from the London School of Economics.[1] Before he became Inspector General of Banks in 1977, he held senior positions in Finance, and was Director of Capital Markets, dealing with matters more abstruse and frustrating than Rubik's cube. He has a reputation for working hard, and knowing his subject. Forget stupidity and forget ignorance. Try caution. Career civil servants do not forge brilliant careers by talking off the cuff, making judgments or courting controversy. Their idea of a truly successful interview is one in which nothing whatever is communicated. A fawn could take their correspondence course in concealment. William Kennett was doing what he does best – passing the potato.

In fact, that is the work for which the entire office seems designed. Kennett told me, "Over the years this office has assumed a kind of ombudsman role and (if we received a complaint) we would undertake an inquiry to find out what the situation is and if the complaint is real, we would attempt to rectify it." Could he give me an example? Well, there were many, but none came immediately to mind. Let us then, I suggested, take the example of the behaviour of the major banks in British Columbia. In 1974, Phyllis Young, then Minister of Consumer Services for the province, advised the businesses of the province, including banks, to make sure that the contracts they used in lending matters did not violate provincial law.[2] The banks, in effect, told her to blow it out her ear; they were not bound by provincial law, only federal law. This was not merely a matter of semantics; British Columbia had erected a series of consumer protection laws that were much stronger than anything on Ottawa's books. For example, under federal law, if you get behind in payments on a car, the lender can seize the car, sell it for a bargain-basement price, and then sue you for the difference between that price and the loan, plus costs.[3] In British Columbia, the lender can seize and sell the car, or sue you; he can't do both. Provincial statutes also provide better protection against someone entering your home in the middle of the night to seize chattels.

All the Big Five banks, and the Bank of British Columbia, used loan forms that ignored B.C. law, and complaints to the banks made no difference whatever. Finally, in October 1977, Rafe Mair, Young's successor (after a change of government from NDP to Social Credit), wrote a blistering letter to Jean Chretien, then the federal Minister of Finance.[4] He complained that the banks were in contravention of four British Columbia statutes, to wit, the Sale of Goods Act, the Conditional Sales Act, the Bills of Sale Act, and the Debt Collection Act. Chretien replied with a straight-arm; he said that it "is the policy of most of the banks to make every effort to comply with the Provincial legislation." Mair returned to the attack on November 22, in a high dudgeon. He wrote, "The bald fact is that 'policy' differs very much from 'fact,' and quite clearly, the banks are not telling you the truth." He then quoted from a chattel mortgage document used by the Canadian Imperial Bank of Commerce that excluded the application of provincial laws. In effect, when the borrower signed up for the loan, he removed himself from the protection provided by those statutes. Mair also complained that the Bank of Montreal and the Bank of Nova Scotia were using a form of guarantee that appeared open-ended. The guarantor thought he was guaranteeing a specific loan, but in fact he was signing "a promise to permanently underwrite any loan with the specific institution that may be undertaken by the primary borrower at any time in the future." Mair rumbled, "We take the view that in using these forms in a consumer transaction, banks are acting unconscionably."

Again nothing happened in response to Mair's complaint, even though his government began to take action against the banks. In one case where the Bank of Commerce had repossessed a truck and camper, sold it, then sued the debtor for the difference between the resale price and the amount owing, the Director of Trade Practices assumed the conduct of the defence on behalf of the consumer. The Commerce dropped the case.[5] But this kind of case by case activity was not likely to provide overall protection, so Mair went public in an interview with the Vancouver Sun.[6] He accused the banks of shady consumer practices, threats, deceit and outright blackmail, and argued, "If it was Four-Flusher Finance doing these things instead of banks, they would be tarred and feathered and run out of town on a rail." While he attacked all the Big Five, and said that the Bank of British Columbia was marginally better than the Big Five, he differentiated among them. "In terms of the nature of violations, the Bank of Nova Scotia is worst. The Canadian Imperial Bank of Commerce is second because it's biggest in B.C. and affects most people."[7]

The banks' position remained that they were not bound to obey provincial law. In due course, however, the pressure of public opinion did begin to work, and in April 1979, the Bank of Nova Scotia announced, with much to-do, that it was introducing new consumer loan forms in British Columbia, which were easier to understand, and in conformity with provincial law.[8] It had taken three years, the bank explained, to develop the forms.

You might think that a man called the Inspector General of Banks would be considerably wrought up over something like the battle between British Columbia and the banks under his charge. Nope. Kennett told me, "On that B.C. thing, it was not exactly our responsibility." That was at least an improvement over what he told the Vancouver Sun when the battle was at its height. To them, he said that he had no power "to direct a bank to behave." He went on to say that it was his practice to turn complaints of a minor nature over to the banks and, "More difficult problems involving large clients in contractual obligations are normally settled in direct negotiations between the client and the bank, or finally in the court."[9]

There's a comfort. If you get into a battle with a bank and go to the government Watchdog, he will decide, first of all, whether it is a major or a minor problem. If minor, he will deliver it, and you, into the hands of the bank you were complaining about in the first place. If major, he will wash his hands of it. The B.C. case fell into the major category. Kennett passed the potato.

His explanation is that his concern is to protect the Bank Act, and to carry out the duties imposed on him by the Bank Act. Period. That Act stipulates that the Inspector General should be someone who, in the view of the Minister of Finance, has "proper experience and training," and that he "shall not borrow money from a bank unless the Minister is first informed in writing."[10] It gives the Inspector one overwhelming responsibility, just as he says: "The Inspector shall be responsible generally for the administration of this Act."[11]

So the question for the Inspector, whenever a discussion of the banks comes up, is: How does this affect the Bank Act? His eighteen-member[12] staff is divided into three groups; an inspection division, which goes over each bank's books annually; a compliance division, which makes sure that the banks get the required returns in on time, and the research and analysis division, which researches and, um, analyses. What the Inspector General's office is providing, essentially, is a service *for* the banks, not a watch over them.

The Inspector cannot inspect the banks' books the way, say, the Comptroller of the Currency does in the United States. There, a staff of 1,800 examiners operates under the strictures of the Handbook of Examination Procedures. There, a bank inspection is a lightning raid, which must be carried out "in a manner that will preserve the element of surprise."[13] The inspection team assembles near the bank entrance before opening time, enters the bank, and seals all records with a small sticker bearing the words "National Bank Examiner's Seal." As each teller arrives and goes to his or her personal safe in the bank vault, an examiner goes with him or her, takes possession of the vault and checks its contents. Every dime in the bank is counted, every unsecured loan is examined, and spot checks are made on secured loans, to ensure that the bank has not accepted several square miles of moose-pasture as prime real estate to back a note. The atmosphere of these inspections is tense, sometimes hostile. Where possible, every branch of the same bank is entered at the same time for simultaneous inspections. In the case of some large banks, this is not possible, but as many branches as can be inspected simultaneously are done. The Comptroller of the Currency only bothers his head about federally chartered banks, representing about one third of all U.S. banks. Those with state charters are checked by state examiners who, again, are much more thorough than the minions of the Canadian Inspector General have time to be. New York State has 325[14] examiners on staff for its share of the non-federal banks, or eighteen times as many as the entire staff of the Inspector General's office. It may be argued that the Americans must have a much more rigorous inspection system than ours, because the Americans have banks that go bankrupt, and we don't. The argument merely underlines the point that the service isn't provided on behalf of the consumer, or the depositor (whose account, in any event, is guaranteed by federal deposit insurance in either country), it is provided for the security of the banks.

Our banks do go through tough inspections, but these are conducted by the bank itself. The difference is that in the United States, inside bank inspections are merely for openers. The Comptroller is not satisfied to leave the job to the bankers; he insists on running his own checks as well. In Canada, the banks examine themselves and report to the Inspector General that everything is lovely; they send in the reports required by the Bank Act, and his staff go over them. There is something marvellously Canadian about this process. Have you been cheating lately? Nosir. Well, send in a report, and we'll check it out. The Inspector can enter any bank, lock up its files and rummage its drawers, but that would only happen if something dreadful had been reported about the bank; it is not, as in the United States, part of the routine. A Canadian banker with extensive experience in the United States puts the difference this way: "When the inspectors arrive from head office in Canada you expect to be put through the hoops. You know they are going to be looking for sloppiness, mistakes and, of course, crookedness. If they catch you doing something wrong, it will go on your record; it can do you a lot of harm. But this is your head office, your bank, doing the checking. In the States, it's quite different. You have the feeling, in some banks, that the feds are out to get you. There's a real adversary relationship. In Canada, you are being looked over, all right, but you're being looked over by fellow members of the club."

The Banque Canadienne Nationale, now part of the National Bank, had a scandal in 1979 that involved senior bank officers authorizing about $51 million in loans based on greatly inflated property values.[15] The Montreal Gazette, and an internal investigation by the bank's staff, discovered the situation.

The manager of an Ontario branch of the Toronto-Dominion Bank made off with $400,000 by way of fraud, forgery and uttering. The bank caught him.[16]

The Canadian Imperial Bank of Commerce lost $10 million from a downtown Toronto branch over a period of two years, and didn't even know the money was missing until police fraud squad officers told them about it, after the arrest of a bank employee. A bank spokesman told a reporter, "How the money went missing without anyone finding out about it is a question that a lot of people here are asking."[17] That's nice.

In all these cases, not merely did the Inspector General's office not do the job – it wasn't supposed to. He is not an Inspector General – not with eighteen troops under his command – he is more like an Inspector, Junior Grade, or an Occasional Auditor. His staff is being expanded, but so is his workload, with the influx of foreign banks under the new Bank Act. He has a new office of foreign banking, but for home-grown institutions, the job, and its narrow scope, remain as before.

However, the Bank Act contains one of those catch-all clauses so beloved of legal draftsmen. This one says, "The Inspector, from time to time, but not less frequently than once in each calendar year, shall make or cause to be made such examination and inquiry into the business and affairs of each bank as the Inspector may deem to be necessary or expedient."[18] He can go barrelling into any bank and take charge of any and all assets to satisfy himself that the provisions of this Act "having reference to the safety of the interests of the depositors, creditors and shareholders ... are being duly observed and that the bank is in a sound financial condition."

I once asked a senior official of the Department of Finance what the Inspector would do if he discovered that the head of one of the banks had decamped to Brazil with a few billion dollars. He didn't know. "There is no annual report, and as far as I know, no official reporting procedure. I suppose he'd tell the Minister of Finance." That sounded odd, so I asked him to check and phone me back; he did, and repeated the answer. But, in fact, the Act does say: "At the conclusion of each examination and inquiry (the Inspector) shall report thereon to the Minister."

An Odd Arrangement

If the Finance Department doesn't know about this provision, it appears that the Inspector's inquiries have assumed the nature of an annual ritual, and his reports the nature of filing-for-the-record. They are not public, and they don't deal with issues raised by the public. If the Inspector chose to, he could obviously examine any part of any bank's activity, on the grounds that it impinged on the safety of its depositors or creditors. And if he didn't have the staff to take on the job, he could hire outside help – that's where the "cause to be made" wrinkle comes in. Occasionally, he does just that. When a western lumber company went bankrupt in 1977, and blamed the Bank of Montreal for its troubles, one of the lumber company owners complained, repeatedly, to the Inspector General. He sent a lawyer out to check into the situation and duly concluded that he had better leave the matter to the courts (which eventually decided in favour of the bank).[19]

The machinery is there; it just isn't being used, and the Inspector doesn't – despite the "ombudsman" reference – really think it should be. His job, as he sees it, is to keep an eye out for irregularities such as Le Groupe La Laurentine of Montreal acquiring 42.56 per cent interest in the Montreal City and Savings Bank in mid-1980. He investigated that, when Le Groupe picked up another block of shares, and announced that while the action was not illegal, it was "breaching the spirit" of the Bank Act, because it gave one shareholder too much control of a bank.[20] (The Act provides that a bank must not officially record a share transaction of more than ten per cent, so that if one shareholder holds more than that share of a bank, he will have no voting rights at the annual meeting, not even the ten percent, although the actual purchase of shares is not illegal.) That's what the Inspector is keen on: not whether the banks are breaking the law in British Columbia, but whether someone is fooling with the system.

It is the system, after all, which pays his salary. The Bank Act says that the expenditures of the Inspector General's office, which amount to about $700,000[21] annually, "shall be recouped after the end of each fiscal year ending March 31 . . . by an assessment on the banks based on the average total assets of the banks, respectively, during the year ending March 31." The banks do not pay the Inspector directly; he is paid out of the Consolidated Revenue Fund, and that fund is repaid by the banks. The Act won't let him borrow money from a bank;[22] it will allow this roundabout way of having him owe his salary to the banks. This lunatic provision is no fault of the Inspector's; he had nothing to do with it, but it does put him in an embarrassing position. The Ministry of Finance cannot understand why anyone would worry about the fact that the Watchdog is being paid by the wolves (or potential wolves). The Official Spokesman's version goes, "It is an odd arrangement, but it seems to work. He is both watchdog and government adviser. I'm told it's a very practical arrangement. Basically he is autonomous, with responsibility to the government to administer its regulations and responsibility to the banks to ensure that everybody is treated the same. The industry is quite happy, the government is happy and Bill is quite happy with it."

You will note that in the list of those who are happy there is no mention of consumers, creditors, depositors or bank shareholders, all of whom come under the Inspector's care in the actual Bank Act. They are part of the great unwashed, not part of the banking community. The idea of having, say, restaurant inspectors paid for by the restaurants, on a sliding scale according to their size, or plumbing inspectors paid indirectly by the plumbing companies, would not wear well with the Canadian public. For the Inspector General of Banks, however, well, we come back to the mythology of banking, and the thousand acts of blind trust that make the business what it is. To cavil at this arrangement, I was told by a senior Finance official, was "to call into question the integrity of a very fine man."

No it isn't; it is to call into question a dubious practice.

There is one other such arrangement in the federal regulatory service; the Superintendent of Insurance is compensated indirectly by the insurance companies,[23] proof that idiocy in these matters is not confined to one instance.

What is worrisome about the way the Inspector is paid is the concern that it may reflect reality. Not that Kennett considers himself an employee of the banks, by any means, but that he considers himself part of their community. You will recall that in the Unity Bank case, W. R. Scott, the then Inspector General, gave his stamp of approval to Richard Higgins, the prospective Unity president, on the basis of one interview and the fact that he had "no reason" to doubt that Higgins was a man of spotless reputation. He could have picked up reason to doubt without doing an awful lot of work, but the banking community, officially at least, had not blackballed Higgins; ergo, he was okay.

Kennett is a suitable successor to Scott. In his appearances before the Senate Banking Committee on revisions to the Bank Act, it was sometimes hard to figure out whether he was speaking about the banks or on behalf of the banks.[24]

He argued, as the banks do, for allowing them to plunge into the mortgage market without restriction, and suggested that any limitation in this area would mean that "The trust companies can make a larger profit to cross-subsidize their estate, trust and agency business, which is not doing very well." In short, to deny the banks deeper penetration of mortgage financing could raise costs for Canadian homebuyers by removing the protective curb of bank competition. Uh huh. Putting this line forward, Kennett noted that it was an argument that could be made; in the context, it was clearly an argument he was making. He also embraced, without reservations, the banks' ambitions to get into the leasing business, and pronounced himself "disappointed" when some limitations were imposed. He also agreed with the banks that trust companies should be required to keep reserves – "I can't see the argument that they should receive special treatment," he told me – and was unhappy because an amendment the banks thought they had won, to loosen their own reserve requirements, was postponed. The Bank Act insists on minimal reserves on term deposits, even if they have been committed to the bank for more than one year. The banks think this is overly cautious, and lobbied fiercely to get the requirement dropped. They thought they had won, but a last-minute change kept the reserves in the law. (We will meet this again in the next chapter.) Discussing this last subject with Sonita Horvich of the Financial Post on January 10, 1981, Kennett noted, "This is a battle we have not lost."

By "we," it was clear that Kennett meant "them" – the banks. When Bud Cullen, the Liberal chairman of the House of Commons Finance Committee, the committee which had denied the banks their demand, read the interview, he was considerably upset. He wrote an angry letter to Pierre Bussieres, Secretary of State for Finance, and the man in charge of shepherding the Bank Act through Parliament, asking what the hell. Bussieres was only able to reply lamely that he would "confer with" Kennett about the interview. The Inspector was not available at the time – he was over in Japan, promoting the expansion of Canadian banks into the Japanese market. He was successful, and the Financial Post was able to report "The go-ahead for Canadian banks followed recently concluded negotiations between Canada's Inspector General of Banks, William Kennett, and the Japanese monetary authorities. (Until now, the banks have been limited to representative offices in Japan.)"

There were those rude enough to want to know why Kennett was off in Asia, negotiating for the banks – was he their watchdog or their travelling salesman? And, while the subject of the Inspector General was open for debate, the question of his salary came up. Some Members of Parliament wanted to know why Kennett was paid under what Bob Rae, then finance critic in Ottawa for the New Democratic Party, called, "this odd arrangement." When Kennett returned to the capital, on February 8, 1981, it was to find himself, for the first time, embroiled in a public controversy. Carol Goar of the Toronto Star[25] phoned him to ask if he stood behind his "we" quote, and Kennett explained that it was "an unfortunate quote . . . All I meant to say was that I expect the reserve requirement will be dropped."

Goar noted that "For the average Canadian, who takes for granted that the government is keeping watch over the huge, profitable banking industry with Solomon-like impartiality, the Kennett affair raises several questions." The most important of these, and the one to which there is still no satisfactory answer, was Goar's first one:

"Whose interests matter most to our federal regulators — those of the public or those of the banks?"

Nothing came of Kennett's brief fling in the limelight. The Inspector General is still paid, indirectly, by the banks, he is still an effective representative to government for the banking community, and he is still passing the potato. About all that happened as a result of his momentary exposure is that he became even softer-spoken than before. Oh well, maybe that's just as well, because the banking lobby, has been accused of many things, but nobody ever called it shy.

12
Clout

> *"What the banks do on a regular basis is quietly attempt to identify where a newly elected Member of Parliament banks. This is done so that if the banks want to provide information to an MP — lobbying it may be called — one of the ways they can do it is directly through the bank where he or she does business."*
>
> Earle McLaughlin, *October 1980*

Earle McLaughlin was Chairman of the Royal Bank at the time he gave an interview to the Canadian Banker, organ of the Canadian Bankers' Association, from which the above quote was taken. In May of that year, a small disturbance had arisen in Parliament when it was revealed that the banks were circulating bank managers to get information on Members of Parliament. The Bank Act revisions were moving through their final stages when D. H. Beattie, Manager of Consumer/Commercial Banking Services, had sent out a letter to "All Winnipeg Branches" trying to find out something about two newly elected New Democratic Party MPs. This is what the letter said:

"Last year, we, along with the other banks, were asked to provide information concerning close contacts which members of the banking industry had with Members of Parliament. As a result of the February 18th election, The Canadian Bankers' Association is updating their information and have again solicited our support.

"Accordingly, we should appreciate hearing whether you, or, where applicable the Assistant Managers have any business or personal contact with the two newly elected Federal Members of Parliament for Manitoba, Messrs. Cyril Keeper and Laverne Lewycky.

"In your reply, it would be appreciated if you could elaborate on the extent of the relationship, if any. In the event the manager of one of the other chartered banks in your area, in your opinion, has a better or closer relationship with the Member involved, please so indicate. If you know where the MP in your area conducts his banking, this information also would be helpful."

That letter reflects either a touching naivete or an immutable arrogance, and the banking community has never been known for naivete. There was another way to put the material in the letter, clearer but more dangerous. It might have asked "Have you got anything on these jokers? How much money do they owe, and to whom? What's the best way to bring pressure on them, to bring them on-side for the Bank Act revisions?" When Lewycky received a copy of the letter – presumably sent by someone who wasn't high on that kind of approach – he raised the matter in the House, charging that his privileges as an MP had been breached. Nothing came of it. The Speaker gave him no comfort, and Robert MacIntosh, President of the Canadian Bankers' Association, sent out a press release saying that his group was just bringing its directory up to date and that "Absolutely no financial information is sought or provided." In an interview, he said with that refreshing frankness for which he is known, that the idea was to help the CBA with its lobbying – "We want to put our point of view across."

McLaughlin was queried by the Canadian Banker later in the year, in one of those no-holds-barred interviews you might expect from a house organ. "Did you feel any embarrassment over that or do you see it as a storm in a teacup?" McLaughlin replied, "It's a storm in a teacup."

How would you feel if your friendly bank manager called you in one day and said "I note that we are holding your mortgage for $50,000, and you're asking for an extension of your overdraft to $10,000. Fine, fine. Now, tell me, how do you feel about this crazy business where they are refusing to lower our reserves?"

Couldn't happen? Then why do the lobbyists compile these lists? If they want to know who the MPs are, that information is contained in the daily newspaper. If they want to know more about them – their backgrounds, marital status, how they feel about economic policy, even how they feel about the banks – that information can be had from the relevant political party, along with copies of key speeches. Or, there is always the mail; MPs love to set forth their views. What the Canadian Bankers' Association is after here is information that may help it to influence MPs. As McLaughlin said, "If that member happens to be appointed to the Trade and Finance Committee, for example, or something in banking is coming up before Parliament that's not well understood, then it might be beneficial to spend an hour with the MP when the member is home in his or her constituency to provide background information. And who can do that best? Amongst the banks, it's the MPs' own bank." There's nothing like a little chat with the man who holds your demand note, and can dump you into insolvency, for clarifying the mind and aiding understanding.

I shouldn't complain, really, because whatever excesses the banking lobby is up to these days are nothing compared to its past. Parliament may be unduly influenced by the bankers today — I believe it is — but at least we have made progress. The first Bank Act, that of 1871, was literally written by the banks, and George Hague, General Manager of the Bank of Toronto, boasted proudly that "We were really a joint committee of Parliament and banks." He noted that bank representatives, "Sat in conference, day by day discussing the clauses of the proposed Act one by one ... Many of the directors of the banks and several of their presidents were Members of Parliament, some in the Senate, some in the House of Commons. These, of course, sat with us from time to time."[1] Among the MPs with dual loyalties on this rudimentary bankers' committee were the rascally Francis Hincks, who was at the time a director (later president) of City Bank as well as Minister of Finance, and Louis Davies, President of the Merchants Bank, and Minister of Fisheries.

That first Act was drafted, for the most part, by the Bank of Montreal. It put the banks of the Maritime provinces under federal control, and opened up their area to the central Canadian banks, which promptly turned the region into a milch-cow for the businesses that were the chief customers of the Ontario and Quebec banks.

An official banking lobby was established by the Bankers' Association in 1894, with Z. A. Lash as official lobbyist. His job was to shoot down any bills that threatened the bankers' interests. Sir Edmund Walker of the Bank of

Commerce commented in 1895 that when "objectionable clauses" were introduced, "The attention of the proper authorities being called by Mr. Lash to these features they were removed."

The Canadian Bankers' Association was officially incorporated in 1901, and handed the right to pronounce on the fitness of any prospective bankers seeking charters. Like giving the Montreal Canadiens control of the annual draft in hockey. By World War I, the bank lobby had expanded to five lawyers and a clutch of parliamentary agents whose job it was to herd friendly MPs into Parliament to vote down unfavourable proposals, and to lean on waverers who seemed to be drifting away from the bank line. In the Senate, the lobbying was carried out directly on the debating floor; at the invitation of Sir James Lougheed, government leader in the Senate, the CBA's lawyer sat inside the rail and interrupted debate, supplying information and argument to support his client's case.[2]

The banks were given, not merely a veto on banking, but effective control over the Finance portfolio. Under the first Bank Act, there was no provision for the banks to keep reserves, but in 1890, Conservative Finance Minister George Foster proposed to establish such a reserve. Prime Minister Sir John A. Macdonald would have no part of it; there was an election coming up, and he didn't want to upset the banking community. Another of Foster's reforms – to make the notes of any bank redeemable at par by any other bank – met the same fate, and Foster went into the bankers' books as the wrong kind of man to have in the Finance portfolio. They would keep that in mind. In the meantime, the Conservatives were defeated, the Liberals elected, and Wilfrid Laurier, the new Prime Minister, proposed to make Sir Richard Cartwright his Minister of Finance. A delegation of bankers called on Laurier to threaten that if he went ahead with the appointment, they would call enough loans to cause a financial crisis. They wanted their own man, W. S. Fielding, in the Finance portfolio, and they got him, too. When the Conservatives came back to power in 1911, and George Foster was again proposed as Finance Minister, the banks moved in once more with a firm nolle prosequi and Foster was shifted instead to Trade and Commerce, then considered to be "a political scrapheap."[3]

Every substantive proposal to change banking legislation, unless it came from the banks themselves, was shot down, including proposals for such elementary precautions as a compulsory annual audit of the banks for the protection of shareholders and the maintenance of transfer and registry offices by each bank in every province where it did business.

One of the tasks the banking lobby gave itself was to eliminate competition, particularly the wasteful competition in interest rates; instead, the banks would compete through the proliferation of branches. Thomas Fysche, a leading banker of the 1890s, declared that the only reason competition appeared in banking whatever was because of "the lack of proper organization. When the latter is achieved we may regard the rapid disappearance of competition with comparative equanimity."[4] Having a strangle-hold on chartering, as the bank lobby did, certainly helped the process along.[5] Between 1867 and 1900, five banks were added to the Canadian system; between 1900, when the banks got control of chartering, and 1914, the number of Canadian banks was reduced by fifteen.[6] Mergers, consolidations and failures – many brought on by the unscrupulous manipulations of the bankers themselves – produced a banking system in which, essentially, a few huge banks located in central Canada siphoned money out of the East and, later, out of the West, for the benefit of the middle of the nation. Attempts to reform the system by establishing regional banks were blocked by the CBA, with its veto power. The right of mortgage companies to raise money through deposits was taken away – and only recently restored. Government savings banks, which competed for private savings with the commercial giants, were gradually removed from the picture, and the local banks on which Maritime commerce had been built were destroyed. Central to all these developments was the control the bankers were able to exercise in Ottawa, over critics and putative reformers. For decades, for example, it was normal for a majority of the members of the Senate Banking Committee, the committee that initiates changes in the Bank Act, to consist of bank directors who were also Senators. The most recent renewal of the Bank Act, in December 1980, marks a watershed of sorts – bank directors on the committee did not take part in discussions on the legislation, although former directors, such as Sen. Hartland Molson, were active, and the process was chaired by Salter Hayden, an honorary director of the Toronto-Dominion Bank.

To understand how crucial these amendments can be, consider briefly what happened in 1967. There had been a Royal Commission into banking before this dicennial review of the Act, and this body, the Porter Commission, reported in 1964, calling for "a more open and competitive banking system." Among its recommendations, the Commission included withdrawing the right of the Canadian Bankers' Association to operate the cheque-clearing system, allowing foreign banks to enter Canada — but not to accept deposits here — and, for the first time, providing a legal definition of banking as a way to keep the banks from straying into other areas. None of these recommendations had the support of the banking community, and none was followed, but a number of changes which the community did want were turned into law, in what the then Minister of Finance, Mitchell Sharp, called "A Blueprint for Competition." A great humorist, Sharp.

Until 1967, banks had been limited to 6% per annum in the interest they could charge, a provision that effectively curbed their consumer lending — it simply was not economical to put out loans at that rate. The ceiling was lifted temporarily in 1967, and permanently in 1968. Describing what happened after the ceiling was removed, Stanley Davison, Vice-Chairman of the Bank of Montreal, told me, "We creamed the finance companies." Robert MacIntosh, President of the CBA, claims, "You, the Canadian consumer, are the winner," because the banks saved us from the exactions of the finance companies, who were charging as much as 12% per annum in 1967. Now the banks are charging as much as 25% for consumer loans; because the finance rates are even higher, MacIntosh argues that consumers are ahead of the game.

The other major change in the Bank Act in 1967 allowed the banks to enter the mortgage loan field in a major way, again for the first time. Until 1967, they were barred from most conventional mortgage lending, and effectively limited to holding residential mortgages guaranteed under the National Housing Act. Until the interest rate ceiling was lifted, they had no desire to get into mortgages more heavily; indeed, they withdrew from the field as soon as these interest rates climbed over the 6% limit. The new Bank Act not only removed this constraint, it allowed them free access to conventional mortgages with the only limit that mortgage loans should not exceed ten per cent of their deposit liabilities, plus the banks' debentures (that is, the total of the deposits they were holding plus the total of debenture bonds, which are notes backed by the full credit of the corporation). At the same time, restrictions on the amount of debentures a bank could issue were eased by removing the requirement to hold reserves against them.[7] There were no limits on the mortgages held by the banks' mortgage subsidiaries.

The effect, again, was galvanic; the banks swarmed into the mortgage market, multiplying their portfolio twenty-two-fold between 1967[8] and 1980, from $825 million to $18.6 billion,[9] taking over much of the market from the traditional mortgagees — the life insurance companies, mortgage firms and trust corporations. Again, MacIntosh claims, the public has been the winner, but he has to argue, again, that mortgage rates would be even higher today except for the competition of the banks, a dubious proposition.

Whatever competition the 1967 revisions introduced, it was not competition for the banks; rather, they were allowed to expand and consolidate their hold on a financial market that was becoming ever-more restrictive, while the near-banks, which had been threatening their role at the centre of the economic world, found themselves in trouble. The banks didn't have everything their way in 1967. Until that time, it had been common practice for the bankers to meet to discuss the setting of rates. This was done quite openly; although it smacked of collusion, it was quite legal. The 1967 revisions barred this practice. Not that that made much difference; striking similarities in the rates remain. The revisions also required the banks to provide more information to borrowers about the real cost of loans, and they were required to provide more detailed reporting to the Inspector General.[10]

Reserve ratios were raised, too, but wound up being lower. That was because the law distinguished, for the first time, between time deposits, which can be withdrawn only after giving notice, and demand deposits, which can be withdrawn anytime. The old reserve ratio was eight per cent; under the revision, the ratio on demand deposits was twelve per cent and on time deposits, four per cent. That worked out to an average ratio of six-and-one-half per cent – the banks were ahead of the game again, as billions of dollars came floating out of reserve.

Also in 1967, legislation provided for federal deposit insurance on the deposits in banks and near-banks, guaranteeing each account up to $20,000 in the case of a business failure in the financial institution.[11] Provincially chartered institutions – such as credit unions and trust companies – gradually came under the same protection from provincial governments. This provision did not affect the competitive market, since all players wound up in the same place, but it did provide reassurance for depositors.

In short, what was to be a Blueprint for Competition became a licence to print money. The banks were better off than ever, while their rivals became dust beneath their chariot wheels. Oh well, next time.

Next time was to have been the revision of 1977, and if you care to ask why the banks should only have to face the possibility of legislative change once every ten years, while other industries may be brought to heel at any time, I can give you no sensible answer. The banks say that it is to provide stability in the industry. It certainly does that. It also limits the possibilities of reform.

Before the 1977 revisions could be written into law, a certain amount of restiveness developed in the political world in connection with the banks. They seemed to be making more and more money, while everyone else made less.

In 1964, the Province of British Columbia had launched its own proposal to start a bank, with B.C. owning twenty per cent of the shares.[12] It was not to be. First, the Senate Banking Committee derailed the proposal by recommending that no charter be issued until after the 1967 Bank Act revision. Then that revision prohibited ownership by any government of the voting shares of chartered banks, and limited non-voting ownership to ten per cent. When the Bank of British Columbia did get going, it was a wholly-private institution, but B.C. citizens, and westerners in general, were sore as a boil.[13]

At a Western Economic Opportunities Conference in Calgary, held in June 1973, the four western premiers issued a joint statement that said flatly, "The oligopolistic position of the Canadian chartered banks results in higher interest rates than are justified, a more conservative lending attitude, and less flexibility." And, directly to the point, "The branch banking system, characterized by the five major Canadian chartered banks with branches coast-to-coast and head offices in Central Canada, has not been adequately responsive to Western needs."

To add to the fun, another Royal Commission – this one into Corporation Concentration – reported in 1978 that "In Canadian markets, the major banks compete with each other as oligopolists."[14]

You might have expected, in the circumstances, that the new Bank Act would come down on the banks like a ton of bricks. Not a chance. That Act was written by the same coalition of Finance bureaucrats, Bank of Canada experts, CBA lobbyists and Senate Banking Committee wizards that composes all such revisions, and while the banks didn't win everything they wanted, they were able to derail proposals that might have done them real harm, and to gain advantages that will give them even more clout in the future. "Just you wait," huffs Carne Bray, President of the Association of Canadian Financial Corporations (one of the lobbies competing with the CBA), "They're going to take over the whole damn shooting match."

The Lobby at Work

The process of drafting new legislation began long before the 1976 White Paper on Banking set down the government's intentions. Top officials of the CBA, and senior officers of the banks, met with Finance officials, made speeches, and granted interviews to friendly newspapermen in which it was allowed that, generally, the banks were being treated pretty shabbily in this country, and the public was suffering as a result.

It is the normal business of lobbying to whine, and the bankers did it well. Whining, wining and dining are the three essential functions. The CBA did not provide ladies of the evening for MPs, or produce compromising pictures, or offer bribes, that is not the Canadian way. What they did was to "tell the bank story" in advertisements, news stories and, face to face, by buttonholing MPs. The

CBA spends about $6 million a year, and with that kind of budget, it is not hard to "tell the story." Much of this work was carried out by Robert MacIntosh, who was the Executive Vice-President of the Bank of Nova Scotia until he became the full-time President of the CBA as the Bank Act revision was coming down to the wire in 1980. (The presidency of the CBA had not been a full-time job, but instead was rotated among bank presidents. Gordon Bell, the Bank of Nova Scotia president, and MacIntosh's boss, took on the CBA presidency on condition that MacIntosh would do the lobbying on the Bank Act. Then MacIntosh became full-time CBA president in June 1980.)

MacIntosh is a tall, rumpled, ruggedly handsome man who, despite a lifelong career in banking, and the possession of a PhD degree in economics, carries a whiff of John Wayne in his wake. He doesn't say "A bank's gotta do what a bank's gotta do," but the phrase seems to be trembling on his tongue. He said to me once, "We're not perfect, by Jesus, but we're goddam good." Bankers are not supposed to talk like that, but MacIntosh does. He is noisy, impatient and outspoken. He attacks, with libellous vigour, anyone who criticizes the banks. The Jack Mintz incident says a lot about both MacIntosh and the way the bank lobby works.

Jack Mintz is an economist, currently teaching banking at Queen's University in Kingston. In 1974, he undertook a study for the Economic Council of Canada on the rates of return in Canadian banking. The idea was to examine the profits of our banks and compare them to other financial institutions, both here and in the United States. Mintz, a dark-haired, cheerful young man recalls, "I was completely objective. I had nothing against banks, and no idea what I was going to learn. As I got into it more and more, the evidence began to pile up that Canadian banks were making a lot more than their competitors, a lot more than banks in the United States, and a lot more than retail trade. You began to look for reasons why, and it came out to one explanation, and nothing else. Canadian banks didn't face any real competition."

So that's what Mintz said, first in a discussion paper for the ECC, and then in an official study, "The Measure of Rates of Return in Canadian Banking," which was to be released as an official ECC report, with all that implied. The Measure — keep it short — was dynamite, even if heavily wrapped. As Tom Sawyer noted about Pilgrim's Progress, "The statements were tough, but interesting." Mintz described the banking system in Canada, and the trust and mortgage business, and compared the Canadian system to the American one. He found that Canadians were being victimized, that the banks make more money than other, similar institutions, and he found that they were not the only gainers – the government gained, too, he said, because it got a slice of the action through taxes on the excess profits (the banks fixed that later). He was even willing to put figures – admittedly tentative ones – on what these extra costs were. He did that by working out what the banks would have made, and the taxes they would have paid, in a competitive market. He concluded that "Canadian bank shareholders between 1968 and 1973 earned total excess after-tax profits of at least $219.7 million (based on the after-tax profit rate of trust and loan corporations) to at most $478.5 million (based on the after-tax profit rate earned by retail trade)."[15] The extra taxes gained by Canadian governments came to somewhere between $197.3 million and $425.7 million, so the total burden on Canadian consumers of banking services was a minimum of $417 million and a maximum of $904 million. He also concluded that "With competition among many firms, services to banking consumers could have been less costly," and suggested "removing legislative barriers" to entry into the banking business to bring about such competition.

One of the people who did not like Mintz' study was MacIntosh, who was then a member of the ECC, representing the banks. "It was a lot of crap," is what MacIntosh says today. When I asked him about Mintz, he said a great many things that could not appear in print in any nation with libel laws, and the nub of his remarks was to suggest that Mintz didn't really understand Canadian banking, or American banking, or much of anything else. Today, MacIntosh can afford to belittle Mintz; in 1979, when the paper was about to come out, it was another matter. He objected, and objected loudly, to the ECC bringing out under its prestigious imprint a study that said such damaging – and, in MacIntosh's view, wrong – things about Canadian banks. MacIntosh left the ECC at the beginning of 1979, but his objections were taken up, and when the study was released, it carried a foreword that said: "The findings of this study are the personal responsibility of the author and, as such, have not been endorsed by Members of the Economic Council of Canada." Before this time, no ECC study had carried such a disclaimer. The Mintz report was to have been the subject of a lead article in the ECC Bulletin for January 1979, and indeed, 10,000 copies of such a bulletin were printed. The headline read "Bank Profits Show Market Power," and a subhead, "More Competition would benefit customers." The bulletin was rewritten to take out the offending material, and the 10,000 copies were destroyed.

Sylvia Ostry, then the Chairman of the ECC, could explain all that. She said that the disclaimer appeared on the Mintz document because of a new policy, adopted in January 1979, to distinguish between consensus documents, on which virtually all members of the Council were in agreement, and "other Council publications," where there might be some disagreement.[16] It just happened that this policy was implemented for the first time in the Mintz case. As to the destroyed 10,000 bulletins, well, Ostry wrote in a letter to an inquiring MP, "The contents of the proposed February Bulletin were examined in the light of the Council's guidelines on publication and it was concluded that the article summarizing the Mintz Study was inappropriate for the reasons outlined above. An article featuring a more timely and newly released study on energy conservation was substituted in the Bulletin." Actually, it wasn't the February Bulletin that was involved, but the January one, and it wasn't proposed, it was in print.

Never mind. Mintz' dynamite was dunked in a bucket. The study was released, but received little notice – the disclaimer made members of the Parliamentary Press Gallery, who might have spread the word, nervous. A leading article in the Bulletin would have set them off, all right, but that had been scrubbed. Mintz went back to Queen's, where he is still studying banks, and smiling rueful smiles about what happened. "I thought I was just bringing an important bit of information to the world," he says. "Boy, was I naive." He adds, "I learned something about the banks' clout."

MacIntosh and the CBA were not entirely winners in this exchange – the report still came out – what they did, in essence, was to avoid losing, and that can be said, as well, about the way the amendments to the Bank Act worked out.

Those amendments were delayed, repeatedly, by changing governments, until what was to have been a 1977 amendment became, eventually, the Bank Act of 1980. Along the way, there were a couple of other developments in the banking field that required the earnest attention of the banking lobby. One of these was a proposal, introduced as legislation in 1977, to require much fuller disclosure of interest charges by lenders, including banks. The lobby went into action, the MPs were called to order, and the bill died.[17] Then there was agitation to apply the rules of competition set forth in a much-debated Restrictive Trades Practices Act to the banks.[18] Robert Bertrand, who was a tough, and controversial, Director of Combines Investigation when this was under discussion, told me, "There was no way the banks wanted me to be looking at them. We did a couple of in-house studies, and they turned up some very interesting stuff. But in the end, the banks were none of our business. They got themselves specifically exempted from Competition Law." Instead, the banks are controlled, or not, under the Bank Act.

All of this was merely a warmup for the main bout, which involved wheeling platoons of lobbyists from banks, trust companies, finance firms, leasing and factoring companies, car dealers, credit unions and consumer groups. They descended on Ottawa in droves, handed out press releases in reams, testified before committees in bundles, and left in tears. When it was all over, MacIntosh and the CBA had most of what they wanted, and the rest could Go Fish.

The White Paper

Between the 1967 revision of the Bank Act and 1977, when it was due for another re-write, the banks multiplied their assets three-fold and their profits four-fold, but it was not enough, and the way they told the story to the Ottawa mandarins, they were the victims of cruel fate. They were still limited in their access to the mortgage market, they had to bear the burden of reserves, from which the trust companies were free, and they could not get into the lucrative leasing and factoring fields, like the foreign banks. This was because the foreign banks were not banks in Canada, and that was pretty unfair, too. These pleas fell on sympathetic ears in Ottawa – for the banks, there are no other ears in the national capital – and the White Paper released in 1976 gave them most of what they wanted:[19]

1. The near-banks would be required to hold reserves, and to join a new Canadian Payments Association, which would take over the cheque-clearing functions of the CBA. Until now, the near-banks had paid a fee to have their cheques handled by the bankers' group. Now, they would be invited – or, rather, forced – to join the club. The membership fee was reserves.

2. Reserve requirements would be changed, although the principle of differentiating between time and demand deposits would be retained. The reserve on demand deposits would remain at twelve per cent, while that on time deposits would be two per cent on the first $500 million and four per cent on the remainder of a bank's holding. The White Paper felt that "Most trust and mortgage companies . . . and small banks will attract only the two per cent reserve requirement." That would hold, of course, only as long as they remained small.

3. Banks could be chartered by letters-patent, as well as by Act of Parliament. This would ease the entry of small banks into the market and help "to ensure a healthy level of competition."

4. Foreign banks operating non-banking subsidiaries in Canada would be required to turn themselves into banks "because of the additional competitive and innovative forces that they can bring to bear in the relatively highly concentrated Canadian banking system." There would be some curbs on their growth. Their total liabilities would be limited to twenty times their authorized capital, and increases in that capital would be subject to approval of the federal cabinet. "The policy, subject to review, will be to limit total operations of foreign banks to fifteen per cent of total commercial lending."

5. Banks would be allowed into leasing – renting out equipment, including cars.

6. They would also be allowed into factoring – taking over accounts receivable for a share of the debt collected.

7. The ten per cent limit on banks' holdings of residential mortgages would be lifted.

There were other changes, too, such as a provision for greater financial disclosure, some curb on the banks' power to control competing firms and a limit on their ability to sell data processing services, but the gist of the changes is found in these seven points. Looking over the White Paper, Allen Lambert, former President of Toronto-Dominion, was able to purr, with an unconscious reflection of history, "There were not many surprises. The paper followed fairly closely the recommendations of the Canadian Bankers' Association."[20]

Other elements of the financial community were not so pleased, and their screams of outrage marked the beginning of a four-year campaign. Lobbyists, for and against the new Act, shoaled through the corridors of power, distributing smiles and press releases. MPs received letters, calls and visits. Any newsman in the capital without lunch money could feed for free just by evincing an interest in the Bank Act. There were hearings in the Senate, and then in the House, which tacked pieces onto the legislation, and then took them off again. The Trudeau government presented a bill which was substantially what the White Paper called for, with a couple of important exceptions, one detrimental to the banks, and one in their favour. First, there was a provision that bank employees could not be directors of outside corporations except in "special circumstances." There went the network. Secondly, there would be no reserve against time deposits with a term of more than one year.[21]

But this bill got bogged down in the parliamentary process, and never passed. When the Trudeau government was defeated, the incoming Tories put a bill into the hopper that was substantially the same, but they were defeated in turn, before anything could come of it. Finally, the Liberals were re-elected, and introduced a new version which went through new committee hearings. These were among the liveliest ever held in Ottawa. In part, that was because the credit unions, trust companies and financial firms lobbied just as aggressively as the banks, and in part it was because Bud Cullen, Chairman of the House Committee on Finance, invited witnesses for and against the bill to the same sessions. Thus we had Ben Turpin, an Ottawa car dealer, mixing it up with Robert MacIntosh, the gong-voiced bank lobbyist. Turpin said that what the banks were aiming to do was to take over the auto-leasing market by undercutting current prices, and then raising them again when they had control. He said that when you went to your friendly bank manager for money to lease a car, he would ask you why you should not, instead, lease from the bank itself. The banks, using their knowledge of customers' financial arrangements, and their leverage on customers, would wipe out the profitable leasing business of the auto sales firms. But the banks were not going into the repair business; instead, their leased cars would be dumped back on companies, like his own, for servicing. Consumers would suffer and the car firms would suffer while the banks, who could get their money more cheaply than their rivals, would mop up the gravy. MacIntosh replied to deny that the banks would damage the auto-leasing companies, and to claim that consumers would gain, because leasing prices would come down. He produced statistics which differed from those being profferred by the auto-lobbyists, and the session degenerated into something of a shouting match. When it broke up, I approached a number of the MPs on the committee, and they seemed agreed that MacIntosh had not been impressive. His view of the matter was that the leasing firms were "Cry babies – all they're afraid of is a little competition"; but that was not what Turpin was afraid of – he feared a lot of competition, in a system that might put him out of business and the banks even more firmly in the driver's seat. MacIntosh lost that one. The House committee recommended an amendment, which became law, limiting the banks to leasing only those vehicles weighing more than 46,000 pounds – effectively debarring them from car-leasing, although they are free to walk into the rest of the lucrative leasing field.

That incident showed that MacIntosh was not as effective before the MPs as before the senators. The atmosphere in the Commons committee was quite different from the clubby tone the bankers are used to when dealing with their chums in the Senate Banking Committee. There, when the subject of outside directorships held by bank officers came up, the senators quivered with rage. The whole idea of worrying about a conflict of interest on the part of a banker smacked of sacrilege; it was an insult, unnecessary and demeaning; banks were perfect, why fool with them?[22]

Senator Cook: "It is only fair to say it is a criticism made by those who are not bank directors."

Senator Beaubien: "Is it not fair to say that over the past fifty years Canadian banks have behaved better and turned in better performances than many other institutions? If that is the case, why put in regulations when they have done so well?"

The MPs were not quite that credulous, but they were appallingly ignorant. In Canada, parliamentary committees do not have expert staffs to generate evidence of their own, as in the United States. They are dependent on the lobbyists, and on the material the government chooses to bring before them. The government kept trotting out William Kennett, Inspector General of Banks, and Gerald Bouey, Governor of the Bank of Canada, who had nothing but nice things to say about the banks.

Richard Lafferty is a Montreal investment dealer and gadfly, who has made something of a career of attacking the banks (he is the co-author of an unpublished book called "The Public Indictment of the Pillagers and Concubines", which is about the banks and their business links; the title gives you some of the flavour of the man.) He asked, and then demanded, to be called before the House committee, but he was given the brush-off. Too bad. He wanted to recommend that "banking" be defined in law, bank officers be barred from serving as outside directors, and foreign banks be allowed to compete in Canada on the same basis as native banks. He also wanted the banks to produce much more information for shareholders, including the salaries of top officers, and proposed that "The business activities of banks shall be confined to normal banking services." Finally, he hoped to get into print his observation that "Anyone who is in business and who is or has been critical of the banks knows how they use their muscle to silence the critics of the system. It is evident from the way the politicians conduct themselves that they have effectively infiltrated the political arena." Committee Chairman Bud Cullen straight-armed Lafferty with the observation that there was not time to hear him, and the committee went with the evidence it had, to wit, the competing claims of the lobbyists topped off with a dollop of government expertise, tilted heavily in favour of the banking establishment.

When it was all over, and a new law was in place, here is what happened to the major recommendations:

1. A Canadian Payments Association was established in law to take over the cheque-clearing business. It is in the process of formation, but the near-banks will be able to decide whether or not they want to join an organization bound to be dominated by the chartered banks, or continue merely to pay a fee-for-service. They will not have to pay maintain reserves in either event. The argument that the trust companies had an unfair advantage over the banks because of their reserve exemption collapsed in the face of overwhelming evidence that the near-banks are in financial difficulty, while the banks are piling up record profits, year after year. The near-banks won this one, and the banks have already begun to mount a campaign to reverse the decision. (The Bank of Nova Scotia's Monthly Review for January 1981 complained that reserve requirements are forcing up interest rates, indirectly.)

2. The main reserve requirements have been cut substantially. Over the next four years, the reserve on demand deposits will drop from twelve per cent to ten per cent, and on term deposits from four per cent to three per cent. Several kinds of deposits are removed from reserve requirements, such as money in Registered Retirement Savings Plans. The banks were not able to get an exemption for term deposits on loan for more than a year – that was the "fight we have not yet lost" Bill Kennett was talking about in Chapter Eleven – but they are still trying for that. The reserve drop is an enormous victory for the banks. They get no interest on money held in reserve by the Bank of Canada, and they think that is unfair. (On the other hand, the government keeps $100 million in each of the major banks, for which it gets no interest, either. This is to cover government cheques, which must be cashed free, but the money allows the banks to expand their loans base. It isn't free money, but it helps.) A drop in the reserve requirement will turn loose a lot of new money for the banks. In October, 1981, they were holding $21.62 billion in demand deposits and $123.78 billion in notice deposits. In effect, they will get two per cent of the former – $432 million – and one per cent of the latter – $1.23 billion – turned back for their use. It can then be put out

on loan with the usual multiple — ten times for the demand money, twenty-five times for the notice money, so this small change will add over $35 billion to bank assets. It will also, just in case anybody cares, reduce the margin of safety in banking.

3. The letters-patent approach to chartering has been adopted. It will make the Minister of Finance — in effect, the Inspector General — the sole judge of who should, or should not, be allowed to set up in the banking business. In a business already so dominated by the Big Five, it is hard to see how this change will make any difference to the oligopoly.

4. Foreign banks have been brought into the banking system, and will be required to keep reserves. They will be limited in growth in a number of ways. First, as in the White Paper, they will be restricted to assets worth twenty times their authorized capital, with increases in that capital subject to the approval of the Minister of Finance. Then, they will be limited to a total of eight per cent of the assets of the Canadian banking system — a much harsher limit than that envisioned in the White Paper. At present, this means that all the foreign banks in Canada can grow to about $14 billion[23] in assets, or about one-sixth of the size of the Royal Bank. Finally, they cannot open more than one branch without the permission of the Minister of Finance. Originally, the entrance of foreign banks was to open up the doors to competition in Canadian banking. Indeed, it was to be the major factor in providing competition. Now, the banks are able to view the intruders with remarkable equanimity. The Bank of Nova Scotia's newsletter reviewing the Bank Act changes comments, "Foreign-owned banks will probably not attempt to penetrate the retail banking market to any great extent."[24] And the President of the Mercantile Bank noted cheerily that "By getting caged, they're less danger to anyone here in the country. They're less competitive today than they were a year ago."[25]

5. Banks were allowed to enter directly into the business of leasing large equipment — although they are still barred from auto-leasing. They are bound to become the dominant force in this market, since they have ready access to (relatively) cheap money and to knowledge of who is in the market for leases — their customers. The

notion that the bankers will not exploit the information on their files to try to steer business to their own leasing subsidiaries – the banks' official position – is like the story about the Easter Bunny – interesting but improbable.

6. They are also allowed to go into factoring. Indeed, the range of businesses the banks are not allowed to get into may soon be shorter than the list of the kinds of service they can perform. If this means that they will provide more competition in the market, so be it; there is a strong body of opinion that the banks will keep charges down until they control the market and then jack them up again.

7. The limit on bank holdings of residential mortgages was left, after due consideration, at ten per cent. There is, of course, no limit on the mortgages their subsidiaries can hold. The mortgage and trust companies mounted a war on this one, with a demand that banks be kicked out of the mortgage field altogether; the banks were able to retain the status quo.

Of the two key changes added after the White Paper, the banks won one and lost one. They managed to get the limitation on outside directors reduced to gibberish. The Act now says that no bank officer can join the board of a company where that board is already more than twenty per cent composed of members of that same bank. Under this definition, every single member of a company board could be a bank officer, though they could not all come from the same bank. There is no corporation I have been able to find that will have to make any change in its board as a result of this "reform." The network is safe. However, the banks lost the battle to have reserve requirements removed on term deposits of more than one year, as we have seen. Again, what the banks saw as a loss was the maintenance of the status quo.

In sum, the banks gained far more than they lost. The muzzle placed on foreign-bank competition and the lower reserve requirements more than make up for the minor setbacks the lobby received during the legislative process.

In case you wonder why the banks always seem to win, I have no one sentence answer. It is true that they are, by far, the most important donors to political parties in this country. Each of the Big Five gives $50,000 a year to each of the Liberal and Conservative parties – though not a dime to the NDP.[26] You expect something in return for that kind of outlay. It is also true that the bankers, led by MacIntosh, spend a lot of time ensuring a favourable press. Not only do they advertise heavily, both individually and as the CBA, they talk to friendly journalists in friendly tones. In June 1981, when the furor about exploding bank profits was at its height, Rowland Frazee, Chairman of the Royal Bank, and Robert Utting, Vice-Chairman, threw a cosy little dinner for a group of Ottawa journalists to set them straight on the subject.[27] It resulted in nice coverage.

It all helps. So does the business of contacting bank managers and asking them to keep tabs on the local MP, for buttonholing purposes.

But it is my feeling that none of this matters nearly as much as the overwhelming fact that Canadians have been taught, over the decades, to revere their bankers, to assume that the bankers know what is best for the country, and to conclude that whatever the bankers want in the way of a Bank Act is just about what they should get.

As the Bank Act drama was winding down, the Globe and Mail ran an article about the lobbying process, which began, "Robert MacIntosh, President of the Canadian Bankers' Association, is singing the Bank Act blues, because the banks have been out-lobbied by various other interest groups."[28] The unsigned article went on to picture MacIntosh as being "dismayed" by the way he had been out-slickered, and to leave the reader wracked with sympathy for the poor dear "licking his wounds in Toronto, wondering what went wrong."

I like to think that when MacIntosh saw that one in the paper, he laughed and laughed.

13

There Is Some Corner Of A Foreign Field That Is Forever Mortgaged

"I don't know why Canadians are upset about bank profits. We've stopped screwing Canadians. Now we're screwing foreigners."

Bank of Nova Scotia Executive, *November 1981*

I was standing on a street corner outside the Bank of Nova Scotia in Kingston, Jamaica, being called an "imperialist" and a "foreign pig" and a number of other things I couldn't make out, and didn't particularly want to, when the thought occurred to me that there are a lot of drawbacks to the rapid expansion of Canadian banks into the world market. The young gentleman with the weird hairdo, loud voice and savage temper was inviting me to leave, forthwith, and to dispose of all Canadian banks — the subject of our casual conversation — in a suitable receptacle, although that is not how he put it. It is hard lines indeed for a Canadian abroad to find himself assailed as if he were an American, forsooth, or a citizen of one of the other nations normally classed as "imperialists" or "bloodsuckers," or "foreign devils," in the liturgy of the restless local populace. But there it is: Canadian banks are world-class institutions; world-class insults go with the turf; and there is something to be said for the argument that our banks, when they go roaming the world in search of markets for money, may be creating as many problems as they solve.

For better or for worse — and there is something of both in this development — the foreign thrust of our financial institutions is an accomplished fact; indeed, if present trends continue, within the decade our Big Five banks may well have more assets outside Canada than within our own borders.

In the Appendices, Table 9, which outlines the size of the investment our banks have developed over the past decade, in dollars and as a percentage of their assets, shows that foreign growth is even more impressive than domestic growth, and is becoming a larger and larger share of our bank activity. A decade ago, when the total assets of our banks ran to $60.6 billion, foreign assets accounted for twenty-six per cent of that, or $15.6 billion. By the end of 1981, all assets had multiplied a whopping 5.6 times, to $343 billion, but the foreign sector had multiplied 8.9 times, to $138.9 billion. Our banks had almost twice as much money invested abroad in 1981 as they had in total assets in 1972, and the foreign segment had grown to forty per cent of total assets. Keep it up, and we will have a foreign banking community with a Canadian base. Today, our banks have 300 branches abroad, and a "correspondent relationship" – means they do business together – with more than 5,000 financial institutions around the globe. Big.

Table 10 shows that the Big Five are all heavily into foreign ventures, but some are more deeply involved than others. The Royal Bank and the Bank of Nova Scotia are the big players, followed in order by the Bank of Montreal, the Bank of Commerce and Toronto-Dominion. The Royal Bank, in its 1981 Annual Report, showed that it had earned $177 million of its $492.5 million profit abroad, or thirty-six per cent. The Bank of Montreal made $115.6 million in profit from foreign operations, more than thirty-two per cent of its total profit. The Bank of Nova Scotia earned more abroad than it did at home in 1981 – of a total profit of $224 million, $122 million came in from outside. Foreign operations provide this large and increasing share of the take-home pay because, although the lending margins are narrower outside Canada than they are inside – the spread between the price of buying and selling money in Europe is often less than one per cent – overhead costs are much lower, since much of the expense is borne in the home office.

Table 11 shows that the Canadian banks concentrate

their efforts in the same sectors of the world. In order, our areas of activity rank this way: Europe, the United States, Latin America and the Caribbean, Asia and the Pacific, and the Middle East and Africa. The Bank of Montreal and the Bank of Nova Scotia are more heavily involved in the Caribbean than the others, for historical reasons, but by and large, the banks travel in a pack.

There are advantages to Canada in the world-reach of our banking community, a reach which the bankers always hasten to point out stems from the same giant size which often causes such controversy at home. The first advantage of size is that Canadian companies operating outside the country have ready access to funds from their own banks. One of the reasons Canadian development firms have done so well in the United States (although they were forced to pull back somewhat in the chilly economic climate of 1981 and early 1982) is that they have taken their banking connections abroad with them.[1] Cadillac Fairview of Toronto built up more than $650 million worth of real estate assets in the United States, much of it purchased with the help of Canadian banks, and, incidentally, sometimes in the teeth of American resistance. A $118 million commercial and residential development in Portland, Oregon brought complaints from a group called SOLD – for Save Our Livable Downtown – which suffered the usual fate of those who go up against developers; they lost. Whatever Americans think of this sort of thing, it is plain that the Canadian corporations are pleased. Angus McNaughton, Chief Executive Officer of Genstar Limited, a Canadian developer with $250 million worth of projects under way in the United States, put the point this way in a seminar of real estate operators:

"What we have found is that certainly the Canadian banks understand us and certainly know us better than the U.S. banks. So in some cases they are more competitive. . . . The last deal we did down there was a $100 million transaction where we borrowed $100 million U.S. from a Canadian bank. There are not too many American banks that can make one loan of the $100 million. So that is another advantage of the Canadian banks."[2]

That's one way to put it. Another was suggested to me by an American banker in New York: "Your guys come galloping down here with bank backing and start to throw their weight around. Canadians are always whining about U.S. interference in your economy, but that's exactly what you're doing to us." I blush to admit that I replied, "Good for us." The presence of a large Canadian bank in a foreign market means, in many cases, that Canadian funds are not shifted abroad to finance foreign projects; they can be borrowed abroad by the bank itself. In Canadian real estate development in the United States, for example, five Canadian firms built up a U.S. investment of $1.5 billion on an injection of $100 million in Canadian funds – about eight per cent of the total.[3] The rest was raised on the spot. Again, Canadian firms buying in foreign markets use the banks to provide credit, and Canadian firms selling abroad can arrange payment through the banks. The Royal Bank has established a separate subsidiary, Royal Bank Export Finance, to provide funds for Canadian exporters.[4] Instead of having to wait for the locals to come up with the cash, the exporter can sell his accounts receivable to the bank, at a discount, and the bank will collect. There are six billion dollars in Canadian receivables outstanding abroad at any one time.

A second advantage of the foreign operations of our banks is that they earn money abroad, some of which finds its way back home, to help improve our balance of payments. The banks are as close-mouthed about this as they are about most of their dealings, so there is no reliable measure of the impact of these foreign earnings. Clearly, however, if the Royal Bank earns $177[5] million abroad, and wants to pay dividends, and put money into its Rest Account, it is going to have to bring some of this back.

Finally, the Canadian banks gain us access to foreign banks, foreign governments and foreign firms. It has become normal for large international loans to be put together by syndicates of banks, to spread the risk, and the business, around. At this writing the Royal is involved in ninety-five such syndications in the European market alone, and these total $14.6 billion in U.S. funds. The Bank of Nova Scotia is a partner in sixty-four syndicates with $14.1 billion in loans, and the Bank of Montreal in fifty-three syndicates lending $13.7 billion.[6] A list of the top twenty banking syndicates in Eurodollars has the Royal in eleventh place, the Bank of Nova Scotia in twelfth and the Bank of Montreal in fourteenth (five American banks head the list).[7] It is a matter of national pride as well as national convenience that our banks play this kind of role abroad.

Three Drawbacks of World Banking

It may also be a matter of national concern on three counts. The first has to do with the inflationary aspect of international banking, a subject dealt with at length in the next chapter. The second is the financial aspect of such banking – many of these loans are hanging by a thread; without the glue of faith which is the common bond of banking, we would already be facing a crisis of mammoth proportions in many areas of the world. The third is the political (some would say moral and ethical) aspect of our activities abroad. We have an uncomfortable habit of finding dictators to press money on.

It will help us to deal with these matters, which are reflected quite differently in different areas of the world, if we know, first, a little about how we got into the world market, and what we are up to in each of the major areas.

The Start — West Indies Banking

Canadian banks began to roam offshore even before they began their internal expansion. The "maritime" banks, as the Bank of Nova Scotia and the Royal Bank were called, followed Canadian trade to the Caribbean and to the United States long before they moved into western Canada. The first agency of a Canadian bank was established in New York City in 1855, twelve years before Confederation, and the Bank of Nova Scotia opened a branch office in Kingston, Jamaica in 1889, a year before there was any branch of that bank in Ontario.[8] In the 1880s, the economy was severely depressed in eastern Canada (for which Maritimers blamed the new-fangled Confederation, with its dominant role for central Canada), and that led to a search for new markets. At the same time, the West Indies were looking for places to sell their sugar and fruit. The fact that many of the islands were British in ownership and English-speaking made them a natural place to turn – besides, there was not the fierce competition that we faced in American markets. So the West Indies became our first area of expansion; it remains the only area of the world where Canadian banks play the lead role. Daniel Jay Baum, a Professor of Law and Administrative Studies at York University in Toronto, and the author of The Banks of Canada in the Commonwealth Caribbean, calls the West Indies flatly, "an area of Canadian financial domination."[9] The process began in the 1880s, when Thomas Fyshe, chief cashier for the Bank of Nova Scotia, was persuaded by an American stock-broker friend to visit Jamaica, and liked what he saw. The bank's expansion to Kingston was the result, and the beginning of a process that has put 122 Scotia branches into the West Indies, centred on Jamaica. The Royal Bank ventured south after General Manager R. L. Pearse made a trip to Cuba at the behest, and with the financial backing, of some American friends, just after the Spanish-American war.[10] In fact, the Royal acted as agent for the so-called "army of Liberation" that took over Cuba.

For some time, the two banks concentrated on building up their Caribbean empires, each within its own sphere of influence – Nova Scotia in Jamaica and the Royal in Cuba. By the beginning of World War I, the two banks had expanded to Puerto Rico, Trinidad, British Honduras and British Guiana. There was some overlapping, as Nova Scotia moved into Cuba, drawn by the Royal Bank's rich profits there. Indeed, the business was so profitable that in 1919 Canada seriously considered taking the Commonwealth Caribbean off Mother England's hands, and running it ourselves (No one asked the British how they would feel about it). However, Sir Robert Borden, then the prime minister, quashed the notion. It would require too large an outlay of capital, and besides, there was the problem of the natives, what he called, "The difficulty of dealing with the coloured population, who would probably be more restless under Canadian law than under British control and would desire and perhaps insist upon representation in Parliament."[11] If the natives were going to want the vote, to hell with them.

Between the wars, the Royal expanded into other West Indian islands and then into Central and South America, while the Bank of Nova Scotia tended to concentrate on Jamaica, Cuba, Puerto Rico and the Dominican Republic. No other Canadian banks got into the act until after World War II, when the Bank of Montreal, which had until then been content to concentrate on foreign exchange operations, rather than foreign branches, formed a joint banking venture, called BOLAM, with the Bank of London and South America (thus the name, Bank of London and Montreal). The Bank of London already had operations in Colombia, Venezuela, Ecuador, El Salvador, Guatemala and Nicaragua, and the new joint venture moved into Jamaica, Trinidad, the Bahamas, Venezuela, Honduras, Grand Cayman and elsewhere. The Bank of Commerce followed, expanding a small holding of three Caribbean outlets in 1955 to sixteen by 1962.

The onset of nationalism in the West Indies in the late 1960s and early 1970s led to demands that the Canadian banks offer shares locally, or sell off part of their holding to local governments. In Cuba, the Castro government bought out all foreign banks, including Canadian ones, in 1960.[12] In Jamaica, where the banks had been operating as branches of the Canadian parents, they were required to become domiciled on the island, and to offer shares to Jamaicans, in a process that began in 1966.

In essence, it was our Caribbean experience that put Canada into international banking; that was where we built up our expertise, learned how to deal with foreign governments, mastered the mysteries of operating in a number of currencies at the same time, and earned the profits that made us hanker for other foreign adventures.

We were in the role of colonizers; our interests, like those of other colonizers, were our own, and not often those of the host country. West Indian banking laws, when they were written, were written with our help and advice, and for our benefit. The Jamaican Bank Act of 1960 was based on a study conducted by Graham Towers, former Governor of the Bank of Canada. Professor Baum calls this law "the prototype" of West Indian banking laws. It left discretion in most areas of banking entirely up to the Minister of Finance, who had a convenient habit of acting in a way that benefited the banks. Until local sentiment, and local laws, made us change, we were content to use white, or near white, help in the banks, and to lend the money we took in according to our own lights. Tourism yes, agriculture no. Money was found for consumer loans, and indeed, it was imported from Canada to supplement local deposits to finance cars, TV sets and other luxury goods, much more readily than to develop local industry. William

Demas, a Trinidad economist, complained that "Not only does the system permit the external borrowing to finance consumption; such borrowing is used to finance imports of luxuries or semi-luxuries when there is a large amount of domestic unemployment and when the glaring necessity exists to mobilize domestic resources for development."[13]

How the Banks Dodged Control

The Canadian government had the power to bring the Canadian banks to heel, to force them to behave as "good corporate citizens" in other lands, as we were always urging the American government to force U.S. firms in Canada to behave, but we have already seen that Canadian banking law is written, in the main, for the banks. The inevitable result is described by Professor Baum this way: "The overall and firm impression with which one is left after reading the (Bank) Act is that its drafters did not intend to control the foreign operations of Canadian banks, or that if they intended to, they failed to do so."[14]

In the circumstances, it is not surprising that rising West Indian nationalism was accompanied by attacks on the Canadian banks. They were, and are, so conspicuous. The white Canadian bank manager lives, often, in a white stucco house surrounded by a white palisade; he drives in a chauffered limousine, he herds with the white and near-white upper crust, he lends money to the deserving, which is to say, those who have a reasonable expectation of paying it back, as opposed to those who desperately need it, and he inspires the kind of dislike that led to mob violence in Port of Spain, Trinidad, in 1970, after West Indians were charged with smashing up a computer installation in Sir George Williams University in Montreal.[15] The protests in Trinidad focused with unerring aim on the Canadian banks in the capital. That led to a grumbling speech by Donald Fleming, a former Canadian Finance Minister and then Managing Director of the Bank of Nova Scotia Trust Company in the Bahamas, in which he warned that such actions "seriously damaged the entire area, including the country, in the eyes of investors abroad."[16]

The banks were among the targets of Prime Minister Michael Manley of Jamaica, before he lost the 1980 election. His dilemma was that to obtain the financing he needed for a collapsing economy — which was being withheld by banks, and by the International Monetary Fund because they didn't approve of Manley — he would have to agree to a great many conditions, such as cutting government spending, which were bound to increase local unemployment, already running at thirty per cent. Mismanagement, bad luck and sharply increasing oil prices put Jamaica at the mercy of outsiders, but Manley wasn't willing to follow the strictures of those who were putting up the money.[17] His government led Jamaica close to the verge of bankruptcy, and close to the embrace of Fidel Castro in communist Cuba, before an election replaced him with Edward Seaga, a man of more conservative bent and amenable disposition.[18] The crisis passed with an infusion of funds, but the underlying difficulties remain and are shared by most of the West Indies. In brief, the area is broken into dozens of financial shards which might, in time, with the right leadership, make a single economically viable unit that could compete in the world. There is no sign of such a development, and the role of our banks remains uncertain. We are making money, but we are not making friends, and we are not likely to.

In Grenada, the Royal Bank was accused of "promoting destabilization" in the economy by Prime Minister Maurice Bishop, and the Bank of Commerce has pulled out of the left-wing nation entirely.[19] While the bank cited economic reasons for the pullout, the locals claimed — and the bank denied — that a major reason was the fact that the firm's employees decided to form a union.

The West Indies do not form a huge part of the Canadian banking system's assets. At the end of 1979, our banks had assets in Latin America and the Caribbean of $17.03 billion.[20] The sum is large by local standards, but not by Canadian banking standards; one Canadian banker told me bluntly, "If it gets to be too much trouble down there, more than it's worth, if we get more nationalization and a few more riots, well, to hell with it, we'll just pull back and let them see how they like it on their own."

Embarrassing Questions

Canadian banks are active in Latin America, although not to the same degree as in the Caribbean. The money tends to flow, not surprisingly, where the banks feel comfortable, and where they seem to feel comfortable is in Brazil — where the Bank of Montreal recently bought Banco Brascan de Investimento, S.A.[21] — in Argentina — where the Big Five poured in more than $1 billion in 1979[22] — in Chile, and in Guatemala. What these nations have in common is repressive regimes, a fact that brings members of the Taskforce on the Churches and Corporate Responsibility out to the annual meetings of Canadian banks to ask embarrassing questions. In 1982, members of the Taskforce, whose annual budget of $47,301 would scarcely buy the olives for the martinis of the bank boards it goes up against, expressed "horror and indignation"[23] at the Bank of Commerce meeting, because that bank is lending money to Guatemala, where thousands of citizens have been murdered in recent years by their own government. A handful of nuns and hangers-on were not going to deflect the Commerce from its appointed rounds, and the protest got nowhere.

However, the Taskforce has won one victory — although not in Latin America. The Toronto-Dominion Bank announced in early 1980[24] that it would no longer be making loans to the government of South Africa or any of its agencies. Apartheid has been condemned repeatedly by the Canadian government, and there are restrictions — more honoured in the breach than the observance — on commercial dealings with that nation; but the banks, until this time, had steadfastly stonewalled any attempt to curb their activities there. Deals in any foreign land, they said, come under the rubric of client confidentiality. While it is customary for the banks to boast of their foreign conquests — the business pages are littered with headlines that say "Canadians Make It Big In Hong Kong"[25] or "3 Banks, EDC in financings worth $1 billion to Mexico," or "Canadian banks bullish on Australia's resource prospects,"[26] you don't find any that read, "Racist Regime Cheers Canadian Funding." I can't imagine why not.

In private, senior bankers will admit that their loan policies abroad are guided by political, as well as commercial, considerations. "Of course we know about the politics of the countries where we lend money," one executive said to me. "We'd be stupid not to." Each major bank has an intelligence unit, composed of half-a-dozen experts in statistics, economics and, yes, politics. Each bank divides the world into lending areas, and establishes "country quotas" for every nation where the bank is doing, or proposing to do, business. The size of the quota depends on a number of factors, but at the head of the list is "political stability." Stable countries are favoured, countries where stability is threatened – as in Jamaica in 1979 and 1980 – lose priority. There is nothing exceptional in that.

Where the problems arise is when the political information seeps into the economic area, as inevitably happens. Banks don't like socialist regimes, since any such regime is likely to have the nationalization of foreign banks on a list of Things To Do Right Away. On the principle of "the enemy of my enemy is my friend," the banks are attracted, in turn, to all the nice colonels and generals and field marshals who tend to congregate around the corpse of democracy or racial equality in foreign lands. Too bad, but there it is. If Canadians disapprove – and I think they should, although I am far from certain that they do – we should press our views on the government, as well as on the banks, because it is the government that sets the tone and establishes the ground rules – and should do so.

When the Globe and Mail asked Bank of Montreal Chairman William Mulholland about South Africa, he replied, "If the public hospital authorities of South Africa wanted to borrow money to build rural hospitals and you had a policy against lending to South Africa, what the hell would you achieve? They (the opponents of such loans) would argue that you're putting pressure on the government because the death rate, the infant mortality rate and all the rest is higher. I'm not prepared to do that."[27]

There is a quotient of peach-pits in this argument. If what Mulholland is saying is that the banks are on the lookout for loans that will save the downtrodden, opportunities abound in the Third World, where the banks are notable by their absence. But he does touch an important, and complex, argument. The Bank of Nova Scotia, as it happens, has a loan out to finance black medical education in South Africa. It is also an agent for the South Africa Chamber of Mines in the sale of the Krugerrand, that popular golden coin dug out of exploitative mines to support an exploitative regime. Should the bank distinguish between these two activities, on the grounds that one is good and the other bad? If so, who is going to set down the rules of good and bad? And on what grounds?

When the Chilean regime of Salvador Allende was first elected to power, all the western banks, including our own, withdrew from Chile, and the economic chaos that resulted was a factor in the subsequent military coup, Allende's murder, and the installation of an oppressive gang of thugs. Then the banks went back in. But leading the exodus and the re-entry were government and quasi-government bodies. It was the Canadian Export Development Corporation, a government body with some members from the private sector, that oversaw a massive shift of funds from Chile to Brazil between 1970 and 1972, when Allende was in power.[28] The banks were merely following government's lead. The same can be said of South Africa. If we don't want to support an apartheid regime, why are we allowing Canadian manufacturers to sell engines which they claim are for civilian use but which end up in tanks? Tank engines classified as truck motors do not make a noble argument that Canada abhors repression.

Or, take Guatemala. The Bank of Nova Scotia has $5 million tied up in the Chixoy hydroelectric plant being erected by the unsavoury Guatemalan government.[29] It became involved at the behest of the Inter-American Development Bank, in which the government of Canada is a shareholder. Whom do you picket? The bank? Ottawa? Or Washington, where the Inter-American Development Bank decisions are really made?

Banks are not the people to decide moral issues in foreign lands. Our assumption should be that they will react, as every business reacts, in light of their own self-interests, and that they will put profitable stability at the head of any list of requirements for financial support. They will react to public relations campaigns like that of the Taskforce, if they are pursued vigorously enough. The Toronto-Dominion Bank didn't back out of South Africa because it suddenly became conscience-smitten, but because it wasn't doing a whole lot of business there, and the bad publicity wasn't worth the effort.

An attempt to come to grips with this thorny issue must begin by assembling far more facts than are now available to the public. The truth is that we don't know which banks are lending, where, or how much. We only know what the banks choose to tell us. The Taskforce has argued that the banks should be required to provide information on any loans to governments or government agencies abroad in excess of $1 million (though not, in deference to client confidentiality, information about private loans). That would at least set us off in the right direction.

One of the things such a provision would bring to light is that a number of the arrangements our banks are involved in look pretty shaky. Brazil, for example, if it were a neighbourhood restaurant, would have been declared bankrupt years ago. Its foreign debt tops $50 billion, inflation is 121%, and it has trouble even paying the interest on outstanding loans.[30] How deeply are our banks involved? Dunno. Will they be repaid? Dunno. If something goes wrong, and the Brazilian loans go down, who will bear the burden? That we do know; one way or another, you and I, in tax write-offs, or government aid, or higher charges. One of the less cheerful aspects of our banks' foreign involvement is that, because of the secrecy surrounding so much of what goes on, the public can be quite misled by reading the banks' financial statements. A loan from the bank, you will recall, is an asset on the books, just as a deposit with the bank is a liability. Therefore, if the bank loans $100 million to the principality of Kumquat, that appears on the good side of the ledger right up until the moment when it becomes apparent that the money is never going to be paid back. Then the bank sets aside a sum to meet the shortfall, and the asset becomes a liability.

What we need is a lot more information than the banks are prepared to give us, and that is a rule that applies to the area where the banks have their greatest involvement – Europe.

Too Many Eggs in One Basket-Case?

Canadian banks had assets in Europe at the end of 1979 of just under $30 billion.[31] It is safe to say that since that time, the figure has doubled (not hard to guess; the foreign assets of our banks are more than doubling every four years, and Europe is the single largest area of investment). Much of this money is at work in Switzerland, France, Italy, the United Kingdom, West Germany, Scandinavia, Holland and elsewhere, building bridges, financing exports to Canada and imports from Canada, constructing schools, mortgaging factories, and performing all the thousand tasks of useful banking. The Bank of Montreal is part of a syndicate lending $175 million to Spain to build a railway.[32] The Royal Bank has just bought Banque Occidentale pour l'Industrie et le Commerce (Suisse), in Switzerland.[33] The Bank of Nova Scotia has just opened a precious metals trading operation in London. And so it goes. We are busy as beavers in Europe.

But we also have a lot of money — sorry, again, nobody knows how much — at work in Eastern Europe, and some of it looks dubious indeed. Canadian banks have $400 million out on loan in Poland, and the Bank of Montreal, while declining to say what its involvement was, announced in early 1982 that it was raising its provision for loan losses by fifty-nine per cent, up to $185 million, in large part because of "turbulent political and economic developments, notably in Poland."[34]

Poland has been a basket case for years, unable even to pay the interest on its ever-mounting debt, but it is not alone. Our banks are also involved in Romania, which owes $10 billion to western lenders (compared to Poland's $27 billion) Czechoslovakia, Bulgaria and Hungary.[35] None of these loans is exactly gold-plated, but we don't know how much they are, or what would happen in the case of a default. Technically, many of these nations are bankrupt, since they cannot meet repayment schedules, but, thanks to the miracle of faith in banking, when the creditors ask for their money and don't get it, or even a reply (that is what happened the last time we broached the subject with Poland), the debt is simply "re-scheduled." Interest is added, and the subject is dropped for a time. Some praying takes place, too; it's called "closely watching," as in "International bankers are closely watching Romania's deteriorating current-debt repayment problems," which was the polite way the Financial Post put it when Romania defaulted late in 1981.[36] Romania owes about $14 billion to the West, the largest single share of which — $1 billion — is Canada's, money being advanced to build two Candu nuclear power plants. The Bank of Montreal is involved, among others, through the aegis of the Export Development Bank. If Romania has gone bust — which appears to be the case — we're going to whistle past the graveyard. "Ottawa is keeping a close eye on the situation," the Financial Post reported. Great. With that and twenty-five cents, you can make a phone call — though not to Romania.

Perhaps it would be less nerve-wracking for us if we just refused to talk about what's going on. When the Globe and Mail lifted an article from the Economist on the gloom enwrapping Eastern Europe, an incensed letter-writer asked a series of questions to which neither the editors of the Globe and Mail, nor anyone else, has answers:

"If these banks have lent untold billions to Russia's satellites, are they a safe place for me to keep my money?

"What bad-debt provisos do these banks carry on these crazy loans?

"What will they do if one of them (or all of them) simply renegs on his loan? Will they go to war to collect?

"Do these banks really and truly believe that they will ever be repaid?"

The letter-writer, W. R. Sachs of Toronto,[37] is obviously lacking in that simple faith which Tennyson claimed was more than Norman blood, and which is so essential to uncritical support of the banking system.

The subject of the European money-market and the dangers thereof will come up again in the next chapter; for the moment, it is enough to say that our banks are making a lot of money in Europe, and expanding rapidly, and engaged, no doubt, in many good works, but they are also running heavy risks, in a belief that in the end, no foreign government will completely repudiate debts entered into in good faith, or, if they do, that our own government will ride to the rescue. We'll see.

Yankee Doodle Dollars

In the meantime, let's talk about the United States, a place where the news, for Canadian banks, is good.

All of the banks conduct their operations according to a series of manuals produced at head office for the guidance of the troops, not unlike a very large, complicated, paint-by-numbers set. The Royal Bank's Lending Manual U.S.A., a secret document marked "For Royal Employees Only," contains this riveting declaration:

"We are not interested in developing and pursuing small or one-time transactions. The basis of our efforts is to participate in large financings that are likely to lead to a lasting and growing relationship. At the risk of turning away some profitable business, we should not pursue transactions that do not meet these standards."

All this yim-yam about meeting the needs of the small investor, the ordinary citizen, the man-with-a-dream is so much banana-oil. What the Royal Bank is after, when it cuddles up to the American market, is the multinational corporation with dollars in its jeans and expansion in its eye. I don't have the manual of any American bank operating in Canada, but I am willing to bet the instructions have a similar ring.

Oh, yes, and how about this:

"Every effort should be made to avoid loan transactions that necessitate heavy day-to-day involvement with the borrower or require a heavy burden of administration. We are not set up for that kind of business."

Forget that film clip from the ad that shows the friendly bank manager talking things over with the client — Bill and the wife. Get it in, get it signed, keep it simple, and latch onto the interest. Clap hands and a bargain. Needless to say, this is not the way Canadian banks present themselves to the Americans; the public talk is all soothing and syrupy. I've said it before and I say it again: the banks are great kidders.

Americans Worry about Us

There are dangers in this kind of approach — or, more specifically, dangers in being caught at it — but no one can quarrel with the fact that our banks are doing very well in the United States, so much so that the Americans are beginning to worry about us. I had a long chat with a senior officer in the Federal Reserve System in Washington, which keeps a much closer eye on American banking than anyone keeps on Canadian banking, and he said, "Frankly, your banks are making mincemeat out of some of ours ... They have the size, the experience and the expertise to walk into even a major American city, set up shop, and start taking business away from the state banks. Some jurisdictions are getting quite worried about it. They don't like the idea of too much control being in the hands of corporations that are not domiciled here. The day may come when we have to do something about it."

Now, there's a switch; Americans worrying about Canadian economic domination. But they do, or at least some of them do. When Canadian banks became active in financing a number of corporate takeover battles in the United States in mid-1981, American politicians made their displeasure clear. Our banks were not bound by U.S. rules that require fifty per cent of the money involved in a takeover to be put up by the purchaser himself – instead of by way of a bank loan. American buyers were swarming to our wickets for such financing. This furor cooled when the banks pulled back, but they remain active in a wide range of fields.

The Canadian banks are centred in New York – the financial hub of the nation – California – a second financial centre in a fast-expanding area of the country – and Houston – which is becoming the centre of energy investment, but they have representatives and agencies virtually all across the country. Our banks have two great advantages over most (though not all) American banks. The first is size. In many states, each bank branch is required to be a separate company. In some states, a holding company may own the branches, which then become, loosely, one large bank. In other states, notably New York and California, "full-branching" as it is called, is legal, just as it is in Canada, but only within the state. There are no nation-wide banks. Even where full-branching is permitted, there are many more banks competing against each other than there are in Canada. This may be good for the consumer but it makes it easier for our banks to walk in and walk out with the business. John McIntosh, who worked for the Royal Bank in Houston before leaving to join Barclays, explains:

"Under Texas law, no bank can devote more than ten per cent of what is called its authorized capital to any single project. And in Texas, there are bank holding companies, but no full branch-banking, so there aren't any really big banks, not what we would call big. So, you are an oil company and you want to raise $120 million in a hurry to put together a deal. You go to a Texas banker and he says, 'Well, that sounds mighty fine. We'll just put together a syndicate and look after your needs.' Which, eventually, he will do. Or you go to a Canadian representative agency, which is what I was, and he says, 'I'll get going on the paperwork right away.'"

That paperwork, incidentally, should be completed for all but the largest loans within seventy-two hours. A typical arrangement — we are again peering at the Royal Bank's Lending Manual — provides the Canadian Lending Manager in a U.S. city with a $1 million limit. He can lend that much on his own say-so. Between $1 million and $3 million, the application must go to the Assistant General Manager for the Region (the United States is divided into three regions for credit purposes). Between $3 million and $5 million, approval must come from "Any two Assistant General Manager/Regional Executive." The Senior Vice President and General Manager can lend up to $10 million. Above that, the loan must come back to Canada for approval, and even then, "When dealing with requests for credit a serious attempt is made to limit turn-around time to seventy-two hours."

There are American banks that can match this size and speed, but they are not many, and that in brief is why our banks are doing so well in the development business, energy, and takeover financing in the United States. Every Canadian bank is expanding rapidly south of the border, and the future prospects look rosy indeed. We may not be lovable, but we are good.

Asia and the Pacific

The same may be said, although on a much smaller scale, concerning our activities in Asia and the Pacific. The Bank of Commerce is heavily involved in real estate financing in Hong Kong, and so is the Bank of Nova Scotia. The Commerce has a partnership with Hong Kong developer Li Ka-Shing in a joint venture called Canadian Eastern, and that relationship has led to access to Communist Chinese banking.[38]

We are also active in our sister commonwealth, Australia. The Bank of Montreal is the lead underwriter in an Australian offshore gas project, and the Royal Bank has been named financial adviser to the Western Australian State Energy Commission for a major gas pipeline project. The appointment was not universally popular; the Financial Post talked to a Perth businessman who called it "absurd."

Elsewhere in the same general region of the globe, the Toronto-Dominion, the Bank of Montreal and the Bank of Nova Scotia are all involved in defence loans to Thailand, which may or may not turn out to be a good thing. A number of American banks shied away from the business, fearing to be labelled "merchants of death."[39] Finally, our banks are expanding in Japan; now that the new Canadian Bank Act allows Japanese banks to set up shop here, we have been given a go-ahead there.

These are not major developments, not yet; all our banking activities in the Far East do not amount to much more than one-third of the commitment to Europe, but the potential is clearly there, and will be exploited. A trading nation, we are trading in money where we used to trade in beaver skins.

Pious Hopes and the World Bank

The last and least of the world areas where Canadian banks have penetrated is the lumped-together region of the Middle East and Africa. Our involvement in Africa, except for South Africa, has tended to follow the Canadian banking policy towards all the Third World areas, which is to exude pious hopes and let it go at that. By and large, the commercial banks have left lending to the International Monetary Fund and the World Bank, although there are some exceptions in water projects and energy developments. Canada participates in both the IMF and the World Bank, but both are, essentially, creatures of American policy. In theory, the International Monetary Fund is the United Nations agency for carrying out the exchange stabilization programs hammered out of Bretton Woods in 1944, and the World Bank is the lending arm of the same body.[40] In fact, the Americans, who put up most of the money, lay down the ground rules for both bodies, neither of which has been notably successful. (John Kenneth Galbraith noted of the IMF that "It could deal admirably with small problems but not with large ones.") Successful or not, they are the people who struggle with the crushing burdens of Third World finance, usually by holding meetings in posh hotels from which underlings emerge from time to time to issue bulletins counselling patience among the starving, and forebarance among their creditors. Our banks have been content that it should be that way, pious hopes aside. A recent move to have the commercial banks become more involved in Third World finance has been criticized – correctly, in my opinion – as likely to cause more problems than it solves. Who is going to foreclose on India? Normal bank loans are not what these nations need, but they are what the commercial banks are designed to provide.

As to the Middle East, where money is not the problem – not for states, anyway – perhaps the most interesting involvement was the fling our bankers had in Iran, before the deposition of the Shah. For a time, it looked as if the Canadian investments – and those of the United States, among others – had been taken hostage, and the banks maintained a decent reticence over how much was at risk, or, as bankers say, "exposed." It appears to have been quite a lot. Euromoney Magazine, putting together the results of advertisements in financial papers, a conservative estimate, concluded that the Commerce was involved in eight loans totalling $1.4 billion,[41] Toronto-Dominion in six loans totalling $14 billion and the Royal Bank in three loans totalling $260 million. The banks were not individually in for these amounts; they were partners in syndications that covered these amounts. Their actual share has never been made public. For a time, this money, whatever it was, trembled on the brink, but now Iran has stated its intention to honour the notes, and the banks can breathe easier again.

We are not used to being Hated

What this hasty spin around the world on the track of Canadian banks indicates is that, in financial terms, they are doing well and growing fast; in political terms they are involved in, and involving us in, some problems of morality and practicality – we are not used to being hated, and it won't do our trade any good; and in economic terms, we may be getting in over our heads, especially in Europe. The time has come to look at that problem in light of the

difficulty it portends for our most pressing economic
need, which is the need to come to grips with inflation.

14
Whose Balloon? Inflation And The Banks Abroad

"The odds, and I don't mean that in a betting way, are that everything is not going to go at once."

Eric Ferguson,
Assistant General Manager, World Trade, Royal Bank.
January 1982

Helmut Mayer was obviously torn between irritation and amusement, between a desire to chuck me out of his swank office overlooking Centralbahnstrasse in downtown Basel, Switzerland, and a concern that if he did so, I would go pedalling my noxious worries somewhere else. In the end, politeness and prudence won over the natural desire of a busy man to be rid of a pestering questioner, and he filled me to the brim with confidence-inspiring quotes. "This is a most complex question," he said. And, "The argument you advance is most naive." And, "You really can take my word for it, the situation is well in hand." It was the last one that finished me off. That is what the central bankers were all saying when the world economy was collapsing in rubble in the 1930s; it is what the market seers were saying before the Franklin Bank cave-in of 1974; it is what the busy people in control, or not, always say when someone asks them a rude question like: Do you people know what the hell you're up to? It is the sound of soothing assurance, not the substance of argument. I am willing to admit that Helmut Mayer, who is the expert on the Euro-dollar market for the Bank for International

Settlements, knows much more about what goes on in the complex world of the gnomes of Zurich than I do, or ever will, but I still think that market carries appalling dangers for all of us.

I had gone to the Bank for International Settlements (the BIS) for answers to a lot of worrying concerns raised by Thomas Velk, an economist and Associate Professor of Banking at McGill University in Montreal. Velk thinks the Euro-dollar market is an inflation-machine, and that world banks, including our own, are fanning the flames of a fire they may never be able to put out. He is an acknowledged expert in international banking, a former consultant to the Board of Governors of the Federal Reserve System in the United States, the author of a number of papers on the international repercussions of what he calls "the new goldsmith banking," and a worried man.

His argument goes roughly like this:

Banks, as we have already seen, are limited in the amount of money they can create out of thin air. If you are able to persuade your friendly neighbourhood bank to lend you $100,000, it will not pass the money across the counter. Instead, a few keystrokes in the old computer, and the money is yours. You could get cash ff you really wanted to, but it would be a nuisance. Cheques are handier. So the bank doesn't need much money in its vault to back the money it creates in the computer. However, the reserve requirements imposed by those niggardly types in government do provide some constraints. The bank must have a dime on hand for every dollar in domestic assets — remember that your loan is an asset to the bank — and that means that if it lends you $100,000, it is using $10,000 of its reserve. Once it reaches its maximum, it can only increase its lending power by bringing in new deposits or adding to its capital base, socking more into reserves, and widening the circle.

But what if there were no reserve? What if the only constraint on creating money was what the economists call its "fungibility," which means, roughly, its interchangeability with other bits of paper? Anything that is acceptable as money is money — playing cards, wampum, coconut shells, or pictures of a log-boom on the Ottawa River backed by a photo of the Queen and a large "1" in each corner. The early goldsmith bankers, Velk says, discovered in the Middle Ages that they could issue bits of paper worth far more than the gold they kept in their vaults, because few of their customers would want to haul the heavy metal around with them. So a piece of paper representing a claim for gold became money, and the banker held onto just enough cash to cover actual clearing transactions (as they have come to be called; they are also known as clearing losses). The banker and the depositor both profited, because the money market expanded, aiding commerce. In time, central banks and governments established rules to limit the creation of fairy gold, but now, says Velk, "Modern private bankers have found a major loophole in the fabric of central bank policy rules: the minimum fractional reserves, and the governmentally produced reserve ... relate only to 'home town' money, and provide no constraint at all to a banker who wishes to create foreign money."

Thus, a Canadian bank can only create a certain number of Canadian dollars, but it can create Japanese yen without number as long as someone else is willing to accept them, as long, in short, as the creations are "fungible." The Euro-currency market is the result of this giant loophole; it is what one American writer has called a "Ponzi scheme on a global scale."[1] In the Ponzi scheme, a large number of people are persuaded to give a little money to the operator of the scheme – the stakes-holder; some of these are rewarded extravagantly, so more are enticed into the scheme with its promise of ever-expanding wealth. When the limit is reached and the pyramid comes crashing down, the original stakes-holder is nowhere to be found. In the banking version of this scheme, the bank accepts deposits, lends them to customers, and then lends the same money to other customers, over and over again. Interest is paid on the deposits, and earned on the loans; new depositors are thus persuaded into the system, and the cycle is repeated. Everything goes well as long as the system continues to expand, but if it ever falters, it will fall in on itself like a collapsing star. How could it falter? Easily. The essence of Euro-market reserves is that they depend on market forces. In good times, everyone is content with fairy gold, or its equivalent, and not much of that. In bad times, only sound money payable in New York or Washington will serve – and there had better be plenty of it. When the need for reserves is greatest, they are scarcest. It's a classic problem for free-market banking. So far, bad times have not happened in the Euro-dollar market. So far.

That market came about in the most ordinary way; it was the result, as even its most enthusiastic boosters will admit, of a desire to escape from supervision and control. It began during the 1950s when the Russians began to deposit dollar holdings in London, because they were afraid that, in those Cold War days, they might wake up one day to find that their money had been restricted or frozen in the United States. To protect against this, they bought dollars outside the United States, which the U.S. Treasury was bound to honour, but which it could in no way control. Other nations found there were advantages to keeping dollars outside the United States, and joined in. Then, in 1957, the United Kingdom, to protect its own dwindling reserves, prohibited the use of sterling as a medium for international finance. The British banks stood to lose all their business in this line unless they took action, so they offered to finance trade with U.S. dollars. It soon became clear that a marvellous new financial instrument had been created, free of the confines of regulation, and the Euro-currency market was off and running.[2]

Suppose, for example, that you are a car-maker based in France anxious to buy Italian steel to make autos in West Germany. You can go to a bank in Belgium and borrow $1 million to buy the steel, simply by having it denominated in, say, U.S. funds. This is done by the simple device of writing onto the loan papers, "In U.S. funds." The Belgian bank now has a note on its books that you owe it $1 million in U.S. funds, which will be repaid, with interest, over, say, five years. That is an asset. To offset that asset, there is a liability, namely, your ability to draw on those funds. You write a bank draft on them and deposit it in a West German bank, where it will earn interest until you draw it out, usually in segments tied to the delivery date of the steel. You pay for the steel with cheques written against the West German account. The steel supplier will in turn use your cheques, which become the base for yet more transactions. If someone calls around for the U.S. dollars, the whole business is in peril; but that's not really likely – cash doesn't earn anything. Velk explains, "Even if someone went to your bank and said 'I want this paid off in

U.S. dollars,' your Belgian banker would say 'Sure, but you realize a U.S. note will only pay eleven per cent in interest, and you realize the Americans send currency inspectors around to check on these deals.'

"The guy will say, 'Oh, oh.' Then the Belgian banker will say, 'Why don't I give you a note on the Midlands Bank instead? They pay fifteen per cent, and the British don't send out inspectors the way the Americans do.' The guy will say Yes, and no U.S. funds will ever leave home."

The Euro-currency market depends on modern communications. Money deposited in New York can be used in Hong Kong, money created in Paris can bob up in Australia, instantly. Restless dollars wing through the air with the speed of light, nosing out investment opportunities wherever they exist. They must never be allowed to rest; a million dollars lying around, even overnight, can lose two or three thousand dollars in unearned interest. So the bazaar never closes, the lights are always burning, the money always flying. The velocity of money counts just as much as its weight, just as the speed of a river counts as much as its volume in swelling a lake; $100,000 re-spent five times has the same impact as $500,000 spent once. Even if the Euro-currency market were controlled, it would have an impact on inflation because of its velocity. But it is not controlled.

The U.S. Comptroller of the Currency, who does have agents stationed around the world to chase down U.S. currency transactions, has difficulty tracing transactions until the funds leave the magic circle of the Euro-currency market. As soon as the money is repatriated, it becomes visible, but as long as it stays abroad, it is free of the meddling of Washington bureaucrats. Even if American money could be controlled, U.S. dollars are not the only Euro-currencies. Obviously, since we are creating money with the flick of a finger, it can be created in any denomination, but the demand for escudos is not excessive. So Euro-currency consists of U.S. dollars, German marks, Japanese yen, Swiss francs, French francs, Dutch guilders, and British pounds, deposited in banks outside of the country of origin and used by those banks as they would use any other deposit. Go forth, these banks say to their currency, and multiply. The U.S. dollar is by far the favourite creation, and probably – nothing is certain, in this area — accounts for close to half of the Euro-currency extant. And how much is there extant? Well, nobody knows. Tom Velk thinks it is "Somewhere between $1 trillion and $2 trillion U.S. dollars, although it may be higher."

A trillion dollars is a stack of thousand-dollar bills sixty-seven miles high. It is a lot of money, and its presence on the world market cannot help but be inflationary, not only on its own account, but because of the effect on other currencies. Currencies are fixed in value according to the key currencies in the Euro-market — the U.S. dollar, the franc, the pound, etc. In effect we have, through linked exchange rates, a single world currency; adding to it in any of the key currencies will tend to increase prices everywhere.[3]

What makes Euro-currency so confusing, as well as so difficult to control, is the fact that it involves transactions from nation to nation, bank to bank, company to bank, company to company, bank to government and government to bank. Some of these are reported, many are not. To keep down the clearing losses in major transactions, the banks have been forming themselves into consortia capable of dealing in a number of currencies at once, and the largest of these consortia, which holds perhaps $100 billion worth of currencies, and is centred on the Bank of America, has made single loans of more than one billion dollars.[4] When that kind of money is whizzing around, it is hard to keep track of. Add the fact that speculators dabble in the market through offshore banks, which are often little more than a brass plate on a door in Grand Cayman or the New Hebrides. These offshore havens are created because they are not required to pay any tax on their profits; nor do they provide any information to anyone. They are sheltered behind laws that make the divulgence of any information about the banks a criminal offence.

Then add in the fact that, in many nations known as the LDCs (Less Developed Countries), which account for perhaps $100 billion in Euro-currency loans, some of the money may be used for arms purchases, or direct investment that never appears on the books even of the purchasing country.

Euro-currency is not entirely immune to national monetary policies. Interest rates in this market rise and fall with the London Interbank Offering Rate, or LIBOR, which moves up and down according to other rates, which are in turn subject to national economic policy in all the nations that follow the LIBOR rate. But this is an indirect control. Direct control, such as that imposed by the U.S. Comptroller of the Currency, who is both trying to protect the U.S. dollar and keep on the lookout for tax dodges, does exist, but only to the extent that the Comptroller can identify the transaction and conclude that it involves his responsibility. The two major weapons for controlling U.S. money have been Regulation Q and Regulation D, which are regulations of the U.S. Banking Act of 1933 and its amendments.[5] Regulation Q forbids U.S. banks to pay interest on money deposited for less than one month. This regulation prevents depositors zipping in and out of markets overnight to speculate in money. It worked so well that it was one of the reasons for U.S. depositors moving to the Euro-market, where their bankers obligingly went to serve them. Regulation D is the American reserve regulation, which puts reserves of anywhere from ten to twenty-two per cent on domestic deposits.[6] Neither of these restrictions applies to the foreign branches of American banks, which is why the large ones hastened to set up in London and Paris and elsewhere to play the Euro-currency game. The largest single currency in the world is free of constraint beyond American shores, a fact that has piled up large profits for the banks of many nations, but which is also piling up problems.

Nobody Knows the Trouble that Looms

The three crucial questions that must be asked about the Euro-market are these:

1. How large is it?
2. How inflationary is it?
3. How dangerous is it?

As to the first, no one knows. The Bank for International Settlements (the BIS), which is based in Basel, and represents the central banks of the world, has made some attempts to find out. It keeps track of central-bank-to-central-bank transactions, through which, it hopes, most of this money must sooner or later pass. As a kind of sidecheck, it also watches the "tombstones," those ads in the financial papers and magazines that boast of deals struck around the world. Obviously, not every financial deal is one the participants want to boast about, but when they do, it can be traced. Finally, the BIS has access to the World Bank's Debtor Reporting System. There are a number of holes in the tables compiled by the BIS. Since only nations that borrow from the World Bank are required to notify that body of their transactions, its listings are incomplete — South Africa and most of Eastern Europe are left out, for example.

Another problem is that the World Bank does not report on debts that mature in less than one year, nor debts which have not been guaranteed by the borrowers' government. All short-term government debt, and all private sector debt except that which receives some form of government guarantee, are left out. In nations where state-controlled enterprises have the ability to enter the Euro-market on their own, there is even some question as to whether the government involved knows what it has borrowed. Sometimes the state agencies report, sometimes they don't.

But if the available figures are incomplete, even those that exist are startling.

The BIS reports show that the "Narrowly defined Euro-currency market" stood at $177 billion in U.S. dollars at the end of 1974. By June of 1980, it had swollen to $540 billion — more than a three-fold growth in less than six years.[7] This figure is a gross under-estimation. When I asked Jean Kertudo, an economist at BIS, about this he said, "Everybody is guessing. We try to guess better than other people, that's all." He was not willing to guess how much money there is in the Euro-currency market outside the figures BIS sees, except that "Obviously it is not insignificant." A senior official at the International Monetary Fund in Washington was a little more forthcoming. He said, "It's obvious that we're not looking at half the problem." And he added, "Maybe it's just as well, because if people knew what a cloud of unsupported debt was hanging out there, they might get nervous."

Some American banks, who are heavy players in this market, have done their own estimates, and Morgan Guaranty Trust estimated the Euro-currency total at $890 billion at the end of 1978.[8] At current growth rates of about thirty per cent per annum, that would put it over two trillion dollars today.

Not one of these figures is reliable, and if that gives you any comfort, God bless.

The second question — how inflationary is the Euro-currency market — obviously depends on the first. The more money there is zipping around the circuit, and the faster it moves, the more inflationary it is. Tom Velk says there are four cylinders in this inflation engine, each reinforcing the others: individuals borrow from banks, and their spending rises; governments borrow from banks and spend more; governments borrow again so they can run inflationary get-elected campaigns while having enough (borrowed) money on hand to keep exchange rates from falling, and that money, re-cycled, starts the whole process again. Euro-money is not just hand-to-hand money, the kind individuals and firms spend, it is bank-to-bank money, government-to-government money, bank-to-government money and government-to-bank money. This money is super-inflationary and super-volatile; its existence encourages the production of still more hand-to-hand money. The heavy thinkers at the BIS, who are always issuing soothing reassurances, say there is nothing to worry about, because it is possible to exercise national control over the money, and because, sooner or later, it must be repatriated. In short, Helmut Mayer says, Tom Velk and others of his ilk are bothering their heads about a phantom. In his explanation to me, Mayer argued, "Each of these dollars must come home, Mr. Stewart. It is quite wrong to say they are created out of thin air. There must be some backing for them, and that backing provides the reserve requirement." If U.S. funds are manufactured to buy steel in Italy, sooner or later those funds will appear as dollars, and travel back to the United States. I said I couldn't see this; banks only need a fraction of the cash on hand to meet the liabilities on their books, even when denominated in their own currency; obviously when the money was moving through a number of currencies, the requirement would be less. In practical terms, it would be non-existent. That's when Mayer told me I was naive. So he loaded me down with a number of papers he had written on the subject, which were tough sledding, but which set forth the argument that all is being looked after on the European front.

They have neat titles like "Credit and Liquidity Creation

in the International Banking Sector", and "The Behaviour of the Euro-Markets and the Problem of Monetary Control in Europe" and "Maturity Distribution of International Bank Lending". Very sophisticated stuff. What these papers all say, in the end, is that "The Euro-market does not perform like a separate and independent national banking system but primarily as a link and channel between the national markets. The quality of the impulses it transmits is not determined by the market itself but by the policy in the national markets."[9]

Velk says yes, of course *something* is used as a reserve asset, but that something is itself a matter of choice. And the thing chosen can and does change with circumstances. The chosen Euro-Reserve asset now used is a bank loan from another Euro-bank — fairly cheap and easy to get. The reserve demanded during a crisis is something much more substantial. In the old days it was gold. Today, the ultimate asset is probably a deposit in New York guaranteed by the U.S. government. Something that is simply impossible to get, if we are talking about a U.S. government guarantee of the entire 2 trillion Euro-dollar market. The real issue is the safety and security of the promises which are the real stuff of the financial agreements which underlie all banking. Nobody can keep his promises during a general financial panic and the dilemma is that's just when it's most important that promises *be* kept.

In rejecting this argument, Mayer argues that the Euro-currency game is merely an extension of what is happening in Washington and Ottawa and London and Zurich, so it can be controlled by monetary measures applied in those places. In fact, trying to establish any kind of control over this market won't work:

"Efforts to apply to the Euro-market the same kind of instruments that are used to control domestic banking systems will in many cases not yield meaningful results, and to the extent that such measures succeed in making the transmission channels less efficient they will tend to give rise to the emergence of new types of channels. While it is true that the Euro-market may help to spread diseases, its control cannot be used as a substitute for domestic monetary health."[10]

The great thing about this argument is that it gets the BIS off the hook. If there is nothing to be done, they are the lads who don't have to do it. So the notion that some sort of reserve should be established on Euro-currency, a notion widely bruited about among those who are concerned about the world's trillion-dollar debt, can be ignored. Even if you could get a reserve system in place, the banks would find a way to slither around it; after all, didn't they do just that in setting up the Euro-market in the first place? They are such cunning devils it doesn't pay to try to outwit them.

I don't find that very reassuring. When you take out the metaphors, Mayer seems to be saying that any interference with money-creation is bad, because it slows down "transmission," which is to say, the movement of money. So it does and so it should; slowing down the movement of money lessens its inflationary impact. Mayer argues — in a very sophisticated way, of course — that the speed of the Euro-market is what allowed it to absorb the billions of petro-dollars that came pouring in after 1973. But those billions don't begin to explain the enormous growth of that market, even by BIS measures. The real answer, according to Mayer, is to control inflation in the national markets; this will automatically control it in the Euro-currency sphere:

"If policies in all the major industrial countries were effective in fully controlling inflation, this would bring the advantages of a floating rate system to bear and would largely obviate the need for official intervention in the exchange markets."[11]

Well, yes. And if Santa Claus really did bring all the presents at Christmas, you and I could save a heap of cash. In minimizing the inflationary impact of the Euro-currency, Mayer has to argue, first, that that push is not all that great, and secondly, that it can't be controlled anyway. Somehow that doesn't make me feel any better.

It's just possible that governments don't want to control the market. They are among the biggest borrowers. From the city of Laval to Hydro Quebec and the Bank of Canada, policy-makers have discovered they can deliver on election promises without having to raise taxes, by going to the Euro-banks. In the end it doesn't work, of course; the debt plus interest has to be paid. With every government from Algeria to Zaire borrowing and lending in the market at once, the final effects are unstable exchange rates, world inflation and higher taxes.

Which brings us to the third question: How dangerous is the presence of all this newly created money? Very dangerous, on two counts. One is the danger that investors, bankers, customers, depositors or all of them at once will begin to look at the Euro-market and wonder what's holding it up. That breach of faith will send them scurrying to their banks to cash in their bits of paper while they still have some value in some currency, and when that happens, somewhere around one trillion dollars' worth of currencies are going to turn up missing. We will have history's biggest bank-run. That's what happened, on a small scale, to the Franklin National Bank of New York in 1974. The bank, the twentieth largest in the United States, sustained huge losses in foreign-exchange trading, and more losses due to the finagling of an Italian financier, Michele Sindona.[12] That led to a run on the bank; the Federal Reserve System stepped in with low-cost loans of $1.7 billion, but the run continued. Finally, the Federal Reserve stepped in to protect the dollar by assuming Franklin's foreign-exchange position. Then the European-American Bank bought out the Franklin, so that it did not technically go bankrupt, it just disappeared. It was the largest bank failure in U.S. history. None of the bank's depositors lost money, which is reassuring, but the difficulties of a comparatively small bank required the entire U.S. banking system to ride to the rescue, which is not reassuring.

The second danger is that, because there are so many outstanding transactions involving bank-to-government deals, the time may well come when, instead of just putting off the creditors, a substantial number of debtors begin to tell the banks to drop dead. It has already happened. North Korea borrowed half a billion dollars from a consortium of French banks in the early 1970s. The North Koreans used the money to bring in goods from the West, and then simply refused to honour the notes.[13] There was nothing the banks could do about it. Zaire managed to lay its hands on $400 million in private international loans — backed, in theory by its immense copper reserves.[14] But the nation is in shambles, and when the time came to collect, there was nothing in the Zaire till. The lending banks could only gulp and renew the loan.

In Indonesia, a default was avoided narrowly when the national oil company, Pertamina, borrowed $6.2 billion abroad, and could not repay even the interest.[15] Once again, the banks were persuaded to stand by, after frantic intervention by the U.S. embassy, which feared that the collapse of Pertamina would bring down the entire local economy.[16]

Poland went bankrupt, in the technical sense, in December 1981, when it could neither meet interest payments on its debts nor provide any plan to do so in the future.[17] The way around that problem, which might well have produced a panic run on the banks involved, was to ignore it. The New York Times talked to a French banker who put the point nicely: "You've got to be cynical. Everyone knows Poland is in default. But if we say so, we admit that we're bad bankers who made loans we never should have made."[18] The Bank of Montreal set aside some extra money to meet the certainty of a default, and forgot about it.[19] Ask for the same break for yourself and see what happens. The costs of Poland's bankruptcy will be paid for by bank customers from Toronto to Des Moines.

All over the world, from Romania[20] to Brazil,[21] from Turkey (which is broke, but managed to get a $1 billion loan from a U.S. banking consortium anyway)[22] to Mexico[23] (which has much oil, little cash) loans are being struck by bankers and private individuals on the hope that, in the end, something will be done to meet the crisis before it is too late. So far, we have not come to grief, which is what the drunk who fell out of the fortieth floor of a hotel said when he passed the twentieth floor. But there is a calamity hanging out there, waiting for a time and place to happen.

Bankers are famous for their prudence, but in the Euro-currency market, they have dispensed with caution. They are violating two basic rules of economic care. The first is the one that says that the velocity of money is as important as its volume; the more the banks move the stuff about, the more inflation they cause. In effect, they devalue the currency, penalize savers, reward spenders and give the roulette wheel another spin. As long as they look grave and responsible, nobody seems to care. The second rule is the one that says there should be some form of commodity — reserves, gold, cash, jewellery, something – behind created money, just in case somebody someday wants to carry away something tangible.

It is not hard to see why the bankers have taken the devil-may-care line. They are cleaning up on the Euro-currency market; its huge sums and high speed mean that transactions involving even tiny margins of profit will produce vast earnings. They are counting on somebody else to step in and clean up the mess. There is a chance, however, that they are sowing a whirlwind that will be beyond the power of anyone to bring under control.

Canadian banks are into the Euro-currency market. They are members of the consortia, they are busy setting up splendid headquarters in the financial capitals of the world, they are locating in tax havens and they are working side by side with Bank of America, Chase Manhattan, Citibank and the others. This is a peculiar position from which to lecture the rest of us on the perils of inflation, but banks don't expect to be bound by the rules they would like the rest of us to follow. You may want to ask your friendly bank manager, the next time he tells you you should never get in over your head, what his bosses are up to in Poland and Romania, and how smart they looked in Iran and Brazil. He may blush – I doubt it, but anything's possible – and he will certainly explain to you, as Mayer did to me, that these things are far more complex than they seem, and that he would be happy to explain how solid these arrangements are, but you probably wouldn't be able to follow his logic. Too true. Bankers have a logic all their own.

This becomes evident when we examine the role of the banks in promoting inflation at home.

15
Whose Balloon?
Inflation And
The Banks At Home

"Bankers are just like anybody else, except richer."

Ogden Nash, *1934*

At the annual meeting of the Canadian Imperial Bank of Commerce in January 1982, Russell Harrison, the Bank Chairman, wanted to make it perfectly clear that he supported the government and the Bank of Canada in their ongoing squeeze to curb spending. He said, "I feel that the federal government deserves recognition for its determination not to abandon the struggle against inflation. To do so would, in my opinion, have negated all our present efforts to come to grips with our inflation problem."[1]

Heaven knows Harrison was doing his best; he had a loan from his own bank for $166,136, it is true, but he was only paying 6.25% interest on it, or about one-third the rate other mortals are required to pay.[2] Just playing his part in the battle to keep expenses down. At the same time, Harrison's bank — with which I have no dealings whatsoever — was importuning me to spend more money in a letter that practically begged me to drop in and twist the manager's arm. "At this time of year," it said, "you may be thinking of the things you would like to do in the months ahead. Your costs may include that long awaited vacation, or perhaps purchasing materials for some special project at home. Such costs can be comfortably within your means with the help of a COMMERCE BANKPLAN LOAN. We can also assist you with the purchase of a new car, colour television, furniture, or appliances for your home. Just call or come in, and we'll be glad to show how a Bankplan Loan could help you get the things you need."

Over at the Bank of Montreal, William Mulholland agreed that the nation's first priority is to hang tough and dampen the fires of inflation. You know Mulholland, he's the one whose bank ran those huge ads that said:

BANK
OF MONTREAL
HAS REDUCED
RATES ON
PERSONAL PLAN
LOANS
UNTIL MAY 15TH

Toronto-Dominion has also been happy to join in the anti-inflation fight. Its ads read:

TD
REDUCES
PERSONAL
LOAN RATES
FOR 26 DAYS

The Bank of Nova Scotia, whose monthly review bulletins are constantly telling us to tighten our belts, was also at my elbow. They were willing to lend me as much as $20,000 at the drop of a hat through "Scotialine, which provides a line of credit ranging from $5,000 to $20,000. Customers access this line of credit conveniently by simply writing a cheque for any purpose." Never mind the abuse of the English language by people who think "access" is a verb, merely consider what it is I am being offered here — twenty thousand dollars, and all I have to do is write a cheque. By golly, that should teach inflation to take a joke.

There is nothing strange about the fact that banks want to sell money — insurance agents want to sell insurance, car dealers to sell cars, writers to sell books, and we all use whatever techniques we think will work best. The only strange part of the banks' performance is that they have been able to work both sides of the street at once, to persuade us to plunge into debt up to our hocks, and then to raise interest rates, and their own profits, to cure the disease they bring us.

If I, in the guise of a typewriter salesman, were to present myself on your front stoop, or through the screen of your television set, with the argument that, for your own good, and because of your own wickedness, I was forced to raise the prices on all my typewriters, you might treat me with some skepticism. If I were to add insult to injury by claiming that I didn't want to take more money from you, and that in the long run I would be losing money by raising my prices, but that your own dumb persistence in paying the prices I already charged forced me into it, you might be tempted to bung a brick at me.

But if I lay the same malarkey on you while dressed in a banker's apparel and mouthing a banker's assurances — and backed by a phalanx of banker's public relations men and tame economists, complete with charts — chances are that you will accept my rebuke as just, pay up with a grimace, and thank me for sticking it to you so thoroughly. What is more, the daily newspapers will be on the stands tomorrow morning, singing my praises for telling it like it is, and warning off any government that may be tempted to interfere with my profits. I am an ornament to the nation, the papers will say, and to mess with me is to imperil western civilization. Bankers are fond of hammering governments for trying to solve their problems by printing money, which is wasteful, extravagant and inflationary. What do you suppose the bank is doing when it sends you a friendly letter upping the credit-limit on your MasterCard from $1,000 to $1,500? It is creating money, and then trying to collect interest on the creation.

The more money the banks can create, the more they make; the higher interest rates can be pushed, the fatter their profits grow. The same rules that apply to manufacturers of typewriters apply to the manufacturers of money.

This general rule is limited only by the observation that carried too far, the process may backfire. If I jump the prices on my typewriters from $500 to $1,100 at once, I may meet some buyer resistance, even if it works out, as it always seems to for the banks, that all my competitors do the same thing at the same time. But, within reason, every price hike will benefit me. Even if my costs go up, I can always skim a little something extra off the margin.

For the past two years, interest rates have been jumping

up and down, but mostly up. On the upswing, the banks have been able to fatten the spread between what they pay for money and what they charge for it, as you can see in Table 3 of the Appendices. In February, 1979, the Bank Rate was 11.25%, and the Prime just a little above that, at 12%; the spread between the Daily Interest rate, money the bank was taking in, and the Prime, money they were lending to the best customers, was 2.50%. By August of 1981, the Bank Rate had been pushed to 21.24% in the fight against inflation; the Prime was at 22.75% and the spread was 4.25%. As the rates came down, the banks widened the gap between the Bank Rate and the Prime, so that a gap of .75% in 1979 had become one of almost 2% by January, 1982. The spread was 4.50%. In short, the banks were taking every nickel they could out of the market, while protesting that they were leading the fight against inflation.

For this, they have received the fulsome praise of all the right-thinking element in our society, led by the editorial writers and business journalists whose prose and mathematics make reading the papers such a joy. (One small example. The Globe and Mail's Report on Business noted solemnly on December 24, 1981 that, although the Bank Rate had come down, the banks were forced to hold their Prime Rate up, because, "Bank spreads between loan and deposit rates have narrowed and smaller spreads work against reducing the Prime." This was 1. Wrong – the spreads had widened, not narrowed; and 2. Dumb – by not bringing down the Prime the banks were, of necessity, widening the spread.)

In mid-1981, when soaring bank profits had become a matter for public embarrassment, the Royal Bank laid on a press conference in Toronto to explain to a polite audience of journalists how tough life was in the banking business. Sure, people were being forced out of their homes and off their farms because they could no longer meet soaring mortgage rates, but their pain was nothing to that of the financial institutions which had been forced, by cruel circumstances, to take the money from them. Rowland Frazee, the genial chairman of the bank, gave it to us straight from the shoulder:

"Banks don't like high interest rates, and they particularly dislike erratic interest rate changes. They prefer lower, stable rates. Banks experience a short-term profit surge in times of rising interest rates, a short-term profit squeeze with falling interest rates, but are on the whole better off with lower, stable rates."

We all wrote that down, underlining the key words. Frazee also gave us a copy of his company's annual report, which looked back at 1980, and shook his head in dismay. "The world saw political turbulence, economic stress, and unprecedented volatility in financial matters. For bankers it was, frankly, a difficult year."

Land-a-mercy, what a time. The kindly reader may be tempted to put the report down, at once, before suffering more anguish. If he persists, however, all the way back to where the numbers are, he will find that, in 1980, the Royal Bank made a profit of $327.4 million, up twenty-one per cent from 1979. It wasn't called a profit, of course, profit is for vulgar firms like meat-packers; it was called a "Balance of Revenue", and by any name, it was a honey. The Royal Bank made more than double the profit it had made in 1976, four short years before. What is more, its assets grew in 1980 by twenty-seven per cent, which brought another burst of gloom from Mr. Frazee – "This growth cannot continue indefinitely at this rate," he noted. (It didn't; in 1981 Royal's assets swelled another 39.3% and profit another 50.4%, to $492,520,000.) The villain was there in plain sight – "This rapid asset growth, which contributed much of the profit growth, is a reflection not only of the rate of inflation and economic expansion, but also of the continued high demand in Canada for bank credit."

If that doesn't make your blood run cold, you are without decent feelings. However, suppose we were to translate Frazee into some other kind of businessman – head of a development corporation, for example – and suppose that beleaguered man were to come before the assembled press to tell them what a hell of a time it was to be a developer.

"People keep buying my damn buildings," he would say, "forcing the prices up without considering the consequences. At this rate, my company is growing so fast, something's gotta give. Last year was a particularly difficult one for us. We creamed off a profit of twenty-one per cent, and we're worth twenty-seven per cent more now than we were a year ago. I don't know why we stay in the business. Well, I can't sit around here chin-wagging with you guys. There are a gang of widows and orphans out there, demanding to be cheated. God, what a life."

Bankers, for laying their version of this line on us, are saluted as pillars of the community, foundation stones of the national economy, worthy of our esteem and admiration. That is malarkey on a massive scale, malarkey so breath-taking, so successful, so profitable, that we can only stand in awe of it.

Consider the mortgage. Canadian banks are into mortgages in a very big way, and mortgage rates have been shoved up in recent years to unprecedented levels. There was a time, before the banks got into the act, when buying a mortgage was a long-term proposition. You trotted around to the trust company – or mortgage firm or insurance company – filled out the forms and, in due course, were assigned a mortgage for, say, twenty-five years at 7%. The trust company did very well out of the transaction, in its role as mortgagee; the mortgagor did less well, but at least he got his house. (The mortgagee is the one who holds the mortgage, a fact recognized in rhyme: Simon Legree is the mortgagee.) At 7% annually, if he had borrowed $50,000 over a twenty-five-year term, he would pay back $106,017 over the period of the mortgage. But after the 1967 Bank Act amendment, the banks took over a major part of this market. In 1963, all the chartered banks in Canada held less than $100,000 in residential mortgages; a decade later, they held $2.3 billion.[3] From a fraction of one per cent of the market, they shot to twenty-eight per cent; today, they hold more than $55 billion in mortgages.[4] They are now the dominant player in the mortgage game. Their availability – with branches almost everywhere – their easy access to funds and their gigantic size gave them an instant edge on their competitors, which they have never lost.

Today's mortgage is a very different proposition from that of a decade ago. The usual term is one year, not twenty-five, and the rate is, at this writing, 21.50% annually. At this rate, the monthly payment on a $50,000 mortgage is $944.18, not the $353.39 it was a dozen years ago. Between mid-1979 and mid-1981, the rate nearly doubled, from 11.2% to 21.5%. Without investing an additional nickel, the bank will get back $133,512 more on a $50,000 mortgage someone had to renew in 1981. They are the beneficiaries of an enormous windfall profit, which they, of course, deny. Dear, or dear, they say, the cost of money is something terrible, and we have to pay so much for mortgage money ourselves we can barely keep our heads above water. We have, they say, a "mismatch" of funds. That is, we loaned out a lot of money at 11% or 12% or 13%, and that is tied up. Now we have to pay 17%, 18%, even 19% to draw in money. Well, you can't lend at 11% and pay 19% and make money. God knows what we'll do.

The banks certainly have some money out at lower rates than they are now paying. It was money created, as most bank money is, essentially by writing down numbers. Because there is a limit to the amount of money that can be created this way – the limit imposed by reserve requirements – it is true that the banks cannot manufacture new money to replace all their old loans. They could pile up even more impressive statistics if they could replace every 11% mortgage on the books by one at 21%. But it is not generally true that they have to go out and borrow money at 19% to lend it at 11%. When that happens, it is because some bank misjudged its requirements and had to rush into the market for deposits at higher rates while stuck with loans at lower rates. A genuine mismatch. The Continental Bank got into such a bind when it first went into business in 1979;[5] it cost so much to borrow money, the bank couldn't make a profit lending it out. But that situation is not common. Generally, the loans being repaid at lower rates were loaned from funds that cost even less. The key is to compare the right sets of figures. When the banks had to pay 17.75% to attract three-year term deposits in mid-1981, they were able to sell three-year money for 21.75%. The spread was 4%, up from 3.25% a year earlier. (You will find the details in Table 3 of the appendices.) They were gaining, not only because housing prices had gone up and mortgages were larger, but because they had widened the spread. The only way they could get hurt in this situation was for the interest rate to drop precipitously at a time when they were holding a lot of high-rate, long-term money. If they were going to be paying 17.75% over the next three years on a lot of money, but had only been able to get a little money loaned out at 21.75%, and now they could only get 15%, they were going to be in trouble. Some credit unions got into this fix. Far more commonly, and profitably, the banks are able to bring in depositors' money at lower rates and then benefit from a jump in rates. That is why, despite everything they say, the banks do well out of constantly rising interest rates.

When grocers demand "replacement value" for the peas they have on their shelves, we give them the elbow; we should treat banks the same way when they make the same argument. However, the banks may have solved the whole problem for us, with the introduction of the "Variable Rate Mortgage," which will soon be the only kind of mortgage available, by the look of things. This is a mortgage in which the mortgagor pays the same amount every month, but on which the interest fluctuates with the Bank Rate. Thus, if the rate goes up by one per cent, the monthly payment remains fixed, but the additional cost is added onto the mortgage. You could put 25% down on a house, hold a mortgage for 75% and, if rates continue to climb, wind up with no equity in the house whatever. It would belong to the bank. The Variable Rate Mortgage takes whatever risk there was in the mortgage business out of it, at least for the banks. It guarantees the spread and, you may depend on it, eventually it will help to widen that spread even further.

We have been beguiled into ignoring another way in which the banks have been fattening the spread, and their profits. Because newspapers only measure the difference between Prime Rates and Savings Rates, two huge gains made by the banks go unreported. The first is on $17 billion in the banks on which no interest whatever is paid, because it is in current accounts.[6] The spread on this money is whatever the interest rate currently is. As I write this, the figure is 21.5%; that represents, on $17 billion, a tidy $3.6 billion annually. Then, there are the chequing accounts on which interest is paid, but at a fixed, low rate of 3%. That rate was set in May 1973, and has never varied.[7] It applies to about $7 billion today. So the spread on that money is the current interest rate minus 3% – currently, that means a spread of 18.5%, another $1.2 billion annually which somehow gets overlooked.

"Real interest" – the economic rent of money – has historically run at about 3%. That is, if inflation is running at 5% and interest at 7%, the lender is the loser; if inflation is 5% and interest is 9%, the borrower is the loser.[8] By making high interest rates the weapon to combat inflation, we have handed the banks an excuse to widen this gap. In 1981, inflation ran at 12.5%, and interest rates ranged from 16.5% to 22.75%. That is only for Prime loans; the gap was much wider for consumer, credit card and mortgage loans. Such a gap adds to inflation; it cannot help but do so, because it piles onto the ordinary push behind rising prices the extra impetus of an inflationary surge in one of the chief components in every transaction, the cost of money.

That is why I say that banks are in the business of inflation.

Or, consider the credit card. Canadians currently hold twenty-eight million credit cards, and we owe $44 billion on them.[9] In 1979, we owed $34 billion. In 1979, the average interest charge on these cards was 18%; now, it is 24%.[10] On top of a growth of twenty-nine per cent in the money created through these cards, we have added 33.3% to the cost of using them. The banks are the owners of twelve million of these credit cards, 8.4 million Visa cards and 3.6 million MasterCards. That's up from 6.6 million in 1975, a growth of eighty-one per cent. The banks say that they issue these cards as a convenience to the user, but in fact, they issue them so that consumers will spend more, and, they hope, spend beyond their ability to repay, and so have to borrow and pay interest on the loan. Indeed, the banks wax indignant at the people who pay off their credit balances on time, avoiding interest charges. These people are called "free-loaders,"[11] and they excite the scorn of every true banker. Sean McNamara, assistant vice-president of credit card services for Canada Trustco Mortgage Company, which offers Visa cards to its customers, put his complaint in words that should be emblazoned on our hearts:

"We have to find a way to get at the convenience users, that forty to fifty per cent of users who pay up in full every month. I really think that's the unfair part."[12]

The American magazine Consumer Reports has estimated that consumers buy on the average thirteen per cent more than they would if they did not have credit cards,[13] so, to the costs of interest and the costs of servicing the cards can be added the inflationary impetus they have by persuading us to spend more. Then there is the cost to merchants, which is passed on to customers, even if they don't use a credit card. MasterCard charges between 2% and 5.5% to the merchant, depending on the volume of sales. Visa charges between 2% and 5.75%.[14] In nearly every case, the prices charged those who pay cash and those who use a credit card are identical, so the effect is to add another two-per-cent-plus to most sales. Finally, there is the cost of the money used between the date of purchase and the date the credit card payment gets back to the merchant. The individual customer doesn't pay this, so collective customers must. It amounts to another two to three per cent, according to a study by the Economic Council of Canada.[15]

If the banks are really anxious to curb spending in Canada, they have many weapons at their disposal. They could stop running firesales on money, they could stop sending out unsolicited letters to persuade customers who are not in debt to get that way, they could become very much fussier about passing out credit cards — remembering that tracking down stolen cards has become a major cost for police forces, and their misuse has added to costs for all of us. And they could stop raising the credit limits on the cards they put out.

I say they could do these things, but I don't expect them to, because I know, what they dare not admit, that it is the multiplication of money that makes their turnstiles turn and their hearts leap up. If we want to bring inflation to heel, the bankers are the last people we should be asking for advice. Would you consult a tiger on the virtues of a vegetarian diet?

Anyone who chooses to can verify for himself the sincerity of the banks' battle against inflation. All you need is $1.50 to purchase a copy of the Bank of Canada Review — or, better still, read it in the library. There, you will discover, in a table called Monetary Aggregates, that the battle to control the money supply is going well. You will recall that the control is targeted on what is called M1, which consists of currency outside the chartered banks and demand deposits. Between September 1980 and September 1981, this figure actually declined, from $32.43 billion to $31.94 billion. Splendid work, chaps; especially when you consider that inflation was adding twelve per cent to everything in the economy. At the same time, however, if you look at another table, Chartered Banks,

General Loans, you will discover that between September 1980 and September 1981, these shot from $87.6 billion to $113.6 billion — up $26 billion, or twenty-nine per cent. While M1 was being constricted, justifying the jacking up of interest rates, banks were adding $26 billion to inflation at the new, high interest rates. The money banks create is being expanded. They are, I repeat, in the inflation business.

Bank Profits

They are in business to make a profit, and that they do. A great deal of controversy has erupted over the size of their profits, which the banks say is not high enough, and virtually everyone else says is too high. The banks have developed an ingenious argument, to the effect that, even if the government were to take away every nickel of profit they make and apply it to bringing down interest rates, those rates would only come down by one per cent. It's true, too; I worked it out. It is, alas, entirely beside the point. The argument for bringing down interest rates has to do with their inflationary impact, not the banks' profits. If interest rates were lower, bank profits would decline, marginally, but the overall costs of financing the economy would decline substantially. The only reason the profit argument began in the first place is because the banks are making so much while everyone else suffers.

Is it too much? Decide for yourself. Table 12 of the Appendices traces the growth of bank profits since 1970 in selected years. You will note that they have multiplied from $492 million in 1970 to $2.1 billion in 1981 — an increase of 429%.

Actually, I don't think that's too much. In the same period, their assets have grown more than seven-fold, from $46 billion to $344 billion. The major inflationary impact doesn't come from their profit-growth, but from the multiplication of assets — loans. If the banks are making too much, that certainly adds to inflation, but it is a drop in the bucket compared to the costs imposed by the high interest rate policies that generate the profit.

There are a number of ways in which profits can be measured. The banks like to measure them in terms of assets employed, because the numbers look so low.[16] The return on assets employed by Canadian banks ranges from a low of 0.50% for the Bank of Commerce to 0.70% for the Royal. That is, for every $1 in assets at work in the Royal Bank, the profit comes to seven-tenths of a cent. Sounds harmless. The Canadian Bankers' Association uses this measure of profit, because it shows the banks have not moved up that much – totalling nine of the eleven chartered banks in the CBA produced a table indicating the return on assets had gone up only marginally, from 0.55% in 1979 to 0.57% in 1981.[17] There are a couple of things wrong with this measurement. In the first place, it certainly understates profits. Nearly forty per cent of all Canadian bank assets consist of foreign funds,[18] on which the profit margin is much narrower, for the very good reason that our banks face competition abroad, but not at home. Economist Jack Mintz calculates that if Canadian banks are showing a net return on assets of 0.57%, their return on Canadian assets must be nearly twice that high. In the second place, the return on assets figure doesn't mean much unless Canadian banks are compared with other banks. You will find such a comparison in the Appendices, in Table 13. There you will notice that the Bank of Tokyo's return on assets is 0.17, Chase Manhattan's, 0.48, Dresdner, 0.24. Canadian banks occupy six of the top seven places in the list, which suggests that they are doing very well indeed.

Another way to measure profits is by way of the return on equity. This strikes me as a more sensible measure, simply because it is normal business practice. In such a measure – again, there is a table in the Appendices, Table 14 – the banks are right up there with the oil companies.[19] Imperial Oil's return on equity in 1979 was 16.6%, the Royal Bank's, 20.1%; Texaco made 21.2%, the Bank of Montreal 22.4%. The banks are gaining, while many other corporations – including oil companies – are losing. Toronto-Dominion went from 14.91% in 1972 to 22.3% in 1981. However, over the long haul, the banks' return on equity is not as high as, for example, printing and publishing, pipelines, real estate, or hotels and restaurants. In the first nine months of 1981, when banks were piling up an after-tax profit increase of 49.4%, and the general run of publicly owned companies were down 8.6%, a few industries were doing even better than the banks – general manufacturing companies, for example, were up 62.5%

and real estate 84%.[20]

The banks say they don't make enough profit. Bank of Montreal Chairman William Mulholland, citing what he said was a public misunderstanding of "dangerous proportions,"[21] told his bank's 1982 meeting that the collapse of long-term bond markets meant the banks had to have high profits to take over this role, and Toronto-Dominion's Chairman, Richard Thomson, told a radio interviewer that "There are no excess profits...I certainly, for one, wish they were higher."[22]

The rationale, if that is the word used to explain such chutzpah, is that bank stocks are not doing well, despite the high profits, and that, to expand, the banks must go into the market, and they can't do so if there is no demand for their stocks, and the demand for the stocks depends on profits. However, the banks could expand their capital base by transferring more money into the Rest Account, and paying lower dividends – it wouldn't help the stocks, though. Or they could do just the opposite; put less into the Rest Account and pay higher dividends. The real reason bank stocks don't sell like hotcakes is that the market already discounts the huge profits they make – they always make them. If you want to make a quick buck in the market, you go for Moose Pastures Unlimited, or something else that will soar quickly before crashing. Bank stocks are not for gambling, but for steady growth and nice dividends. What all this suggests is that, while the banks are making very large profits indeed, and while they are growing ever fatter, it is hard to argue that they are excessive. Rich, yes, obscene, no.

I think that what excites people about bank profits isn't their size, but the unfairness of a system that produces gold for them and dross for the rest of us. In 1981, while Canada was setting a record for bankruptcies in small businesses – the ones beholden to banks – and farmers were going under at the sharp edge of interest charges, the chartered banks racked up an average increase in profit of 49.8% before taxes and 38.0% after taxes. The banks' explanation, that the profits look so huge because 1980 was a bad year, lasts only until you bother to look up the 1980 profits. They weren't great, but after taxes, profits were up over 1979 – which was a good year – by 11.9%.[23] (In 1982, we are told, the figures will not be quite so fat.)

The Big Five were the particular beneficiaries of the profit surge — with one exception; the Bank of Nova Scotia got caught with a lot of long-term, lower rate loans, and with a higher-than-average loss on bad debts. Before taxes, Nova Scotia actually dropped in profit, from $298 million to $266 million.[24] Thanks to the miracle of tax-wriggling, the bank was able to turn that drop into a gain and came out of the year with take-home pay of $224 million, compared to $221 million in 1980, a net gain of 1.3%.[25] Chicken feed. The Royal Bank's pre-tax profit was up 70.5%, the Commerce was up 99.2%, Montreal up 43.3% and Toronto-Dominion up 53.6%.

Taxes bit into these figures, but not deeply. Indeed, one of the most remarkable aspects of banking in this country is the degree to which the major banks have been able to escape taxes and escape criticism for escaping taxes. In 1970, the Big Five made a total profit of $492,128,000 and paid taxes of $256,363,000, or 52.0%.[26] The tax share remained fairly constant until 1977 when the tax lawyers discovered the miracle of income debentures and term-preferred shares. These are financial instruments originally designed to provide low-cost loans for companies in trouble. Instead of making a straight loan, the bank gives the borrower money in return for debentures or shares which pay interest. This interest is then treated as dividends from a Canadian-owned company, which are not taxable. The idea was that the banks would be able to drop their interest charges by as much as 50% to the borrower, since $10,000 in tax-free money would be worth as much to the banks as $20,000 in taxable income. The banks claim that this is exactly what they did. "The winners," Bank of Montreal Vice Chairman Stanley Davidson insisted to me, "were the companies who got the money. We passed on the advantage we gained."

You can test this proposition for yourself by looking at Table 12 in the Appendices. You will see that as the banks piled into this business — they multiplied their holdings of these instruments from $765 million to $7.2 billion in two years, so that by the end of 1978, 80% of all bank holdings of securities were in one or other of these two forms — their taxes plummeted drastically. In 1979, when the Big Five made a total of $1,272,253,000, they paid taxes of $230,300,000 a rate of 18.1%. Nine years earlier, they had paid $256,363,000 in taxes on earnings of $492,128,000 – while their profits tripled, their taxes shrank.[27]

Eventually, the dodge came to light, and the then Finance Minister, Jean Chretien, moved to act on what his officials called "a pretty hideous kind of situation,"[28] which they calculated had transferred at least $630 million from the coffers of the taxpayer to the pockets of the banks in two short years. The 1978 budget removed the tax exemption. But, alas, it contained another loophole. Instruments already purchased, some of them with terms of up to thirty years, were not affected. (Nor were instruments of more than ten years purchased by non-financial institutions, a loophole that was closed in the November, 1981 budget.) That meant that the benefits continued to flow to the banks, although they will gradually dry up.

I asked William Kennett, the Inspector General of Banks, about this subject, and he was, as usual, unperturbed. "If you close up one loophole, they'll just find another one," he said. I guess he was right, at that. In 1981, the Big Five banks paid income tax of $468,400,000 on profits of $2,109,024,000,[29] a tax-rate of 22.2%. This is equivalent to what an individual making $15,000 a year would pay.[30]

Tax-dodging is not confined to banks, by any means. Over the decades, despite the howls of business about the high and rising rates of tax, the tax burden has been shifted substantially from corporations to individuals. We are all paying more, but individuals bear much more of the burden than they used to. In 1951, companies paid just over half of every dollar collected in income tax; by 1979, they were paying less than a quarter.

I have been wondering if the banks and other corporations are likely to start paying higher taxes voluntarily, as a way of contributing to national contentment, and I have decided that, on the whole, probably not. Their general philosophy seems to be, if you've got it, hold on to it; if somebody else has it, get it, and in any event, don't give anything away. That may not be a charitable philosophy, but as my own manager at the Bank of Nova Scotia put it to me, "We are not in the charity business, and no one would want us to be."

So, if we think the banks are getting away with murder at tax-time, that is a matter for Parliament, and I have little faith that Parliament will do anything about it. The banks will continue to make large profits and pay low taxes. These are not the most severe problems they present us with, anyway. Their capacity to foster inflation through money-creation is far more dangerous to the commonweal than the profits they make. So is their capacity to reach ever further into our lives with computers, the subject of the next chapter.

16
Stick 'Em Up.
This Is A
Recording

> *"The typical take of a computer crime is $430,000, compared with $23,000 for the average bank embezzlement, and $3,000 for the average bank robbery ... Only 23 of every 1,000 computer criminals are convicted, and only one in 22,000 wind up in jail."*
>
> Globe and Mail, *May 15, 1981*

In Washington, the FBI agent was direct. "I guess it's up to the banks to decide what they want to do with computers," he said, "but there are these two worries, the thing about invasion of privacy and the worry about theft. It is awfully easy to steal an awful lot of money. Who do you think is going to pay when things go wrong, the taxpayer or the banks?"

In Montreal, Rowland Frazee, Chairman of the Royal Bank, was equally direct, but far more sanguine. "The computer is here to stay," he said. "We couldn't operate without it, I think there is going to be a great expansion in its use, and the consumer will reap the benefits."

There, in brief, is the nub of the argument about the role of computers in banks; on the one hand, the pitfalls they present, on the other, the promise they offer. Virtually every view of these marvellous number-pushers comes down on one side or the other. Before you decide which side you belong on, you will need some information of a general nature, the kind both sides can agree on.

Nearly every branch of the major banks in Canada is now "on line," and those that are not soon will be. All that means is that the branches are linked, through electric lines, to the data centres where the computers are stored. Since the computer has no idea, when a teller punches your deposit into the keyboard in front of her, whether you are in your own bank, just down the street or half-way across the country, each branch becomes, in the computer's terminal, merely a number in its innards. "Multibranch banking," as it is called, might as well be called "one branch banking," or "computer-linked banking."

What happens when you pass a deposit slip across the counter is that the teller, checking first to see that the computer is not off, or out of service, punches in a series of symbols to get access to the computer, usually through a screen that looks like a small TV screen. The code is usually letters, and usually four in number, to get access at the lowest level. "Soup," for example, may identify a teller. Each teller has his or her own code, which is secret, and stored in the teller's vault; the bank's branch executive officer can get at it, but doesn't normally know it. The codes are changed periodically, in case they have become known. In response to the code, the computer will ask what kind of transaction is required, and the teller will stroke in a symbol for one type of transaction – general ledger, customer accounts, savings, or whatever. Then the account number is entered, and an instruction to, say, enter $300. As the transaction is entered, information on this account will flash onto the screen, indicating the name, address, any notations for special handling and the current state of the account. If there is an error, it should show up at once; if the name on the deposit slip doesn't jibe with the one on the screen, for example, the wrong account has been called. When the entry is complete, the teller can instruct the computer to update the pass-book. That's all there is to it.

The entries are checked the next day against a print-out that comes from the data centre of the bank. If the teller slipped on the keys and entered $3,000 instead of $300, that will be caught when the print-out is checked against the deposit-slip.

So there is nothing mysterious about the computer; it is merely a mechanical aid. It can instantly calculate daily interest on an account, and post the interest automatically. It can move money from branch to branch, or out of the bank to other computer-linked facilities. It can check calculations against each other, providing an automatic back-up to the tellers' work. It can work out foreign exchange transactions, agency fees, commissions or anything else, and keep track of everything it is doing as it goes.

But it does not – at least not yet – change the fundamental instrument of banking, which is the piece of paper – cheque, debit note, credit note, whatever – that sets a transaction in motion. Watching the computer at work, you may assume that it is already in charge; not so. Eighty per cent of all banking transactions are still paper-based, only twenty per cent consist of electron talking to electron.[1]

Let us suppose that you work for an employer who deposits your pay automatically to a bank account. If you have an account at his bank, and he is a major employer, his accounting department will produce a computer tape which, fed into the bank's data centre, will automatically deposit the pay of a thousand employees, and deduct the total from the employer's account. A print-out of all the transactions will be delivered, and a cheque to cover the balance written by the employer. If you deal at another bank, and are allowed to have your pay deposited there (many employers, encouraged by their banks, will not permit this, and require you to open an account, instead, where they bank), then the money will go into your bank's data centre from the employer's bank's data centre as an electronic blip, but it will not go into your account until a cheque has been written by his bank to your bank, and sent around either by the daily messenger service, or by mail. The money will come out of his account at once, but it will not go into yours until the piece of paper changes hands.

The cheque is still king. Every day, Canadians write ten million cheques,[2] which represent $14 billion worth of money. Every night, the banks must "clear" with each other to balance all these transactions. Each bank – or other cheque-issuing institution – is linked by computer with one of the ten regional "settlement points" located in ten major cities across the nation.[3] Here, the regional books are balanced between banks, and the results are telegraphed to the Bank of Canada in Ottawa. Each institution in the system will have a plus- or minus-balance from each region, and a total plus- or minus-balance in Ottawa. Then the bank with a minus balance issues a cheque to the bank with a plus. The Bank of Canada, which is holding reserves from the banks, deducts or deposits funds according to the bank's daily balance to keep the reserves matching the legal requirement. This balancing must all be done by three p.m. of each day. If a cheque is drawn on the Bank of Nova Scotia in Vancouver and cashed at the Bank of Commerce in Halifax, the information covering that transaction will be flashed to Vancouver at once – the money will come out of the account. But the cheque itself must go back to the issuing bank. Every night, ten million cheques, weighing five tons, are sorted and shipped; if all goes well, they should be back in their own home banks within twenty-four hours of being cashed.

Most cheques – ninety-seven per cent of them – carry a magnetic-ink band at the bottom, with a series of numbers on it.[4] These represent the bank, branch, and account number, and they help the sorting process. Automatic cheque-sorters can read these bands at the rate of 2,000 a second and sort the cheques accordingly. Any cheques without the band must be sorted by hand. If you want to slow down a transaction, the way to do it is to tear off or blot out the numbers on the bottom of the cheque; the cheque-sorter will then reject the item, and it will have to be sorted by hand, which may take a day or two longer.

It costs Canadian banks $1.4 billion a year to deal with all these cheques, some of which may be handled as many as fifteen times. The average cost per cheque is between sixty and seventy cents, and for those that must be sorted by hand, as much as $1.50.[5] Your bank doesn't charge you that much, because cheques are used as a loss leader, to persuade you into the bank in the first place. Your bank will charge you between eighteen and seventy cents,[6] or it may give you a special deal because you have a package arrangement – a Key Account, or whatever – that provides "free" chequing. The chequing is never free, but a package account may be a good deal for you, if you write many cheques.

Obviously, the fewer cheques the banks have to deal with, the cheaper it is for them, and the greater use they can make of their computers, the better it is for them. Already, the computer has provided them with an enormous advantage; in the past, each bank had to keep money in "float" – on hand, but not used – to cover cheques that might come in. Because the computer can lift money from a Vancouver account at once on behalf of a cheque cashed in Toronto, there is no need for so large a float. The banks have saved much of their normal float of about $1.2 billion this way.[7] They also benefit because they have the use of the money between the time it is whisked out of one account and paid into another. That is exactly like having interest-free funds on hand. The real advantage of multi-branch banking accrues to them, not to you.

The Bank of Montreal puts out a brochure called "Find out how our bank computer improves service for you," which claims, under the heading:

"What it does

"It keeps your account instantly up to date and gives you, through your teller, immediate access to up-to-the-minute information on your account. For instance, if you deposit $10 in your account and then ask for your balance, within seconds the keyboard will type out your latest balance, including the $10 you just deposited."

If you will cast your mind back to the dim, dark days before computers, you will recall that when you went into a bank to deposit ten dollars and took in your passbook and gave it to the teller, he or she brought it instantly up to date and gave you immediate access to up-to-the-minute information on your account, including the ten-dollar deposit just made. And did it all without a single cathode ray tube; all that was required was Teller (one), Passbook (one), Pen (one) and a little scratching. The account might not have been quite as up-to-date as the computer-driven version, because the bank's books were only posted once a day; but the teller could go and look up transactions easily enough. You haven't gained much; unless you were in the habit of dropping in to one bank-branch to deposit money in another, you probably haven't gained a thing. It's the banks that go dancing into the street with their hair in a braid over the glories of the computer, not the customers.

But life, already sweet, would be even sweeter for the financial institutions if they could eliminate most of the cheques, if the accounts between banks could be settled merely by the exchange of electronic tapes, and if individual accounts could be settled merely by a computer print-out. That is the direction the banks are moving in, as fast as possible. The banks' plan is to have ninety per cent of all transactions handled by computer only by the end of this decade, with the other ten per cent remaining paper-based.[8] Think of the advantages – to the banks – if your bills could all be settled on the spot, by presenting a card that would communicate with the computer. Finally, think of the glory of the day when you could go into a grocery store, load up your cart, check it through the cash-desk, and the items would be automatically priced, totalled, and the cost charged directly to your bank account. Not thrilled? What are you, a spoilsport?

That is the world into which, unless something happens soon, we are all heading, thanks to what is called EFT, for Electronic Funds Transfer, which is just over the horizon. The Canadian Bankers' Association, always one for a joke, has looked at EFT and pronounced:

"The huge and growing volume of transactions makes it necessary to replace manual procedures with computers. And in some of this electronic processing, payments are made without currency or cheques actually changing hands.

"But, this transition will not be completed overnight. It will take time. And the change will not take place until new systems prove themselves to be efficient, economical and able to meet high standards of service. There is one very important and fundamental consideration, as far as the banks are concerned. The traditional bank standards of privacy of customers' accounts will always be maintained."[9]

I hope that gives you comfort. It doesn't do much for me. It has the vague and hollow ring of a politician's promise, in the first place, and in the second, it has nothing to do with the fact that we are already well into computerization, with nothing done about the major concerns the process raises.

The bank credit card is a major tool in this process. It substitutes for cash, and for cheques, in millions of transactions every week. These are forwarded from merchants to the bank, collated by computer, and then billed to you. To turn this operation into an EFT function, all the banks need to do is to turn the credit card into a debit card – a process which our banks have well in hand. You can already use your Visa card or MasterCard to take money out of a bank; the sum is then charged to your account, with interest. To make this credit card into a genuine debit card all that is required is to extend this function. When you use a debit card, you present it to a merchant, who feeds it into a terminal connected to the bank computer. The money is instantly deducted from your account. There is no need for a cheque, or cash. The computer, in due course, will print out an account. This same debit card could be used to buy groceries, withdraw money from a twenty-four-hour automatic teller, pay your rent, indeed, to perform many of the functions now bound up in the separate worlds of cash, cheque and credit card. It could automatically give you an overdraft – charging interest, of course – just as a special bank card will now do. It could replace, or supplement, department store and oil company credit cards. The possibilities are endless. They are also dangerous.

We are not talking now about a "cashless" or "chequeless" society, merely one in which debit cards become the normal way to transact business, a society in which you would be even more at the mercy of the banks than you are at present. The "convenience factor" which banks cite as a major reason for customers turning to credit cards is another way of describing the seductions of easy money. Credit cards invite you to spend more than you would in either cash or cheques; debit cards, with a built-in credit, would extend the process. In addition, credit cards provide you with very little verification, and no recourse. The monthly statement you get from the bank tells you little about the transaction – it carries the name of the merchant (which may not even be a name you recognize; quite often, a restaurant or store deals through another company, which may even be headquartered in another city), the date – which is quite often wrong, because the merchant has not brought his machine up to date – and the amount of the sale – which, again, may be wrong. Sorting out the errors from the modicum of information provided is up to you, not up to the bank.[10] If you don't catch an error within fifteen days, your credit card agreement provides that you owe the money, regardless.[11] In any case of a dispute, the money is transferred first and quarrelled over afterwards.

Toronto consumer columnist Ellen Roseman of the Globe and Mail cites a case in which a man rented a car, for which he bought insurance. He then become involved in an accident for which the insurance company, on a technicality, declined to pay. The car rental company, using his credit-card signature, subtracted $2,000 from his bank account. If he wanted it back, he could sue. When you buy merchandise, if you find it unsatisfactory, and if you have paid for it by cheque, you can stop the cheque. But you can't stop a credit card, and you won't be able to stop a debit card, either. At least with a credit card, you can take the elementary precaution of using two banks, keeping money in one and running the credit card out of the other. Even that protection will be gone.

And what do you do in the case of error? If the bill that comes in is too high, it is up to you to prove it; first the money is removed, then you try to get it back. Anyone who deals with credit cards knows how often errors occur. What if the firm claims that you haven't paid? Or haven't paid in full? A computer record is nothing to go into court with. A report commissioned by the Province of Ontario, and titled, The Challenge of EFT, notes, "At present, disputes over computerized transactions often end in stalemate because the expense of retrieving the relevant information from the innards of the system is greater than the amount in dispute." It's not merely you against the machine; it's you against the machine and all the experts. Or, as the Ontario report puts it:

"The advantages of EFT to banks and near-banks are obvious – increased speed and efficiency ... But EFT, by taking our already-computerized money system a stage further into the electronic future, poses new threats to the consumer's privacy, security from deliberate theft, and accidental loss through the muddles and mistakes which are all too frequent in computerized operation. It may turn him into a small, shaky digit, quivering before a colossal, unfeeling machine."

The computer transfers the burden of proof, in every instance, from the merchant or the bank to the consumer. It seizes the money, then invites you to open the debate. At the best of times, a one-on-one confrontation with a bank is not an even match, but under these circumstances, it is no contest whatever. EFT will simply add to the advantage of your adversaries, and there is no proof whatever that it will bring you an off-setting benefit by reducing costs.

Indeed, since the introduction of computers, virtually every bank transaction charge has shot up, many of them faster than the rate of inflation. If these machines are so marvellous, why are we paying more for services?

As if you weren't at the bank's mercy in enough ways, you will also, under EFT, come under more pressure. What if you are one of those freaks who likes money, the feel of it, the crisp green of it, and who doesn't like to deal with cards, credit-, debit- or otherwise? Too bad. Already, when you go into a hotel and leave blank the space where it says "Credit Card," the man behind the desk looks as if he detects a bad smell. You may be required to pay in advance. You may not be allowed to charge meals to your room. You are certainly going to be sniffed at by the hired help. That is nothing to what you will face when EFT gets really rolling. You may find that you cannot deal in cash anymore. It's too inconvenient. Nobody wants to give you a receipt. You may also find that you can't even pick your own bank. Your employer will do it for you. He is dependent on the goodwill of a bank that performs many services for him, including, in many cases, handling his payroll and some accounting procedures. The bank will put pressure on him to have all employees sign up at the right wicket — its reasoning is that once you have a payroll account with that bank, you will tend to transfer more of your banking there. Sound reasoning. My employer thinks it is a damn nuisance that some of the serfs deal with different banks, but goes along; many other employers do not go along and the outlook is for more, not less, of this kind of pressure. I suppose this is no big deal — especially since, as I believe, there is little to choose between banks anyway — but it is one more instance of the degree to which we are becoming subservient to the machines that are supposed to be our slaves, and one more instance of the narrowing circle of individual choice.

Then there is the matter of the invasion of privacy, on which the CBA tries to be so comforting. The banks already have a great deal of information on file about you, and whatever their policy manuals say, they are often careless about releasing it. As we move deeper into EFT, there will be more and more information on each of us in the bank files. What use will they make of it? Will they sell information to other agencies — if they do, we'll certainly never know. Will they use it themselves, to draw up lists of potential customers for various banking services? They already do that when they send us those alluring invitations to pile up more debt by extending a loan or, at Christmas, to skip one month's payment, and add onto the interest. Banks are involved in an ever-widening circle of enterprises, from mortgages and leases to business advice, investment sales, and accounting services. They naturally want to make use of information gained in one part of their business to help in another. So, with the best will in the world, the extension of today's computing services into true EFT carries a danger with it. And if you believe banks always have the best will in the world, well, bless you, my child, and would you care to buy a wooden nickel?

Finally, there is the question of theft. It used to be that when Steve Suchan or Willie Sutton or whoever wanted to hold up a bank, he loaded up the trusty .38, sloped off down to the corner institution and transacted his business on the spot. There are still some elemental types who insist on curb service, but we frown on them. Only the crudest bank robber says it with a gun. The modern thief does it with finesse, by dipping into the computer during that micro-millisecond when a transaction is in the ether, and millions of electronic signals are buzzing about looking for a place to land.

This is not a subject that our bankers are anxious to talk about. "There will always be robbers, I guess," is about all I got out of Rowland Frazee on the subject. This shyness on the part of a group of men usually known for expressing themselves forcefully is understandable. Little is known about the extent of computer thefts in Canada, and what is known is anything but comforting. Roughly $100 million[12] seems to go missing every year this way, but nobody really knows. Better to forget the whole subject. However, money stolen from the banks has to be replaced, by other consumers, and money spent tracking down the criminals has to be raised, from taxpayers. Even if the banks aren't anxious to discuss the subject, the rest of us should be.

One man who works as a consultant for banks on computers was willing to talk to me about this, off the record. He said that he thought the dangers were "greatly exaggerated." But the more he explained how the systems work, the less reassured I was. "Well," he said, "the case you always hear about is those kids in New York State who got on the telephone and got into a computer system in Canada and screwed things up. In effect, what they were doing was to make a telephone ring in a house. That's all." (The reference is to a case in which three eighth-grade students in Manhattan used a school computer and a telephone to penetrate the files of twenty-one Canadian firms and destroy the files of one in May 1980. No charges were ever laid.[13]) He said that, although computers work through telephone lines, they are "dedicated" lines − that is, nothing else is on that line, and they are guarded by "Security systems you wouldn't dream of." He said it is possible to program a computer so that, "the instant there is an unauthorized use, the computer will scream bloody murder." But − there is always but, isn't there? − "Computers lack common sense. The computer recognizes electronic signals; once you have access to those signals, the computer will respond to a fourteen-year-old kid with a black box in exactly the same way it will respond to the chairman of the bank.

"In a bank, in the old days, if you put a million dollars into an account one day and took it out the next, a teller would say, 'There's something wrong here. This guy doesn't have any million dollars.' But the computer doesn't do that; it just reacts to the impulses it receives. So, yes, you could probably, if you got access, stick a million into an account one day, take it out the next and collect the interest on it − a few hundred dollars. We're working on that kind of thing. It is possible to program a certain amount of common sense into the system, so that the computer will flag unusual transactions."

I don't want to be a gloomy Gus, but it's clear that the people on the other side of the law are doing their work, too, and every advance in computer protection seems to be matched, or more than matched, by an advance in stealing techniques. These are already quite sophisticated. The FBI manual Computer Crime[14] lists no less than five categories of computer theft that apply to banks. To wit:

1. Data diddling

Someone who has access to a computer simply changes information before or during input. A deposit of $300, for example, could be changed to $3,000. In one case, the girlfriend of a female bank employee who worked with the bank's computer took to dropping in on her pal to pick her up for lunch. Her boyfriend, who worked in another bank, knew something about computers, and wrote her out a series of instructions. One day, the young woman came to pick up her friend, who left her chair for a few moments to go to the washroom. The computer was on and ready to be worked. The thief slipped into her chair and, within a few seconds, had transferred $10,000 into an account for her boyfriend. She got up, and threw the notes on computer access into a wastepaper basket. Another girl happened to see her at the computer and noticed her disposing of a piece of paper, so she checked the wastepaper basket. This piece of data diddling didn't work. Many do.

2. Trojan horse

The computer can be programmed so that it will perform unauthorized functions while still carrying on its usual job. This must be done by someone within the institution who takes advantage of the fact that the computer may be performing as many as 100,000 transactions for a single program. The Trojan horse can also be concealed among up to five or six million instructions in the operating system. So a bank's computer, while performing one complex transaction, sets up a special fund and deposits money in it. According to the FBI, "There are no practical methods of preventing and detecting Trojan horse methods if the perpetrator is sufficiently clever."

3. Salami techniques

These involve slicing off a tiny share of each transaction on its way through the computer. In the classic case, called the "rounding down" technique, a bank employee programs the computer so that, when it is calculating interest to several decimal points, it will direct the tiny remainder from each transaction into a special account, which quickly builds up. Thus, if the interest was $1.03441, the 441 — roughly four-tenths of a cent — would normally be rounded down and retained in the computer for application to the next transaction. As soon as the excess comes to one cent or more, it is applied to the next account — thus keeping the books balanced. But the computer can be re-programmed to divert this tiny remainder into the thief's account. The theft will escape any ordinary auditing and, applied to 180,000 accounts, will bring, according to the FBI's figures, a profit of $300 painlessly to the perpetrator, in a few minutes.

4. Superzapping

Every data centre requires a program to bypass ordinary controls to modify or disclose the contents of the computer — what is called a "break glass in case of emergency program." This is known as "superzapping." In one instance, a manager of computer operations in a New Jersey bank was using the superzap program to make changes to account balances to correct errors, because the regular error-correction program was not working. When he discovered how easy it was to make changes without leaving a trace, he diverted $128,000 into the accounts of three friends. He was caught because he got too greedy and took money from an account where it was noticed at once. Normally, the FBI says, the discovery of superzap by technical means is "highly unlikely."

5. Piggybacking

This is also known as "impersonation," and it is a variety of the Data Diddling process. In the most spectacular case, a computer analyst in Los Angeles, bluffed his way into the computer room of the Security Pacific National Bank and, by merely looking over someone's shoulder, learned the password to transfer money to other banks. Later that day, he telephoned the computer-centre, identified himself as a bank official, used the code, and ordered $10.2 million transferred into an account in New York. Then he switched the money to Switzerland. The FBI agent I talked to in Washington contends, "He got too greedy, or he might have gotten away with it; because so much money was involved, the theft was noticed in about three days, and we got him."

There is No Secure Computer

Small thefts often go undetected. And the methods used defy the FBI's neat categories. A customer is working a Citibank automatic teller in New York, and has inserted his plastic bank card to activate the machine. At this point, a stranger at a nearby bank emergency phone waves him away — the machine is broken, he says; don't use it. The man leaves. The stranger then walks up to the open machine and withdraws money from the victim's account.

The automatic tellers, so beloved of the banks, are

bonanzas for thieves. Someone intercepts a bank card in the mail, and uses it to withdraw $3,000 before the loss is discovered. A robber pulls a gun on a man at an automatic teller and uses his card to collect, not only at that terminal, but at every one of the bank's terminals in town.

Donn Parker, a computer security specialist and author of Crime By Computer, told the Los Angeles Times that "It's not currently possible to build an adequate, technically secure computer system."[15]

Aside from the technical problems of detecting thefts is the problem of prosecuting them. Computer thefts fall in the category of "victimless crimes," in most cases, and the perpetrators, who, according to one study, tend to be between the ages of eighteen and thirty-nine and "presentable", are not your everyday thugs. The law is far from clear on what constitutes a computer theft — whether, for example, stealing valuable information from a computer is a theft — and computer criminals tend to be treated with good humour or, even worse, awe. They don't go to jail; they get job offers.

Gaylen Duncan, Executive Director of the Canadian Law Information Council, the man quoted at the beginning of this chapter, told a Toronto conference that not only were computer crimes going undetected and unpunished, but in many cases, unreported. Better to swallow the loss than admit vulnerability. Duncan said, "In the early 1970s it was predicted computer crime would be the white collar crime of the twenty-first century, but I believe it is the entrepreneurial activity of 1984."[16] Not a crime, really, just another way to make a buck.

Computer thefts involve many businesses besides banks, but banks are a prime target.

Banks get the Benefits

If the computer poses so many problems for us — errors, invasion of privacy, theft — why are the banks so intent on pressing ahead with EFT? Quite simply because the advantages flow to the banks and the shortcomings are borne by society as a whole. EFT will tie every one of us closer to the banking network, whether we like it or not; you can't expect the banks to consider that a drawback. It will increase the incidence of theft, and while the banks

17
The Balance Sheet

"The most efficacious and the most immediate means which the Canadians have to protect themselves against the fury of their enemies is to attack them in their dearest parts — their pockets — in their strongest entrenchment — the banks."

Louis Joseph Papineau, *1834*

We have come far enough to draw some conclusions about the Canadian banking system, and to consider some proposals for improvement. However, to set both in context, it will be useful to make some comparisons with other banking systems similar to our own. Therefore, this final chapter will begin with a quick world-tour, pause briefly to summarize what we have learned about the strengths and weaknesses of our own system, advance some modest proposals, and wind up with Stewart's Code — not unlike Hammurabi's Code in its broad sweep, but less bloody-minded — containing instructions on how to cope with banks.

The major banking systems of the world share a number of common characteristics; they are all built on the notions of fungibility, faith and low clearing losses. They are all in the money-creating game, and they all have reserve requirements, of one sort or another, operated through some kind of central bank, usually government-owned. To a degree, all banking systems are characterized by strong links between members of each nation's recognized establishment, through the banks. The complaints registered in Chapters Eight and Nine about the tendency of the well-to-do to favour each other in banking institutions is universal, although carried further in Canada than elsewhere. In Japan, for example, the great private corporations like Mitsubishi, Mitsui and Sumitomo – inheritors of the names and many of the characteristics of the zaibatsu empires on which Japan's wealth was built before World War II[1] – have their own banks and trust corporations which give each other mutual assistance. There, as here, what counts in money matters is having the correct connection.

Like our own banks, all the major systems are moving into computerization, and there is a tendency in every system to consolidate smaller units into larger ones. The virtues of rigorous competition are relentlessly hymned in every modern industrial state, and just as relentlessly avoided wherever possible. The banks are not unique in this respect; the unstated theme of business enterprise everywhere is a prayer for competition in every other industry, and a monopoly in one's own.

However, no other industrialized nation outside the Soviet bloc presents so complete a domination of the banking industry by a handful of firms as does Canada.

Denmark, with a population one-fifth our own, has forty commercial banks and 200 savings banks, as well as a strong admixture of foreign banks now allowed to compete with the native ones. Denmark has a rule that every bank supervisory board – somewhat like our boards of directors – must contain representatives of the general public.[2]

Tiny Austria (population, 7.5 million) has thirty-eight joint-stock banks, ten private banks, 165 savings banks, 1,279 rural co-operative banks, 148 Volksbanken (small business credit co-operatives) ten provincial mortgage banks and a postal savings bank.[3]

West Germany has 5,300 banks,[4] and while three commercial banks tend to dominate the foreign operations of the nation (Deutsche Bank, Dresdner Bank and Commerzbank) they face stiff competition at home from large regional banks like the Bayerische Vereinsbank and the Frankfurter Bank.

Switzerland, whose banks win the admiration of financiers everywhere, has 551 public banks, twenty-five private banks, and twenty-nine cantonal banks.[5] The Swiss sometimes worry about the domination of their banking system by the Big Five — Union Bank of Switzerland, Swiss Bank Corporation, Swiss Credit Bank, Swiss Volksbank and Bank Leu — because they represent over forty-seven per cent of domestic business. That compares with our Big Five, representing ninety-one per cent of all assets. The cantonal banks, financed and controlled by the cantons, hold twenty-two per cent of the nation's banking assets, and their success is an argument for the notion that regionally based banks can be made to work, even in a nation whose regions are jammed together.

France has sixty-seven banks, including such foreign-owned institutions as the Banque Europeenne de Tokyo (a subsidiary of nine Japanese banks), and Barclays Banque. Charles de Gaulle nationalized much of the French banking system after World War II, and Francois Mitterand, upon his election in 1981, began a campaign to carry the process almost to completion over the next few years. The French government is in the process of nationalizing thirty-six banks, bringing the state-owned share of the banking business from the current sixty per cent to ninety-three per cent.[6] Nationalization doesn't seem to have hurt the system so far; one list of the world's top banks puts the Banque Nationale du Paris at the top, with $107 billion in assets, and puts Credit Lyonnais third, Credit Agricole fourth and Societe General fifth. This is the list as compiled by the American Banker; The Banker, a British publication, has two American banks, Citicorp and Bank of America, in the top spots, followed by the three French national banks. Despite the overwhelming government hold on French banks, they compete with each other effectively; indeed, it is hard for an outsider to see what advantage there is in government ownership — outside of the opportunity for taxpayers to share in the profits — because the banks seem to operate exactly like any other business enterprise.

Japan has seventy-six commercial banks, as well as seventy-one Sogo banks — mutual loan and savings institutions which perform many of the same functions — 468 credit associations, 494 credit co-operatives, and a government-operated postal savings system.[7]

All of these systems, like those of Norway (twenty-seven commercial banks, seven savings banks), Sweden (one

national bank, fourteen "other banks"), and Belgium (five
state-owned banks, four development banks, twenty-three
commercial banks, eight foreign banks) provide institutions superficially like our own. Walking in off the street,
we are at home, language barriers aside. We know where
to line up (in Japan, the lineup will be longer than we are
used to, even with the longer lines produced by the
"efficiencies" of the computer in Canada), and how to
transact our business. To get at what separates our own
system from others, we will want to look more closely at
the two foreign systems with which we have most to do —
that of the United Kingdom, and that of the United States.

Banking in the U.K.

The United Kingdom provided the model for Canadian
banking, and our systems have a great deal in common.
However, over the years, we have developed a number of
differences worth noting. The British banks are directed
far more effectively by the Bank of England than ours are
by the Bank of Canada. It can be argued — indeed, I think it
is self-evident — that the Bank of Canada serves the banks
more effectively than it does the government, and sees its
role as an aide rather than a curb to the private institutions. Patrick Frazer, an official with Banking Information
Services in London, who studied the Canadian banks on
behalf of his own employers, puts the difference this way:
"Here, things are done less by the word of law than by
word of the dear old B of E. The Bank of England says,
'Don't go too fast, old chap,' and that's it . . . It is so
powerful, it nods and winks and things happen. The B of E
does everything. It supervises the banks, it is the judge and
jury on any banking matter. You don't have this separation
that you have in Canada with an Inspector General; the B
of E is the Inspector General and the General everything
else. It carries out the bank inspections, wouldn't dream of
leaving that to the banks."

Frazer can't imagine the British bank system getting
into the kind of tug of war that developed in Canada when
developer Robert Campeau tried to take over Royal Trustco
and the Toronto-Dominion Bank stepped in to freeze him
out. "Here," says Frazer, "the B of E would simply say 'He
won't do, old boy,' and the entire financial community

would take the hint. The takeover would be dropped. There would be no need for all that fuss."

Beneath this powerful, government-owned central bank, the British system divides into two main streams, "recognized banks," and "recognized deposit-taking institutions."[8] It is the Bank of England that does the recognizing. There are 300 recognized banks, and an equal number of deposit-taking institutions, and there is no definition of banking except this recognition. Non-recognized banks can't call themselves banks, even if they are banks everywhere else in the world.

The key to recognition lies in one of two qualifications – either the institution performs a wide range of banking services – Midland Bank, for example – or it performs a specialized function on a national basis, and does it well. The eleven London discount houses are recognized as banks, although their main functions are to raise money from the banks on short-term paper and to purchase liquid assets – treasury bills, commercial notes, certificates of deposit – with this money. Similarly, the merchant banks, whose function is to finance industry by way of venture capital – often buying shares themselves – are recognized as banks. Baring Brothers, Hill Samuel and Lazard Brothers are typical examples of large merchant banks. In Canada, we don't have merchant banks, because our banks are severely restricted in the degree to which they can own shares in any outside corporation; here, the functions of the merchant bank are taken over by venture-capital firms and investment houses. As well, in Britain, there are many closely-held, privately owned banks, whereas in Canada, the big banks are all widely-held and publicly traded, even though they are private (that is, non-government) institutions.

The "recognized deposit-taking institutions" are all the trust companies, credit firms, co-ops and building societies – the near-banks. Under the revised banking law of 1979, every deposit-taking institution had to be recognized as either a bank or other deposit-taker by April 1, 1980, or cease taking deposits.

Within the pure banking sector, there is yet another division, between the "clearing banks" and the other commercial banks. The clearing banks are thirteen in number, the six London clearing banks (of which four –

Barclays, National Westminster, Lloyds and Midland – are the dominating firms, and Coutts and Williams and Glyn's are junior), the three Scottish clearing banks (Bank of Scotland, Royal Bank of Scotland and Clydesdale) and the four Irish clearing banks. Wales is covered by the London clearing banks. They are called clearing banks for the obvious reason; they run the cheque-clearing system for the financial community.

To complicate the picture still further in Britain, there is cross-ownership between the clearing banks; Barclays owns thirty-five per cent of the Bank of Scotland, Lloyd's has sixteen per cent of the Royal Bank of Scotland, Coutts is a wholly-owned subsidiary of National Westminster. In effect, the Big Four – Barclays, National Westminster, Lloyds and Midland – occupy central stage in the British banking system, but they are nowhere near as powerful as Canada's Big Five. The combined London clearing banks hold thirty-two per cent of Britain's deposit accounts compared to the seventy per cent held by our Big Five. Competition is not exactly raging, but it does exist.

Nor do the U.K. banks have the cosy relationship our banks have with government. That became clear when the budget of March 1981 imposed a windfall profits tax on gains made because of high interest rates. Our banks claimed they made no such profit, or if they did, they shouldn't be taxed on it, and they were listened to; the British banks were cold-shouldered by the Conservative government.

The British banks are also more limited in the business they are allowed to attend to. They have only recently moved into the residential mortgage market, for example, which has always been dominated by the building societies, a cross between a savings bank and a credit union. Nor do British banks perform the extensive payroll and accounting services our banks are taking on, nor their leasing and factoring functions.

Britain's National Girobank, successor to the Post Office Giro, is a government-owned competitor that provides cheap credit transfer and postal cheque service for account holders, and 22,000 post offices are, in effect, bank branches for small savers who can buy National Savings certificates, premium bonds and other securities that take much of the business away from the commercial banks.

In addition to that competitive spur, the British banks, as of 1981, no longer follow a uniform Bank Rate (in Britain, it was called the Minimum Lending Rate); the general interest rates are now established by individual transactions between the discount houses and the Bank of England, and vary from bank to bank.

Rising to the top of the British banking world, Patrick Frazer explains, is accomplished in one of two ways: "Either the man (women's liberation is no further advanced there than here) joins the bank after leaving school and hangs on until everyone else dies off, in which case he becomes managing director; or he is blue-blooded enough to be brought in at the top to give the board a dash of class." In Canada, by and large, the first approach dominates.

Frazer is a great admirer of the Canadian banks: "In England, there is less doing of the unexpected. In Canada, you can have a bank handling lottery tickets or giving you a toaster. I once saw a sailboat in a bank-window, in support of a sales drive. You wouldn't see that here. Your banks pay more attention to ordinary people. They're more fun."

Fun isn't the word that springs to my mind contemplating Canadian banks, but I'm not a banker.

The U.S. System

American banks, our neighbours, look much like our own, but they are not. There are many, many more of them, for one thing; at last count, the United States boasted 14,712 banks,[9] but that included all sorts — savings banks, trust companies, mutual stock savings associations and industrial banks are all treated as part of the same system. Of these, 4,564 were federally-chartered, and the rest state-chartered. However, being federally-chartered does not allow an American bank to operate federally; no bank is allowed to operate within the United States outside its native state. The word "National" in a bank's title doesn't mean it is national in scope, only that it holds a federal charter. The Americans don't have anything that we would recognize as a national bank. What is more, as we have already seen, most states have "unit banking" laws, which means one bank, one branch, although in some states, holding companies are allowed to control a number of branches. The result is that while some American banks are world leaders – Citicorp, Bank of America, Chase-Manhattan – the average American bank is much smaller than our own, and competition is much fiercer than it is here. While the United States has a "discount rate" similar to our Bank Rate, by which the banks are signalled as to whether interest levels should go up or down, Prime Rates shift much more rapidly than they do in Canada as competing banks try to jostle for a share of the market.

The central banking control is also quite different from our own. The Federal Reserve System is not a single central bank, but the linking of twelve Federal Reserve Banks in each of twelve districts – Boston, New York, Philadelphia, Cleveland, Richmond, Atlanta, Chicago, St. Louis, Minneapolis, Kansas City, Dallas and San Francisco.[10] Each of these banks can issue money – under central control, of course – and the letter in the rosette on the grey side of an American bank note signifies which reserve bank issued it.

Central control of the Fed, as it is normally called, is lodged with a seven-man Board of Governors appointed by the President, and resident in Washington. The Board is responsible, as the Bank of Canada is, for the general conduct of monetary policy. It is the Fed which swallowed the arguments of the monetarists and imposed the tight-money regime which has distorted world finance for the past seven years. The independence accorded the Chairman, Paul Volker, is complete, and written into law. I argued in Chapter Ten that the Governor of the Bank of Canada had managed to squirm loose from effective control, but that was never the intention of legislators. In the United States, the Fed was intended to exercise independent control over the money-supply from the start; it is part of the division of powers that Americans are so fond of, and which has proven as disastrous in this field as in, say, foreign policy. There is a certain irony in the fact that the Federal Reserve Chairman is independent of the U.S. administration, and the Governor of the Bank of Canada is independent of the Canadian government, but Canadian monetary policy is dependent on the policy of the Fed, which has been both dumb and dangerous.

The Fed exercises its policy by controlling reserve

requirements – which are higher than our own, and range all the way up to twenty-two per cent for certain kinds of deposits. It also controls interest rates, both by setting the rate at which banks can borrow from it, and by punishing banks that borrow too much or too often. In 1981, when the Fed was squeezing the money supply, it charged banks that borrowed frequently an extra two per cent.[11]

In the United States the banking lobby managed to get a law passed limiting the interest that can be paid on savings – ostensibly, this was to protect consumers in some fashion; in fact, it protects the banks by putting a lid on competition. (In Canada, when we had an interest-limiting law, it was a law to curb the interest a bank could charge, not the amount it could pay.) Enforcing these interest ceilings is yet another task for the Fed.

The twelve Reserve Banks are owned by the member banks – the national banks in each region and such state banks and trust companies as have chosen to become members. The president, first vice-president and three board members of each district are named by the Board of Governors in Washington; six other board members are elected in each region.

Bank supervision, as we have already seen, is shared between the Fed, the Comptroller of the Currency, and the individual banks. It is much stricter than is the case in Canada. State banks that do not choose to join the Fed are examined by state officials.

More banks do not belong to the Fed than do – of the 14,712 banks, 9,315 are not Fed members. The advantages of belonging are prestige, profits – the district banks make money and share it with their owners – and automatic membership in the Federal Deposit Insurance system, which offers five times the protection of Canadian deposit insurance, with a maximum guarantee of $100,000 compared to our $20,000.[12] (Non-Fed members can join the system by paying a fee; many do.) The advantage of not belonging is to escape the stricter reserve requirements – state reserves are much lower.

The great strengths of the American banking system are its competitiveness, its efficiency, and its regional base. Profit margins are slender and interest rates are more susceptible to bargaining; American banks try harder. I used to think American bank tellers smiled more than ours do, but two years of living in the United States cured me of that delusion; their tellers are as grumpy as our own.

The fact that the Federal Reserve System is organized through local districts has allowed the Americans to hold onto the jump their banking history — with its base in local requirements — gave them. American banks are more entrepreneurial than our own not because of some flaw in our makeup, but because they have always had a banking system in which, if you couldn't get a hand from one bank, there was another standing by, and longing for your business, and from the fact that local development was and remains the raison d'être for most banks. No single region was allowed to plunder the hinterland, as in Canada, nor to turn one area into a savings pool for another — as Canadian banks served up the Maritimes to Ontario and Quebec.

The drawback in the American banking system is that it is not as uniform as our own. The citizen of Musquash, Maine who doesn't care for the administration of Uncle Lou's Bank, Cafe and Billiard Parlour may find he has to travel quite a way to do his banking. He may also find that he can't get as good a deal in Musquash as he could if he lived in Bangor, or New York. Canadian banks offer similar services at similar prices right across the country.

Two Overwhelming Drawbacks

Is the Canadian banking system "better" or "worse" than the banking systems of Britain, the United States, or elsewhere? I don't think any definitive answer can be reached on this score, and I'm not sure the question matters all that much. Our system has two overwhelming disadvantages — its inefficiency and its timidity. It has not served regional development well, it has not served small and medium-sized entrepreneurs well, and it is expensive for consumers. All of these flaws stem from the same source — the oligopolistic nature of the banking system in this country. It does not follow that we should try to turn our system into one resembling that of, say, the United States. We couldn't do it if we wanted to, and it is far from certain that we want to. If we are going to reform Canadian banking then we should start with a realistic notion of what we have.

What we have is a banking system that works quite well. It delivers a wide range of services to business and customers — only the so-called "full-service banks" in the United States are comparable; it is stable; it has not been marked by corruption — at least recently — and it has proven effective in financing Canadian business beyond our own borders. Its shortcomings — high costs, arrogance, uneven performance, an inflationary bias, a tendency to deal with a narrow circle of business associates — are susceptible of reform. If we want to set things right, we should address ourselves to the shortcomings, and leave the main structure of the system in place.

Therefore, my ten-point plan — everyone should have a ten-point plan — to make Canadian banking better cannot be unveiled before rejecting two of the possibilities that spring instantly to mind. The first is the suggestion that Canadian banks, or some of them, should be nationalized. The second is the argument that they should be broken up. Both sound terrific to anyone who gets as mad at the banks as I sometimes do, but neither makes sense in the long run.

If we're going to nationalize the banks, we start with a couple of questions: 1. Which banks will we take? and 2. Who is going to run them? I have no objection in principle to government owning a bank — governments own airlines, trains, hospitals and oilwells, and don't do any worse with them than private owners do. But I can't see us putting up, say, $2,635,147,000 to buy up the Royal Bank, Canada's largest bank (I have taken the 1981 high share price of $32.25 and multiplied it by the 81,710,000 shares outstanding). By the time the lawyers are through, we will be shelling out over $3 billion; even at the Royal's fat rate of profit, it's going to take us years to get our money back. Buying any bank smaller than the Royal Bank doesn't make much sense — not with the stranglehold the other banks have on the market. Setting up a new bank might be cheaper, but I doubt it — again, there is the oligopoly to go up against. Small banks have not done well, so we would have to launch a huge bank. That would bring us to the second question — who is going to run it? If it is the folks who run the post office, I'd just as soon forget it. Nationalizing the banks might provide some spiritual satisfaction, but not much else; the nationalized French banks are not better than our own, and the pattern of nationalized industries everywhere suggests that, in time, the best of them come to resemble private sector corporations so closely that — as with Credit Lyonnais — most people aren't even aware they are dealing with a state firm. To spend billions taking over the Royal or launching a new bank only to end up with the same thing we already have, under government control, would be pointless.

Breaking up the big banks also sounds attractive, at first glance, but it contains the same drawback; it is not good business. If we want to continue to compete abroad — and we have to continue to compete abroad — it would be madness to break up the banks that give us a major advantage in foreign fields. It is their very size that provides the advantage, as the Americans keep reminding us. If we broke them up at home, we would end up allowing them to combine abroad — the trend in many industries, anyway — and that's plain silly. Regrettably, then, we must turn our faces away from the temptation to nationalize and the temptation to go at the banks with a balpeen hammer, and settle instead for a program to reshape what we have closer to the heart's desire. This brings us to my ten points.

1. The dicennial review of the Bank Act should be abolished, and the act should be available for amendment as required — like any other legislation. The provision written into the original Act — whose architects were bankers — was designed to provide stability to the system. The system is oozing with stability; what it needs is some flexibility. The current Act is virtually silent on such pressing matters as Electronic Funds Transfer, and to wait ten years to make the law conform with the onslaught of looming problems would not be wise. The simple solution is to lift the banks' immunity.

2. "Banks" and "banking" should be defined by law, and the definitions should be strict enough to limit these institutions to common-sense versions of what banking comprises. As long ago as 1964, the Porter Commission on Banking pointed to the difficulties in arriving at an acceptable definition while noting that the lack allowed the banks to move increasingly into other fields. In the United States, a bank is clearly defined as an institution, "a substantial part of the business of which consists of

receiving deposits and making loans and discounts." The U.S. phraseology would not apply to Canada, because our systems are so different, but the example shows that it is not impossible to arrive at such a definition. The Egyptians have one; it says simply that a commercial bank is "an institution which accepts demand deposits or time deposits payable within one year."

That would certainly put a crimp in Canadian banks, which is not a bad idea, since the alternative is to let them absorb more and more of the management of finance. They are becoming, in addition to their normal banking role, payroll managers, accountants, bond salesmen, business partners, factors, leasing operators, and pension-fund salesmen. They are coming to dominate three fields — mortgages, consumer loans and the management of Registered Retirement Savings Plans and Registered Home Ownership Savings Plans — where they were never intended to be and where their influence, in my opinion, has been harmful. In the future, their threat to take over the electronic funds system poses an even greater danger. They ought to be defined back down to some semblance of size, and limited to such functions as the handling of savings and chequing accounts, term deposits, loans, the purchase and sale of securities, and safety deposit and safekeeping facilities. Their role in residential mortgages and consumer finance should be limited and perhaps eliminated, and they should be required to withdraw from leasing and factoring. RRSPs and RHOSPs should be turned back to the trust companies — this is primarily a fiduciary function anyway, and their plans have been consistently better than the banks'. Finally, banks should not be allowed to venture into any new fields without a great deal more planning than took place when they were allowed to plunge into mortgage and consumer lending. A definition that starts with the notion that the banks are too big and works backwards would suit admirably.

3. We need a radical change in the rules governing the boards of directors of banks, both to curb the built-in conflicts of interest that now seem unavoidable, and to open up the system. For starters, there ought to be a provision like that in Danish law, that a substantial proportion of every bank's board consist of members of the outside public. The Royal Commission on Corporate Concen-

tration made such a suggestion about bank boards in 1978, and was studiously ignored, but it is absolutely essential that the people who make so many decisions affecting consumers have some contribution from their victims.

In the same vein, there ought to be a severe limitation, if not a prohibition, on the membership on bank boards by executives of client firms. The reasons are obvious, and already detailed in Chapter Eight. They were summarized this way by the Royal Commission on Corporate Concentration in 1978:

"The boards of our major lending institutions are composed almost entirely of persons who have an additional relationship to the bank, usually as the chief officer of a borrower. Inevitably this creates the possibility of a conflict of interest, collective as well as individual, where the directors' obligations to the bank may clash with their duties elsewhere."

4. A parallel change is also required going the other way. Bank officers ought to be prohibited from holding outside directorships. The Porter Commission in 1964 called these outside jobs "unwise and undesirable," but did not suggest a legal prohibition. The Royal Commission of 1978, citing a concern about the conflict of interest, quoted a senior banker as saying "There is no doubt that the potential problem is there," but suggested "restraint" rather than a prohibition. Something that is unwise, undesirable and potentially dangerous requires more than a mild clearing of the throat. These jobs should be taken away from bank executives, not merely to protect them, and us, from concerns about conflict of interest, but to open up the world of finance to others. The narrow circle of bankers, bank lawyers and their chums has not served us well, so it is time to call in some strangers.

5. The office of the Inspector General should be changed and expanded. The lunatic provision that pays his salary indirectly out of bank funds should be scrapped forthwith. He – or she; there is a strong argument for looking for a competent and combative female in this role – should be the Inspector, in a real sense, of banking operations, and conduct regular examinations. He should assume the ombudsman role he claims to have. It wouldn't be a bad start – to place some necessary distance between the Inspector and the banks – to ask him to chuck out all

those beautiful bank pictures on his office walls.

6. Much greater public disclosure should be required from the banks. As it is, they are not even required to comply with normal Canadian accounting practice in preparing financial statements, which means that their reports are even less useful and informative than the average run of corporate statements. Information required for shareholder reports ought also to be made available to the public – as is the case in the United States. Much more information about executive compensation should be made available to shareholders – including salaries, bonuses and special loan arrangements.

The public should also be told about loans to foreign governments in excess of $1 million, so we can get some concrete information about arrangements that affect Canadian foreign policy, but about which we know almost nothing.

We also require much more information about the banks' involvement in the Euro-currency market. We can't get all the information we need from our own banks – one of the scary aspects of this inflationary binge is that even the banks don't know the real size of the money-bubble they have created – but the information they do have at least might give us a place to start.

7. Much more public scrutiny is also required when banks set up for business in this country. The Unity Bank case indicated that banks regard the promises they make when starting up as merely a form of temporary public relations. Under the new chartering system, we will know even less about the people who want to rule our financial lives. There should be provision for one public hearing on every charter application, and that hearing should be conducted by a House of Commons committee, not the Senate Banking Committee.

8. The Bank of Canada Act must be revised to restore responsibility for monetary policy to the Minister of Finance. The present system – passing the buck – has led us to a monetary policy which is both irresponsible, in every meaning of that word, and disastrous. The Bank Rate is a political and economic matter, and ought to be announced in the House of Commons by a minister responsible for its setting and knowledgeable about its workings.

9. Electronic Funds Transfer ought to be stopped in its tracks until we have much more information, and a much greater sense of responsibility on the part of the banks. Getting the machinery to make bits of information whiz back and forth is the easy part; making a profit out of expanding credit is even easier. But we need to know that we have provisions to protect our privacy, and to transfer the costs of the inevitable increase in thefts to the banks before they go one step further. We also require a provision reversing the current assumption that whatever a bank says is correct, and that it is up to the customer to prove that something went wrong inside the computer. Computer-driven systems must be required to provide documentation to customers and to courts, and the vexed question of the legal status of a computer print-out must be straightened out before it is too late, and we find that we have created yet another and larger Big Brother in every bank building.

10. Finally, restrictions on the growth of foreign banks in Canada ought to be removed forthwith. The reason for this radical suggestion – radical coming from a Canadian nationalist, at least – is that there is no other possibility of providing much-needed competition in Canadian banking. The Royal Commission on Corporate Concentration said flatly, "The economic barriers to entry of new banks into the retail branch banking business ... appear to us so formidable that easing of the legal and procedural barriers would not be enough to bring any early increase in competition sufficient to permit a new bank to rival one of the big five." The solution is self-evident – if no home-grown bank can provide competition, allow foreign banks in to take on the job.

The National Bank may not be interested in going up against the Bank of Montreal to provide regional banking in Calgary, but the Bank of America would be and, released from the shackles that now bind it, could bring in enough resources to give the Big Five a run for their money. The bank lobby has so far strangled every attempt to provide competition – while extolling the virtues of the fierce clash which the CBA already sees in Canadian banking. The proposal to bring in foreign banks during the 1980 revision was emasculated. Limited to eight per cent of the assets of domestic banking, foreign banks will remain bit-players and competition will remain a distant dream. Lifting the barriers would provide better service, lower costs and a new attitude on the part of the banks. The obvious concern – that foreign banks would take over the Canadian financial system – is not a real one; our banks are already so large and well-entrenched that the most that could happen is that one or more of the Big Five might find itself in difficulty, and all of them would be required to pull up their socks.

If foreign ownership did become too intrusive, it would not be hard to reimpose some form of restraint, but I doubt if that will ever be necessary. The threat Canadians face is not from foreign banks, but from our own.

Coping with your Bank

You may want to know what to do between now and the time a grateful Parliament implements my ten reforms – bound to take a few weeks – so I have devised Stewart's Code for dealing with the banks as they now exist, and are likely to continue to exist for some time. It consists of seven points.

1. All Cats Look Alike In The Dark

Since the major banks are indistinguishable from each other, except in minor and unimportant ways, disregard all the heavy advertising hype about the advantages of one over the other, and use whatever bank is nearest to you, or whichever one makes you feel most at home. That is most likely to depend on the individuals in the bank, not the brand-name. The Bank of Commerce is not, in fact, any more or less friendly than any other bank.

2. Cultivate The Near-Banks

A credit union is a better place to get a loan than a bank – unless you're in a dreadful hurry. Trust and mortgage companies provide better returns on Guaranteed Investment Certificates, and run better RRSPs and RHOSPs. Don't go to a bank for services that can be provided better elsewhere; you will have the same guarantee of security at a trust company as at a bank and, chances are, you will find the staff friendlier. They're hungrier than bankers.

3. Split Your Credit Cards

Don't ever hold a bank-card at a bank that has your major accounts in it. As we have already seen, in any case of dispute, the bank can simply grab your money and let you sue for recovery. Keep your card in one bank, and your money in another, or in a trust company.

4. Bargain With Your Bank

Remember that each branch is operated as a profit-centre, and if the manager or loans officer can make more money out of you, he will. Find out what a number of institutions are offering by way of rates before you take out a mortgage or other loan, and reject, as a matter of principle, the first offer put before you. Canadians have been brainwashed into thinking that when a bank manager says, "Our rate on consumer loans is twenty-two per cent" that is the word of God. It isn't. That is the bank's first bargaining position; it will not be offended if you make a counter-offer.

5. Get Your Financial Advice Elsewhere

Bankers are free with opinions, but their track record is not good. Anyone who cares to read the monthly bulletins and yearly forecasts put out by the banks will discover that he would be as far ahead to slaughter a pigeon and examine its entrails as to govern his conduct by what his bank manager tells him. The bank is in the business of selling services, and it will proffer advice that aids that purpose. Remember all the bankers who were advising customers to hold off on mortgages when they hit twelve per cent – because they were bound to come down.

6. Scream Like Hell

Banks make errors; they make them often, and they correct them slowly. The customer who waits idly for the bank to correct one of its blunders is in for a long, cold wait. If you think there is something wrong with your savings account, for example, ask to see the Savings Supervisor, and demand an explanation you can follow. Never accept "I'm sorry, but that's bank policy." Bank policy is arrogant and unfeeling. (I can't wind up this book without one more example. The Bank of Montreal deducted $100 from the account of Michel Morgan of Toronto in September 1981, in error. After a number of weeks, and repeated complaints, the bank finally admitted the error and promised to return the $100, but to collect it, Morton had to visit the bank and sign an affidavit stating that she had not written the cheque the bank was trying to charge against her. She resented having to take time to straighten out the bank's mistake, but went to the bank, grumbling. She wasted her visit, because she didn't have an appointment; she was told to come back after making one at a time when the bank could have a lawyer on hand to handle the forms. She balked, and took her complaint to Rod Goodman, consumer columnist for the Toronto Star, who told her that she would have to do what the bank said, and make an appointment at their convenience, not her own.[13] It was the bank's blunder, but it is the customer who is expected to bear whatever inconvenience results.) If you complain early and often and out loud, you will become known in the bank, your account will be marked with a notation – Handle With Care – and you will get better service. You will not be loved, but you will receive better treatment from your bank than most customers. I regret to add one small additional caveat – keep complaining until your complaint comes before a man, unless you know you happen to be in a bank where women employees are in positions of responsibility.

7. Cultivate A Sneer

Banks are not, in fact, the glorious creations of a munificent deity. They are not run by saints nor supervised by angels; they are tough, aggressive, self-centred business enterprises. I don't complain about this; it goes with the territory. I simply mention it as the background to the most important advice any Canadian can be given when he deals with his own banking system. Do not assume that something is correct because your bank says it is so, do not assume that your bank has your own best interests at heart, and do not assume that the banks in general have Canada's best interests at heart. What the banks have at heart is what any well-run corporation has at heart – growth, profits and satisfied shareholders. It is in the bank's interest to conduct itself so as not to offend its customers unnecessarily, but that is quite different from, say, giving you a break on interest rates because the manager admires your pretty eyes and lithesome form. What he admires is a satisfactory performance report, and the way to obtain one is to get as much money out of you as possible while delivering as few services to you as possible.

Your bank is not your buddy.

18
Appendix I

The Tables

1. The 11 Parliamentary Chartered Banks

Bank and Rank	Assets at Oct. 31, 1981
	($ Billion)
1. The Royal Bank of Canada	87.51
2. The Canadian Imperial Bank of Commerce	66.84
3. The Bank of Montreal	63.78
4. The Bank of Nova Scotia	50.13
5. The Toronto-Dominion Bank	44.86
6. The National Bank of Canada	19.16
7. The Mercantile Bank of Canada	4.10
8. The Bank of British Columbia	2.99
9. The Continental Bank of Canada	2.53
10. The Canadian Commercial Bank	1.53
11. The Northland Bank	.52
Total	343.95

2. Growth of the Banks, 1960-1981
Total Assets of Chartered Banks

Year	Assets ($ Billion)	% Change from 1960
1960	16.91	–
1968	36.74	217.2
1970	46.26	273.4
1972	63.22	373.7
1974	91.59	541.4
1976	126.40	747.2
1978	179.81	1062.9
1980	269.88	1595.3
1981	343.97	2033.3

Source: Canada Gazette, various issues.
Note: The chartered banks as a group multiplied in size more than twenty-fold between 1960 and 1981.
Between 1980 and 1981, they grew by $74.09 billion, growth in a single year of more than their entire assets in 1972.

3(a). Interest Rates

Date	Bank Rate	Prime	Consumer Loan	Mortgage	Daily Int.	Spread
Feb. 28/79	11.25	12.00	13.00	11.25	9.50	2.50
Feb. 28/80	14.00	15.00	16.00	13.75	12.25	2.75
Sept. 21/80	11.02	12.25	14.25	13.75	9.25	3.00
Oct. 1/80	11.60	12.75	14.75	15.00	9.25	3.50
Apr. 30/81	17.40	18.00	17.50	16.50	13.75	4.25
July 24	19.89	21.00	23.00	20.00	17.25	3.75
July 31	20.54	21.75	23.00	20.00	17.75	4.00
Aug. 7	21.24	22.75	25.00	21.25	18.50	4.25
Aug. 14	21.07	22.75	25.00	21.25	18.50	4.25
Sept. 4	20.69	22.75	25.00	21.75	19.00	3.75
Sept. 11	20.18	21.75	24.00	21.75	19.00	2.75
Sept. 28	19.63	21.25	23.75	21.00	17.25	4.00
Oct. 19	18.31	20.00	22.25	20.25	15.25	4.75
Oct. 30	18.21	20.00	22.25	20.25	15.25	4.75
Nov. 9	17.62	19.50	21.75	19.75	15.25	4.25
Nov. 16	16.13	18.00	21.00	18.25	13.50	4.50
Dec. 4	15.31	17.25	21.00	17.50	13.50	3.75
Dec. 15	15.18	17.25	20.50	17.50	13.50	3.75
Dec. 22	15.00	17.25	20.00	17.50	13.50	3.75
Dec. 29	14.66	16.50	20.00	18.50	12.75	3.75
Jan. 9/82	14.74	16.50	19.75	18.50	12.00	4.50
Jan. 16/82	14.81	16.50	19.75	18.50	12.00	4.50
Jan. 23/82	14.72	16.50	19.75	18.50	12.00	4.50
Feb. 5/82	14.74	16.50	19.75	18.50	12.00	4.50

Sources: Newspaper tables, Bank of Canada Review (Monthly), Telephone checks with banks.

3(b). Spread on Chequing Accounts

Date	Prime	Chequing Interest	Spread
Dec. 31/79	15.00	3.00	12.00
June 5/80	13.25	3.00	10.25
Jan. 2/81	18.25	3.00	15.25
June 4/81	20.00	3.00	17.00
August 14/81	22.75	3.00	19.75
Oct. 19/81	20.00	3.00	17.00
Nov. 16/81	18.00	3.00	15.00
Dec. 9/81	17.25	3.00	14.25
Jan. 9/82	16.50	3.00	13.50

3(c). Mortgages

Date	Bank buys (term deposits)			Sells (mortgage)			Spreads		
	1 year	3 year	5 year	1 year	3 year	5 year	1	3	5
Sept. 5/80	10.25	10.75	10.75	13.25	14.00	14.24	3.00	3.25	3.50
June 5/81	16.25	16.00	15.75	18.25	18.50	18.75	2.00	2.50	3.00
Aug. 19/81	18.25	17.75	17.50	21.25	21.75	22.00	3.00	4.00	4.50
Sept. 17/81	18.00	17.25	17.00	22.25	21.25	21.50	4.25	4.00	4.50
Oct. 17/81	17.25	17.25	17.25	19.75	19.75	20.00	2.00	2.00	2.25
Dec. 4/81	14.25	13.50	13.50	17.50	17.75	17.75	4.25	4.25	3.25
Dec. 22/81	14.00	13.50	14.00	17.25	17.50	18.00	3.25	4.00	4.00
Jan. 4/82	15.50	16.50	16.50	17.50	18.00	18.25	2.00	1.50	1.75
Jan. 23/82	15.50	14.50	15.00	17.75	18.50	18.75	3.25	4.00	3.75

4(a). Deposit-Taking Institutions

Size by Assets
As of End of First Quarter, 1981

Institution	Assets ($ Billion)	% of Total
Chartered Banks	294.27	74.0
Credit Unions & Caisses Populaires	31.33	7.9
Trust & Mortgage Firms	59.18	14.9
Mortgage Firms Connected with Banks	9.71	2.4
Government Savings Offices	2.99	0.7
Total	397.48	99.9

Sources: Bank of Canada Review, November 1981, and Globe and Mail October 5, 1981 p. B33.

4(b). Deposit-Taking Institutions

**Share of Personal Loans
As of End of First Quarter, 1981**

Institution	Loans ($ Billion)	% of Total
Chartered Banks	32.99	77.8
Credit Unions & Caisses Populaires	6.29	14.8
Personal Finance Firms	1.22	2.8
Government Savings Offices	1.90	4.5
Total	42.40	99.9

Sources: Bank of Canada Review, November 1981, and Globe and Mail October 5, 1981 p. B33.

4(c). Deposit-Taking Institutions

**Share of Residential Mortgages
As of End of First Quarter, 1981**

Institution	Mortgages ($ Billion)	% of Total
Chartered Banks	16.79	22.3
Credit Unions & Caisses Populaires	15.63	20.8
Trust & Mortgage Firms	41.93	55.6
Life Insurance Firms	1.03	1.4
Total	75.38	100.0

Sources: Bank of Canada Review, November 1981.

5. Interest Rates Compared

As of October 28, 1981

| | Savings Accounts | | | | |
| | Monthly | | Daily | | |
	Non-Chqing	Chqing	Non-Chqing	Chqing	Minimum Deposit
Banks					
CIBC	16.75	3	15.75	–	$ 5,000
Montreal	16.75	3	15.75	3.00	1,000
Nova Scotia	16.75	3	15.25	–	1,000
Royal	17.25	3	–	15.25	5,000
Tor-Dom	16.75	3	15.25	15.00	1,000
Trust Companies					
Canada Trust	17.00	3	–	15.75	5,000
Guardian	19.50	6	19.50	–	5,000
Continental	17.50	–	–	–	10,000
National	16.75	3.25	15.75	7.00	5,000
North West	17.50	–	15.50	–	5,000

Sources: Globe and Mail, Oct. 21 & 28, 1981.

6. Bank Directors on Corporate Boards

This list of some famous Canadian corporations shows the penetration of the boards of these firms by bank directors. The list is selective, and by no means complete – it represents merely some of the most outstanding cases. In some instances, the directors shown here are also executive officers of a bank. I have made no distinction in these cases, since what we are examining here is the inter-linking of companies through their boards; titles are not important. **The information is as of 1980**, drawn from the banks' annual reports and directories of directors.

Abitibi-Price Inc.
Royal Bank
W. O. Twaits
T. J. Bell
John A. Tory

Canadian Imperial
Edmund C. Bovey
Marsh A. Cooper
John P. Robarts

Toronto-Dominion
Kenneth R. Thomson

National Bank
Marcel Belanger

Continental Bank
C. Harry Rosier

Argus Corporation
Bank of Montreal
Donald A. McIntosh

Canadian Imperial
Douglas G. Bassett
Conrad M. Black

Toronto-Dominion
G. Montagu Black
Frederick S. Eaton

Bell Canada
Royal Bank
G. Allan Burton
W. F. Light

Bank of Montreal
Lucien G. Rolland
James C. Thackery

Canadian Imperial
James W. Kerr
John P. Robarts

Toronto-Dominion
H. Clifford Hatch
Gerard Plourde
A. Jean de Grandpre

National Bank
J. V. Raymond Cyr
Louise B. Vaillancourt
Marcel Belanger

**Canadian International
Paper Company**
Royal Bank
Paul Pare
Claude Pratte

Bank of Montreal
J. Bartlett Morgan

Toronto-Dominion Bank
Jacques de Billy
Cecil S. Flenniken
Allen T. Lambert

National Bank
Michel Belanger

Canadian Pacific Limited
Royal Bank
Ian D. Sinclair
Paul Pare
Claude Pratte
Alexander M. Runciman

Bank of Montreal
Frederick S. Burbidge
G. Arnold Hart
Lucien G. Rolland

Bank of Nova Scotia
Thomas G. Rust
Frank H. Sherman
Ray D. Wolfe

Canadian Imperial
H. J. Lang

Eaton's of Canada
Bank of Montreal
David Kinnear

Canadian Imperial
Douglas G. Bassett
Conrad M. Black

Toronto-Dominion
Richard M. Thomson
Frederick S. Eaton

Gulf Canada Ltd.
Bank of Nova Scotia
John C. Phillips

Canadian Imperial
E. H. Crawford
Alfred Powis
Robert G. Rogers

Toronto-Dominion
Clarence D. Shepard
John L. Stoik

**Hudson's Bay
Company Ltd.**
Royal Bank
Ian A. Barclay
G. Allan Burton
Mrs. Dawn R. McKeag
John A. Tory

Bank of Nova Scotia
Allan M. McGavin

Canadian Imperial
G. R. Hunter
A. J. MacIntosh
George T. Richardson

Toronto-Dominion
Kenneth R. Thomson

IBM Canada Ltd.
Royal Bank
Paul Pare

Canadian Imperial
W. Darcy McKeough
Andre Monast

Toronto-Dominion
Allen T. Lambert
Lorne K. Lodge

Inco Ltd.
Royal Bank
Walter F. Light

Bank of Montreal
G. Arnold Hart
Lucien G. Rolland

Bank of Nova Scotia
David W. Barr
Donald G. Willmot

Canadian Imperial
George T. Richardson

Toronto-Dominion
Allen T. Lambert

Massey-Ferguson Ltd.
Royal Bank
Alexander M. Runciman

Canadian Imperial
A. A. Thornbrough
J. Page Wadsworth

Toronto-Dominion
G. Montagu Black
Frederick S. Eaton

Noranda Mines Ltd.
Royal Bank
W. P. Wilder

Nova Scotia
E. Kendall Cork
David E. Mitchell

Canadian Imperial
W. Darcy McKeough
Andre Monast

Continental Bank
Adam H. Zimmerman

**North American Life
Assurance Co.**
Bank of Nova Scotia
Kenneth V. Cox

Canadian Imperial
R. Donald Fullerton
Sydney M. Hermant

Toronto-Dominion
Gordon P. Osler

National Bank
Mary Lamontagne

Mercantile
J. H. Taylor

**Northern Telecom
Canada Ltd.**
Royal Bank
Walter F. Light
Clifford S. Malone

Bank of Montreal
Donald C. Harvie
H. J. S. Pearson
James C. Thackery

Bank of Nova Scotia
David W. Barr

Canadian Imperial
Robert C. Scrivener

Toronto-Dominion
Gerard Plourde
A. Jean de Grandpre
W. Maurice Young

NOVA, an Alberta Corporation
Royal Bank
Donald R. Getty
P. L. P. MacDonell
John R. McCraig

Bank of Montreal
S. Robert Blair

Bank of Nova Scotia
Robert L. Pierce

Mercantile Bank
Ronald Southern

Power Corporation
Royal Bank
Claude Pratte

Canadian Imperial
John P Robarts
Robert C. Scrivener

Simpsons Limited
Royal Bank
Ian A. Barclay
T. J. Bell

Bank of Montreal
Raymond Lavoie

Canadian Imperial
Edgar G. Burton
A. J. MacIntosh

Toronto-Dominion
Kenneth R. Thomson

Simpsons-Sears Ltd.
Royal Bank
W. P. Wilder

Canadian Imperial
J. C. Barrow
M. E. Jones
Alfred Powis

National Bank
Michel Belanger

Continental Bank
Harold Corrigan
William A. Dimma

Steel Company of Canada Ltd.
Royal Bank
F. C. Mannix

Bank of Montreal
Thomas M. Galt
J. P. Gordon
D. R. McMaster

Canadian Imperial
A. J. MacIntosh
W. F. McLean

Toronto-Dominion
A. Jean de Grandpre

Steinberg Inc.
Royal Bank
Mrs. Mitzi Dobrin

Toronto-Dominion
Donald G. Campbell
Gerard Plourde

National Bank
J. V. Raymond Cyr

Mercantile Bank
H. A. Steinberg

TransCanada Pipelines Ltd.
Royal Bank
John H. Coleman
Herbert C. Pinder

Canadian Imperial
Russell E. Harrison
J. P. Gallagher
James W. Kerr

Toronto-Dominion
A. Jean de Grandpre
Gordon P. Osler

Union Carbide Canada Ltd.
Royal Bank
Ian D. Sinclair

Bank of Montreal
James C. Thackery

Toronto-Dominion
Jacques de Billy
John S. Dewar

7. Bank Executives on Corporate Boards

This is a partial survey based on positions shown in 1980. In most cases where overlapping directorships are held in wholly-owned subsidiaries of the bank, these are omitted. For example, Cedric Ritchie, Chairman of the Bank of Nova Scotia, was also shown as chairman of twelve Bank of Nova Scotia subsidiaries overseas, and as a director of six others. These are omitted as not showing a significant cross-link. Some sample subsidiaries are shown – in leasing companies, for example – where they seem significant.

1. Royal Bank of Canada

Rowland Frazee, *Chairman*
  Fraser Inc
W. D. H. Gardiner, *Vice Chairman*
  Canadian Utilities
  Cassiar Asbestos
  Federal Pioneer
  Hastings West Investment
  Interprovincial Pipeline
  Scott Paper
  Woodward Stores
R. A. Utting, *Vice Chairman*
  Globe Realty
  Dominion Bridge
H. E. Wyatt, *Vice Chairman*
  Liquid Carbonic Canada
  RCA Canada
Jock K. Finlayson, *President*
  Orion Bank
  PanCanadian Petroleum
  RJR-Macdonald Inc
  Royal Insurance
  Sun Life Assurance
  United Corporations
  Western Assurance
B. D. Gregson, *General Manager*
  Globe Realty
John C McMillan, *General Manager*
  Globe Realty
  J & P Coats (Canada)
  RoyNat
Allan H. Michell, *General Manager*
  Globe Realty

2. The Bank of Montreal

Fred H. McNeil, *Chairman*
  Canadian Canners
  Dominion Life Assurance
  The Seagram Co.
Stanley Davison, *Vice Chairman*
  Canadian-Dominion Leasing

  The Mortgage Insurance Company
  of Canada
J. H. Warren, *Vice Chairman*
  BM-RT Realty Investments
William D. Mullholland, *President*
  Algemeine Deutsche Credit Anstalt
  Kimberley-Clark
  The Standard Life Assurance
  Upjohn Co.
J. D. C. de Jocas, *Executive Vice President*
  BM-RT Ltd.
  La Cie Mutuelle d'Assurance-Vie
  du Quebec
D. G. Payne, *Executive Vice President*
  First Canadian Investments
Carson B. Stratton, *Executive
Vice President*
  Canadian-Dominion Leasing
J. A. Whitney, *Executive Vice President*
  First Canadian Mortgage Fund
  First Canadian Investments
Pierre MacDonald, *Senior Vice President*
  Canadian Arsenals Ltd. *(Chairman)*
  Societe de developpement de la
  Baie James

3. Bank of Nova Scotia

Cedric E. Ritchie, *Chairman*
  Empire Realty
  Scotia-Toronto Dominion Leasing
  The Nova Scotia Corp.
  Adela Investment Co. S.A.
  Canada Life Assurance
  Maduro and Curiel's Bank N.V.
  Minerals and Resources Corp.
  Moore Corp.
  Shroder Darling & Co. Holdings
  The West India Co. of Merchant Bankers
Arthur H. Crockett, *Deputy Chairman*
  Scotia Centre Ltd.
  The West India Co. of Merchant Bankers

Brunswick Square Ltd.
Scotia Realty
Canada Colors and Chemicals
Eastbourne N.V.
Fintra Corp.
Hawker Siddeley Canada
The Nova Scotia Corp.
Siemens Electric
Siemens Overseas Investments
Supreme Aluminum Industries
George C. Hitchman, *Deputy Chairman*
   Scotia Factors
   Scotia Leasing
   Scotia Ventures
   Scotia Covenants Mortgage Corp.
   Algoma Central Railway
   Canborough Corp.
   Canborough Ltd.
   Empire Realty
   Husky Injections Holding Systems
   Ontario Energy Corp.
   Scotia-Toronto Dominion Leasing
J. A. Gordon Bell, *President*
   Bluenose Investments
   R. L. Crain Inc.
   The Nova Scotia Corp.
   Scotia Factors
   Scotiafund Financial Services
   Scotia Leasing
   The West India Co. of Merchant Bankers
Peter C. Godsoe, *Executive Vice President*
   Export Finance Corp.
   The Nova Scotia Corp.
Richard J. Kavanagh, *Senior
Vice President*
   Vancouver Centre Development
Andre Bisson, *Vice President*
   The Fire Insurance Co. of Canada
   Logistec Corp.
   L'Union Canadienne Cie d'Assurances
   Rougier Inc.
   Gestion Revue Internationale
   de Gestion
Robert L. Mason, *Vice President*
   Vancouver Centre Development

4. Canadian Imperial Bank of Commerce

Russell E. Harrison, *Chairman*
   Canada Life Assurance
   Dominion Realty
   Falconbridge Nickel Mines
   Roins Holding
   Royal Insurance
   TransCanada Pipelines

United Dominions Corp.
   The Western Assurance Co.
R. Donald Fullerton, *President*
   American Can Canada
   Amoco Canada Petroleum
   Dominion Realty
   North American Life
John A. C. Hilliker, *Vice Chairman*
   Glen Elgin Investments
   Kinross Mortgage
   United Dominions Corp.
Charles M. Laidley, *Vice Chairman*
   Commerce Factors
   Commerce Leasing
   Kinross Mortgage
   United Dominions Corp.
J. G. Bickford, *Vice President, International*
   Transatlantic Trust
   Canadian Eastern Finance
   Commerce International Finance
   Kuwait Pacific Finance
   Martin Corp. Group
A. Warren Moysey, *Executive
Vice President, Systems*
   Toronto Arts Productions
D. A. Lewis, *Senior Vice President*
   Kinross Mortgage
Gordon T. Ormston, *Senior Vice President,
Real Estate*
   Dominion Realty
   Canlea Ltd.
   Imbank Realty
   McKinnon Properties
   Stornoway Investments
   Commerce Optimation Services
   Delta Hotels

5. Toronto-Dominion Bank

Richard M. Thomson, *Chairman*
   Cadillac Fairview Corp.
   Canadian Gypsum
   Eaton's of Canada
   S. C. Johnson and Son
   Midland and International Banks
   Prudential Insurance
   Texasgulf
   Union Carbide Canada
J. Allan Boyle, *President*
   Regtor Investments
   Torcred Developments
   Toronto-Dominion Centre
   Toronto-Dominion Centre West
   Aetna Casualty
   Costain Ltd.

Excelsior Life
Jannock Ltd.
Robert W. Korthals, *Executive Vice President*
  TD Realty Investments
  Tordom Corp.
  Co-Steel International
  Talcorp Associates
  TD Leasing
R. Glen Bumstead, *Vice President*
  Leamor Holdings
  94027 Canada Inc.
  Edmonton Centre Ltd.
  Pacific Centre Ltd.
  Regtor Investments
  Terbert Investment Properties
  Tordom Corp.
  Toronto-Dominion Centre Ltd.
  Toronto-Dominion Centre West
  Toronto-Dominion Realty
R. R. B. Dickson, *Executive Vice President*
  Euro-Pacific Finance
  Midland and International Bank Ltd.
  Brasilinvest S.A.
A. B. Hockin, *Vice President, Investments*
  Acadia Life Insurance
  Leamor Holdings
  Phoenix Assurance
  Regtor Investments
  Tordom Corp.
  Toronto-Dominion Leasing
  European and Pacific Investment
    Management
F. G. McDowell, *Executive Vice President*
  Toronto-Dominion Leasing
  Zurich Life Insurance

6. National Bank of Canada

Germain Perrault, *Chairman*
  Domco Industries
  Laurentian Mutual Assurance
  Les Ensembles Urbains
Leo Lavoie
  Canadair
  Alliance Mutual Life Insurance
  Canada Reassurance
  Canada Reinsurance
  Tele Metropole Inc.
Michel Belanger,
  Canadian International Paper
  MICC Investments
  The Mortgage Insurance Co. of Canada
  Simpsons-Sears

Gilles Roch, *Executive Vice President*
  Laurentide Financial
  Le Credit Industrielle Desjardins
  Les Immeubles St-Cyrille
Jacques A. Signeuret, *Senior Vice President*
  Laurentide Financial
Richard Lapointe, *Vice President*
  ProCan Financial Services

7. Mercantile Bank of Canada

Walter A. Prisco, *Chief General Manager*
  Sovereign Hotel Operating
  American Hoist of Canada
  Machinery Investment Co. of Canada
  Canadian Superior Oil
John E. Pierce, *Senior Vice President*
  Candev Financial Service
  Commonwealth Insurance
  Ivanhoe Insurance Managers
  Merchant Trust
  Northumberland General Insurance
  Reinsurance and Excess Managers Inc.
  Rolfe, Reeve Group

8. Bank of British Columbia

Trevor W. Pilley, *Chairman*
  BBC Realty Investors
  British Columbia Resources Investment
Arthur Fouks, *Vice President*
  Coralta Resources
Coleman E. Hall
  Devonshire Hall Ltd.
  Granville Ventures
  North West Sports
Donald M. Clark, *Secretary*
  Silver Standard Mines
  BBC Realty Investors
Victor Dobb, *Executive Vice President*
  BBC Investments
  BBC Mortgage
  Johnston Terminals & Storage
  Johnston Terminals
  Transtec Canada
Arnold E. Miles-Pickup, *Senior Vice President*
  BBC Mortgage
  Ventures West
  Westbank Leasing
Leslie J. Fowler, *Vice President*
  BBC Investments
  BBC Mortgage
  BBC Realty

9. Canadian Commercial and Industrial Bank

William H. McDonald, *Chairman*
  Boyd, Stott & McDonald, Ltd.
G. Howard Eaton, *President*
  CCIB Realty
  Financial Life Assurance
Chesley J. McConnell, *Vice President*
  NuWest Development
  Voyageur Petroleums

10. Northland Bank

Robert A. Willson, *Chairman*
  Willson Associates
  Banff School of Advanced Management
Norman A. Bromberger, *Vice Chairman*
  Saskatchewan Co-operative Credit
  Society
  Canadian Co-operative Credit Society

Allan W. Scarth, *Secretary*
  Manitoba Mineral Resources

11. Continental Bank

Douglas Maloney
  IAC Ltd.
  Niagara Finance
  Niagara Realty of Canada
  Niagara Realty Ltd.
  Premier Ltd.
Stanley F. Melloy, *President*
  IAC Ltd.
Allan P. Bolin, *Senior Vice President*
  IAC Ltd.
  Capital Funds
  Niagara Finance
  Niagara Realty
  Premier Property

8. *The Board of the Bank of Nova Scotia*

1. Cedric E. Ritchie, *Chairman and Chief Executive Officer and President*
  Also: *Chairman*
    BNS International (United Kingdom) Ltd.
    The Bank of Nova Scotia Asia Ltd.
    The Bank of Nova Scotia Channel Islands Ltd.
    The Bank of Nova Scotia International Ltd.
    The Bank of Nova Scotia Trinidad and Tobago Ltd.
    The Bank of Nova Scotia Trust Co. (Bahamas) Ltd.
    The Bank of Nova Scotia Trust Co. (Caribbean) Ltd.
    The Bank of Nova Scotia Trust Co. (Cayman) Ltd.
    The Bank of Nova Scotia Trust Co. Channel Islands Ltd.
    The Bank of Nova Scotia Trust Co. United Kingdom Ltd.
    The Bank of Nova Scotia Trust Co. of the West Indies Ltd.
    Empire Realty Co. Ltd.
  Deputy Chairman
    Scotia-Toronto Dominion Leasing Ltd.
  President
    The Nova Scotia Corp.

  Spencer Hall Foundation
Director
  Adela Investment Co. S.A.
  BNS International (Hong Kong) Ltd.
  BNS International (Ireland) Ltd.
  BNS International N.V.
  The Bank of Nova Scotia Jamaica Ltd.
  The Bank of Nova Scotia Trust Co. Jamaica Ltd.
  Bermuda National Bank Ltd.
  The Canada Life Assurance Co.
  Canadian Council of Christians and Jews
  Centre for Inter-American Relations
  International Monetary Conference
  Canadian Service Overseas
  Maduro & Curiel's Bank N.V.
  Minerals and Resources Corp. Ltd.
  Moore Corp. Ltd.
  Shroder Darling and Co. Holdings Ltd.
  The West India Co. of Merchant Bankers Ltd.
Governor
  Adela Investment Co. S.A.
  Olympic Trust of Canada
Member
  Canadian Economic Policy Commission
  School of Business Admin. Advisory

Director
Abitibi Asbestos Mining Co. Ltd.
Brinco Ltd.
CAE Industries Ltd.
The Canada Life Assurance Co.
Carena-Bancorp Holdings Inc.
Edper Investments Ltd.
McGraw-Hill Ryerson Ltd.
Norcen Energy Resources Ltd.
QIT-Fer et Titane Inc.
Rolland Inc.

6. Donald G. Willmot *Vice President*
Also: *Chairman*
The Molson Companies Ltd.
Vice President and Director
The Bank of Nova Scotia
Director
Crown Life Insurance Co.
Hayes-Dana Inc.
Inco Ltd.
Jannock Ltd.
Molson Breweries of Canada Ltd.
Vice President and Trustee
The Ontario Jockey Club
Governor
Ridley College

7. Hon. René Amyot, *Director*
Also: *Director*
Amyot, Lesage, Bernard, Drolet &
Sirois
Northern Quebec Finance Co. Ltd.
Rothmans of Pall Mall Canada Ltd.
Sigma Mines (Quebec) Ltd.
Vice President and Director
Gaz Provincial du Nord de Quebec
Ltée. (also member of executive
committee)
The Imperial Life Assurance Co. of
Canada
Secretary and Director
Canadian Helicopters Ltd.
Credinord Gestion Inc.
Davie Shipbuilding Ltd.
Fidusco Ltd.
Le Fonds Laurentien Inc.
Les Enterprises Bussieres Ltee.
Logistec Corp.
Rimouski Transport Ltee.
Chairman
Centre de Recherches et d'Etude en
Management (C.I.R.E.M.)

8. Lewis H. M. Ayre, *Director*
Also: *Chairman*
Ayre & Sons Ltd.
Director and Chairman
Ayre's Ltd.
Blue Buoy Foods Ltd.
Clayton Construction (1965) Ltd.
Clayton Refrigeration & Diesel Ltd.
Harbour Fashions Ltd.
Holiday Lanes Ltd.
Job Bros. & Co. Ltd.
J. Michael Fashions Ltd.
Newfoundland Telephone Co. Ltd.
Northatlantic Fisheries Ltd.
Director
Colonial Cordage Co. Ltd.
Dominion Stores Ltd.
Labrador Exploration and Mining
Co. Ltd.
Newfoundland & Labrador Hydro
Robinson-Blackmore Holdings Ltd.
Robinson-Blackmore Printing &
Publishing Ltd.
Top Tone Cleaners (England) Ltd.
Member Advisory Board
Canada Permanent Trust Co.

9. Dr. Lloyd I. Barber, *Director*
Also: *President and Vice Chancellor*
University of Regina
Director
Burns Foods Ltd.
Husky Oil Ltd.
SED Systems Ltd.
The Molson Cos.
Regina United Way
Commissioner
Elden Indian Testimony

10. David W. Barr, *Director*
Also: *Chairman*
Moore Corp.
Reid Dominion Packaging Ltd.
Vice President and Director
The Canada Life Assurance Co.
Director
Canadian Investment Fund Ltd.
Canadian Reassurance Co.
Canadian Reinsurance Co.
Inco Ltd.
Northern Telecom Ltd.

11. E. Kendall Cork, *Director*
Also: *Vice President and Treasurer*

Noranda Mines Ltd.
Vice President, Treasurer and Director
Brunswick Mining & Smelting Co. Ltd.
Director
The Casualty Co. of Canada
The Dominion of Canada General
Insurance Co.
E-L Financial Corp. Ltd.

12. Kenneth V. Cox, *Director*
Also: *Chairman and President*
The New Brunswick Telephone Co. Ltd.
President
Bruntel Holdings Ltd. (also chief
executive officer)
Director
Datacrown Inc.
Eastern Telephone & Telegraph Co.
Fraser Inc.
Maritime Electric Co. Ltd.
North American Life Assurance Co.
Chairman
New Brunswick Research and
Productivity Council
Member
The Conference Board

13. Gerald H. D. Hobbs, *Director*
Also: *Director*
British Columbia Telephone Co.
MacMillan Bloedel Ltd.
Okanagan Helicopters Ltd.

14. Rt. Hon. Earl of Iveagh, *Director*

15. John J. Jodrey, *Director*
Also: *Chairman and President*
Minas Basin Pulp & Power Company
Ltd.
Canadian Keyes Fiber Co. Ltd.
Chairman
Campbell & Burns Ltd.
Coastal Insurance Ltd.
Dartmouth Lumber Co. Ltd.
Halifax Developments Ltd.
President
Argyle Securities Ltd.
Avon Foods Ltd.
Bedford Village Properties Ltd.
Blomidon Investments Ltd.
Cabin Baking Co. Ltd.
E. A. Cattley Ltd.
Coastal Enterprises Ltd.
Fundy Investments Ltd.
Hants Investments Ltd.

Hantsport Insurance Agencies Ltd.
Hantsport Securities Ltd.
R. A. Jodrey Investments Ltd.
Minas Investments Ltd.
Parrsboro Lumber Co. Ltd.
Scotia Investments Ltd.
Smith Fisheries Ltd.
Sunset Farms Ltd.
York Securities Corp. Ltd.
Vice President and Director
All Canadian-American Investments
Ltd.
Crown Life Insurance Co.
L. I. Jodrey Investments Ltd.
Director
Algoma Central Railway
Annapolis Basin Pulp and Power Co.
Ltd.
Apple Products Ltd.
Avon Valley Greenhouses Ltd.
Ben's Ltd.
Ben's Holdings Ltd.
Canning Investment Corp. Ltd.
Maple Ridge Realty Ltd.
Maritime Containers Ltd.
Maritime Paper Products Ltd.
L. E. Shaw Ltd.
Valley Investments Ltd.

16. F. Ross Johnson, *Director*

17. Rt. Hon. Lord Keith of Castleacre,
Director

18. Hon. Donald S. Macdonald, *Director*
Also: *Partner*
McCarthy & McCarthy
Director
Boise Cascade
Dupont Canada Inc.
Manufacturers Life Insurance Co.
McDonnell Douglas Canada Ltd.

19. Donald Maclaren, *Director*
Also: *Vice Chairman*
Maclaren Power & Paper Co.
President
Maclaren-Quebec Power Co.
Director
The James Maclaren Co. Ltd.
Thurso Pulp & Paper Co.

20. Rafael J. Martinez, *Director*

21. Malcolm H. D. McAlpine, *Director*

22. H. Harrison McCain, *Director*
  Also: *Chairman*
    McCain Foods Ltd.
    McCain International Ltd.
  President
    Thomas Equipment Ltd.
  Director
    Carleton Cold Storage Co. Ltd.
    Day & Ross Ltd.
    McCain Australia Pty. Ltd.
    McCain Espana S.A.
    McCain Europa S.A.
    McCain Fertilizers Ltd.
    McCain Foods Inc., U.S.A.
    McCain Produce Co. Ltd.
  Vice President
    Valley Farms Ltd.

23. Allan M. McGavin, *Director*
  Also: *Chairman*
    McGavin Foods Ltd.
  Director
    British Columbia Forest Products Ltd.
    British Columbia Telephone Co.
    British Pacific Properties Ltd.
    Hudson's Bay Co.
    John Labatt Ltd.
    Park Royal Shopping Centre Ltd.
    Trans Mountain Pipe Line Co. Ltd.

24. William S. McGregor, *Director*
  Also: *President and Managing Director*
    Numac Oil & Gas Ltd.
  Director
    Canadian Utilities Ltd.
    Felmont Oil Corp.
    Union Gas Ltd.
    Western Canadian Resources Funds
    Ltd.
  Member
    Royal Trust Co. (Edmonton Adv. Brd.)

25. David E. Mitchell, *Director*
  Also: *President*
    Alberta Energy Co. Ltd.
    (also Chief Executive Officer)
  Director
    Canada Cement Lafarge Ltd.
    Noranda Mines Ltd.

26. Sir Denis Mountain, *Director*

27. Helen A. Parker, *Director*

28. John C. Phillips, *Director*

  Also: *Chairman*
    Gulf Canada Ltd.

29. Robert L. Pierce, *Director*
  Also: *Executive Vice President and*
  Director
    NOVA, An Alberta Corp.
  Chairman
    AGEC Security Corp.
    Alberta Ethane Development Co. Ltd.
  Chairman
    Diamond Shamrock Alberta Gas Ltd.
    Pan Alberta Gas Ltd.
  Vice Chairman
    Algas Mineral Enterprises Ltd.
    Energy Equipment and Systems Inc.
    Montana International Resources Inc.
    Steel Alberta Ltd.
  President
    Foothills Pipe Lines (Alberta) Ltd.
    Foothills Pipe Lines (North B.C.) Ltd.
    Foothills Pipe Lines (Yukon) Ltd.
    Foothills Pipe Lines (Sask.) Ltd.
    Foothills Pipe Lines (South Yukon) Ltd.
    Foothills Pipe Lines (South B.C.) Ltd.
    Foothills Pipe Lines (North Yukon) Ltd.
    (also chief executive officer of above)
    A.G. Industries International Inc.
    A.G. Minerals Inc.
    The Alberta Gas Ethylene Co. Ltd.
    Danebro Investments Ltd.
    WAGI International, Inc.
  Executive Vice President and Director
    A.G. Pipe Lines (Canada) Ltd.
    Algas Resources Ltd.
    Q & M Pipe Lines Ltd.
  Vice President and Director
    Foothills Pipe Lines Ltd.
  Director
    Alberta Gas Chemicals Ltd.
    Algas Engineering Services Ltd.
    Algas Investments Ltd.
    Foothills Oil Pipe Lines Ltd.
    Gas Initiatives Ventures Ltd.
    Grove Italia S.p.A.
    Grove Valve and Regulator Co.
    Husky Oil Co.
    Husky Oil Ltd.
    Husky Oil Operations Ltd.
    International Portable Pipe Mills Ltd.
    Pierce Assoc. Ltd.
    WAGI Internatinal S.p.A.

30. Thomas G. Rust, *Director*

Also: *President and Chief Executive Officer*
Crown Zellerbach Canada Ltd.
Director
Canadian Pacific Ltd.
Inland Natural Gas Co. Ltd.
Quadrant Development Ltd.
Seaboard Lumber Sales Ltd.
Seaboard Shipping Co. Ltd.

31. Frank H. Sherman, *Director*
Also: *President and Chief Executive Officer*
Dominion Foundries and Steel Ltd.
Director
Arnaud Railway Co.
Canadian Pacific Ltd.
Canron Inc.
Crown Life Insurance Co.
Knoll Lake Minerals Ltd.
National Steel Car Corp., Ltd.
Wabush Lake Railway Co. Ltd.
American Iron & Steel Institute
Great Lakes Waterways Development Assn.
Trustee
The Ontario Jockey Club
Governor
The Art Gallery of Hamilton
Hamilton Philharmonic Orchestra
McMaster University
Member National Executive
Canadian Manufacturers Assn.

32. William A. Stewart, *Director*
Also: *Director*
Hardee Farms International Ltd.
Ontario Hydro
Royal Agricultural Winter Fair
Silverwood Industries Ltd.
Honorary Director
Canadian National Exhibition

33. Marie Wilson, *Director*
Also: *President*
A. E. Wilson & Co. Ltd.

34. Ray D. Wolfe, *Director*
Also: *Chairman and President*
The Oshawa Group Ltd.
Chairman
IGA Canada Ltd.
Director
Canadian Pacific Ltd.

Confederation Life Insurance Co.
Consumers Distributing Co. Ltd.
Super-Sol Ltd.
Baycrest Centre for Geriatric Care
Canada-Israel Development Ltd.
Canadian Council of Christians and Jews
Food Marketing Institute
Chairman
Canada-Israel Chamber of Commerce
Canadian Jewish News
Member of Council Trustee
Institute for Research on Public Policy

Other Executive Officers

35. W. Scott McDonald, *Senior Executive Vice President*

36. Peter C. Godsoe, *Executive Vice President*
Also: *Director*
The Bank of Nova Scotia International Ltd.
Export Finance Corp. of Toronto Ltd.
The Nova Scotia Corp.
The Canadian Club of Tornto Corp.
The Canadian Council of Christians and Jews
Member of Council
Board of Trade of Metropolitan Toronto

37. Bruce R. Birmingham, *Senior Vice President and Corporate Banking and General Manager (North American intl. reg.)*

38. C. Foster Gill, *Senior Vice President and General Manager (Eastern Canada)*

39. Richard J. Kavanagh, *Senior Vice President and General Manager (Eastern Canada)*
Also: *Director*
Vancouver Centre Development Ltd.

40. Walter P. Meinig, *Senior Vice President and General Manager (Ont.)*
Also: *Trustee*
Spencer Hall Foundation

41. L. A. Shaw, *Senior Vice President, Commercial Banking*

42. Boris Arthurs, *Vice President and General Manager (Saskatoon)*

43. C. Bartlett, *Vice President and General Manager (St. John's Newfoundland)*

44. Andre Bisson, *Vice President and General Manager (Montreal)*
  Also: *Director*
    The Fire Insurance Co. of Canada
    Logistec Corp.
    L'Union Canadienne Cie d'Assurances
    Rougier Inc.
  Chairman
    Gestion Revue Internationale de
    Gestion
    Hopital Notre-Dame
    Quebec Committee Canadian Bankers
    Assn.
  Director
    Centraid-United Way (Canada)
    Chambre de Commerce Française au
    Canada
    Fondation de L'Universitaire du
    Quebec a Montreal
    INSEAD
    Montreal Symphony Orchestra
    Province of Quebec Chamber of
    Commerce
    Universitaire de Montreal

45. R. Cooke, *Vice President and General Manager (Latin American intl. reg.)*

46. Thomas A. Cumming, *Vice President and General Manager (Calgary)*

47. H. L. Fawcett, *Vice President and General Manager (Toronto suburban)*

48. L. L. Fox, *Vice President and General Manager (London, England)*

49. Edwin D. MacNevin, *Vice President and General Manager (Toronto central)*

50. Robert L. Mason, *Vice President and General Manager (Vancouver)*
  Also: *Director*
    Vancouver Centre Development Ltd.

51. Ralph C. McLeod, *Vice President and General Manager (Halifax)*

52. William H. McMillan, *Vice President and General Manager (Ottawa)*

53. Glen M. Morell, *Vice President and General Manager (Saint John, New Brunswick)*

54. W. P. Penny, *Vice President and General Manager, Banking (commercial)*

55. E. Ranft, *Vice President and General Manager (Winnipeg)*

56. Kevin S. Rowe, *Vice President and General Manager (Pacific region)*

57. Robert G. Taylor, *Vice President and General Manager (Caribbean region)*

58. Lorne A. Thurston, *Vice President and General Manager (W. and N. Ontario)*

59. William H. Milne, *Secretary*

60. J. K. Mitchell, *Compt. and Chief Accountant*

9. *Canadian Bank Assets, Domestic and Foreign*

($ Billion)

	Total Assets	Canadian	%	Foreign	%
1972	60.6	45.0	74	15.6	26
1973	75.0	53.3	71	21.7	29
1974	91.6	65.1	71	26.5	29
1975	105.3	74.5	71	30.8	29
1976	121.8	86.4	71	35.4	29
1977	147.5	100.6	68	46.9	32
1978	179.8	117.6	65	62.2	35
1979	221.6	141.7	64	80.1	36
1980	269.9	166.9	42	103.0	38
1981	343.9	205.0	60	138.9	40

Source: Canadian Bankers' Association: Bank Facts 1981.

10. *Foreign Assets of the Big Five*

As of 1979

	($ Billion)	% of foreign
1. Royal	21.0	26.2
2. Commerce	14.8	18.5
3. Montreal	15.7	19.6
4. Nova Scotia	18.0	22.5
5. Toronto-Dominion	10.6	13.2
Total	80.1	100.0

Source: Calculated from annual reports of the banks.

11. Foreign Assets by Region (1979)

	($ Billion)	% of this Bank's Foreign Total
Europe		
1. Royal	8.27	39.4
2. Commerce	6.34	42.9
3. Montreal	4.52	28.8
4. Nova Scotia	6.87	38.2
5. Toronto-Dominion	3.39	25.7
Total	29.39	
United States		
1. Royal	4.03	19.2
2. Commerce	4.17	28.2
3. Montreal	3.54	22.6
4. Nova Scotia	4.14	23.0
5. Toronto-Dominion	2.34	21.9
Total	18.22	
Latin America and Caribbean		
1. Royal	5.46	26.0
2. Commerce	1.86	12.6
3. Montreal	3.79	24.2
4. Nova Scotia	4.01	22.3
5. Toronto-Dominion	1.91	17.9
Total	17.03	
Asia/Pacific		
1. Royal	1.14	6.9
2. Commerce	1.19	8.1
3. Montreal	2.07	13.2
4. Nova Scotia	2.08	11.6
5. Toronto-Dominion	2.40	22.5
Total	11.28	
Middle East/Africa		
1. Royal	.44	2.1
2. Commerce	.39	2.7
3. Montreal	.34	2.1
4. Nova Scotia	.21	1.2
5. Toronto-Dominion	.29	2.8
Total	1.96	

Source: Derived from tables prepared by Pitfield Mackay Ross Ltd.
Globe and Mail January 18, 1982.

12. Profits and Taxes of the Big Five

(Selected Years, 1970-1981)
($ Thousand)

	1970	1975	1979	1980	1981
1. Royal Bank of Canada					
Profit	144,280	287,872	317,130	385,130	656,520
Tax	75,000	134,630	46,300	57,700	164,000
Rate of Tax	51.9%	46.8%	14.6%	15.0%	25.0%
2. Canadian Imperial Bank of Commerce					
Profit	137,019	262,443	239,001	210,735	419,785
Tax	71,500	128,500	37,700	67,404	109,600
Rate of Tax	52.1%	49.0%	15.8%	31.9%	26.1%
3. Bank of Montreal					
Profit	93,325	195,735	285,396	319,353	457,633
Tax	48,763	93,600	56,700	56,113	99,100
Rate of Tax	52.3%	47.8%	19.9%	17.5%	21.7%
4. Bank of Nova Scotia					
Profit	61,889	214,602	241,692	298,861	266,759
Tax	32,900	102,900	60,800	77,700	42,700
Rate of Tax	53.1%	47.9%	25.1%	25.9%	16.0%
5. Toronto-Dominion Bank					
Profit	55,615	175,310	189,151	200,769	308,327
Tax	28,200	84,700	28,800	18,000	53,000
Rate of Tax	50.7%	48.3%	15.2%	8.9%	17.1%

Summary Big Five 1970-1981

Total Profit 1970	492,128
Total Profit 1981	2,109,024
Tax 1970	256,363
Tax 1981	468,400
Rate of Tax 1970	52.0%
Rate of Tax 1981	22.2%

Sources: Calculated from annual reports of the banks.
Note: In the eleven years, profits increased by 429%, while the tax increased 182%.

13. Capital Ratios and Return of Some World Banks

Bank	Ratio	Return on Assets
Royal Bank	32	0.70
Toronto-Dominion	27	0.69
Bank of Montreal	29	0.65
Standard Chartered	24	0.63
Bank of America	29	0.58
Bank of Commerce	33	0.50
Bank of Nova Scotia	30	0.50
Chase Manhattan	28	0.48
Citicorp	30	0.46
Union of Switzerland	17	0.46
Dresdner	27	0.24
Commerz	27	0.20
Mitsubishi	34	0.19
Bank of Tokyo	48	0.17

Source: Derived from material prepared by Pitfield Mackay Ross Ltd., reproduced in the Globe and Mail, January 18, 1982.

14. Return on Equity for Chartered Banks

Year	Return on Equity (%)
1970	11.8
1971	14.1
1972	17.0
1973	14.4
1974	12.6
1975	16.0
1976	15.7
1977	16.5
1978	18.7
1979	17.7
1980	15.8
1981	18.2

Source: Calculated from information supplied in Canadian Bankers' Association Bank Facts/81.

19

Appendix II

Glossary of Terms

asset
   Anything that has monetary value. Buildings, accounts receivable, land, machinery, cash, even goodwill are assets for any corporation. Because of the business it is in, a bank's main assets are the loans it has out to customers, since they represent money owed to the bank.

authorized capital
   The original shares authorized by the founding directors of a bank. A "Schedule A" bank – in effect, any of the eleven parliamentary chartered banks – must have an authorized capital of at least two million dollars. A "Schedule B" bank – any of the foreign banks now setting up – must have an authorized capital of at least five million dollars.

Bank Act
   The law under which Canadian banks operate. It is unusual in that it may only be amended once every ten years.

Bank Rate
   Largely a polite fiction, the Bank Rate is the rate at which the Bank of Canada lends money to any private bank. This seldom occurs, but the rate is important anyway, since it signals to the banks the rate of interest the central bank wishes them to charge. When the Bank Rate goes up, they are to raise their interest rates, and when it goes down, to lower them. By convention, the Bank Rate is set at one-quarter of one per cent above the average rate at which 91-day Treasury bills are auctioned each Thursday.

call loan
   A loan that may be withdrawn – called – at any time, and payment in full required, solely at the bank's discretion. Same as a demand note.

capital-to-assets ratio
   The ratio between a bank's paid-in capital and its assets – in essence, its loan portfolio. Leverage.

chartered bank
   Every Canadian bank is federally chartered (except the Montreal and District Savings Bank, which is chartered by the Province of Quebec) in that it requires a charter to go into business, in addition to the normal articles of incorporation. In

the past, charters were issued only by Parliament, and the creation of each bank required an Act of both houses of Parliament. Under the 1980 Bank Act amendments, a charter may be issued by letters patent; in effect, by the Minister of Finance acting on the advice of the Inspector General of Banks.

constant dollar

The current dollar minus the rate of inflation. If inflation is running at ten per cent, the constant dollar would be worth ninety cents. The dollar, needless to say, is never constant, but economists like to use the term anyway, as a benchmark.

consumer rate

The rate at which consumer loans are charged. It may be as much as five per cent above the Prime Rate.

demand deposit

A deposit in a bank or near-bank that may be withdrawn by the customer at any time. Opposite to a notice deposit.

demand note

A call loan; one on which payment in full may be demanded at any time.

equity

Usually, "shareholder's equity" – the amount the shareholders would have to distribute among themselves if the corporation went out of business. The net worth of the company.

exposure

The degree to which a bank is exposed on a doubtful loan. If Company A has a debt of $100 million to a banking syndicate, and Bank B has advanced $10 million of that loan, Bank B's "exposure" is $10 million.

fiduciary agent

Someone who can act in the position of a legal trustee. A major difference between banks and trust companies is that trust companies can act as fiduciary agents – in handling of estates, for example – and banks cannot.

fiscal policy

Tax policy, as opposed to monetary policy.

fungibility

Interchangeability. A bank note is "fungible" if it is acceptable as legal tender, and can be exchanged for another note of stated value.

goldsmith bankers

The early bankers who converted coins and acted as treasurers and, indeed, as goldsmiths.

Gresham's Law

Bad money drives out good.

leakage

The money required in cash from a bank or other deposit-taking institution, as opposed to cheques, bank-drafts or other bits of paper. More properly, leakage is described as "transaction costs" or "transaction losses."

leverage

The ratio between funds actually employed and the multiplier effect available because the same money can be used over and over. Another way of referring to the capital-to-assets ratio, which in Canadian banks is normally about 32-to-1.

liability

Demands against a corporation's assets, including loans owing, accounts payable, depreciation, etc. Just as a bank's main assets are its loans, its main liabilities are its deposits, since these represent the bank's debts to its customers. In a corporation's balance sheet, its assets and liabilities always balance. This is not because the corporation has no real worth, but because its net worth is always treated as a residual item.

mismatch of funds

The situation that arises when a bank has money out at long term and low rates and must raise new money at high rates. The rate it pays for money and the rate it can get for it no longer match.

money supply

There are three main versions of the money supply, M1, M2 and M3, with some subdivisions. M1, also known as the "narrowly defined" money supply, means all the cash outside chartered banks plus demand deposits. M1-b means M1 plus chequable savings deposits. This definition is sometimes used because it is equivalent to the U.S. version of M1. M2 means M1-b, plus non-chequable savings deposits and personal term deposits and some corporate notice (or demand) deposits. M-3 means M-2 plus corporate term deposits. Each M, as the numbers mount, contains its predecessors. The total money supply consists of M-3 plus Government of Canada deposits in chartered banks.

mortgagee

The institution or person who lends the money on a mortgage. Simon Legree is the mortgagee.

mortgagor

The one who is paying for the mortgage. The home-owner.

near-bank

Any of the non-bank deposit-taking institutions, viz., trust companies, mortgage loan companies, credit unions and caisses populaires.

notice deposit

A deposit on which the holder is required to give notice before collecting. In law, a savings account is a notice deposit, and a bank may require up to ten days' notice for a withdrawal. Opposite to a demand deposit. See term deposit.

outside director

A member of a corporate board who is not an employee of that company. On bank boards, the outside directors are normally executives of customer companies.

paid-in capital

The amount of cash actually raised, as opposed to that promised or authorized, in a corporation's treasury. Paid-in capital includes the original equity plus money from any debentures or other capital issues.

Prime Rate
The rate at which loans will be granted to a deposit-taking institution's most credit-worthy customers.

real interest
The difference between the inflation rate and the current interest rate. If inflation is at ten per cent and interest paid is thirteen per cent, the real interest is three per cent. Historically, real interest has run about three points above inflation, at three per cent.

reserves
There are two kinds of bank reserves, primary and secondary. The bank is required to keep money deposited in the Bank of Canada in proportion to its liabilities. The level of reserves is currently being shifted downwards over a period of time. The new primary reserve will require the banks to deposit with the Bank of Canada ten per cent of demand deposits, two per cent of notice deposits, one per cent of the amount by which its Canadian currency notice deposits exceed $500 million and three per cent of foreign currency deposits of residents of Canada held in Canadian banks. The secondary reserves are variable by the Bank of Canada, and are based on a combination of Canadian currency deposits and foreign currency deposits held by Canadians in Canadian banks. The secondary reserves have historically amounted to about five per cent. In addition, some banks maintain voluntary reserves with the Bank of Canada to provide more flexibility.

The proportion of reserves to "statutory deposits" held by the Bank of Canada as of October 31, 1981 was 4.71 per cent, or about one dollar in twenty.

rest account
A complex measure of bank accounting; in essence, the rest account is a technique of adding to the bank's capital through retained earnings.

retained earnings
The portion of a corporation's profit kept on hand, rather than being returned to shareholders in the form of dividends.

return on assets
A measure of the proportion of profit a corporation makes compared to the assets it shows on its books.

return on equity
A measure comparing the profit with the corporation's net worth.

spread
The difference between what a deposit-taking institution pays for money and what it gets for it. If the Prime Rate is eighteen per cent and the bank is paying fifteen per cent on daily interest savings accounts, then the spread between those two is three per cent.

subscribed shares
Shares which the holder has agreed to purchase at a set price, but for which he has not yet paid in full.

term deposit
Money deposited with an institution for a fixed period of time, anywhere from

twenty-nine days to five years. The difference between a term deposit and a notice deposit is that, in the case of a term deposit, the time-period is fixed; with a notice deposit, a set period of notice is required, but the money may be left on deposit indefinitely. A term deposit is one form of notice deposit. A savings account represents a notice deposit, but not a term deposit.

Treasury Bills
Government IOUs, sold in batches of one million dollars, with maturities of 91 days, 182 days and 364 days.

underwriter
The firm, or combination of firms, that undertakes to market the securities of a corporation.

20
Notes

I have interrupted the text for chapter notes only where it was not possible to explain the derivation of facts in the body of the text; in most cases, the reader anxious to discover my sources will find them readily enough inside each chapter. It should also be noted that a book of this sort always contains some instances of information gathered from people — chiefly bank employees — who add a natural reticence to the consideration that being identified might mean being discharged. Rather than inserting a weasel phrase like that generally employed in newspapers — "It was reliably reported," or "It was learned from unidentified sources" — I have chosen to present information of this sort as my own. What follows, then, is the absolute minimum of chapter notes.

Chapter One

1. Money, Banking and the Canadian Financial System, by H. H. Binhammer, Third Edition, Methuen, Toronto, 1977, p. 114.
2. The Bankers, by Martin Mayer, Ballantine, New York, 1974, pp. 72-73.
3. Canadian Public Policy, Summer, 1976.
4. Press Relations Office, Ministry of Transport, March, 1982 and Royal Bank, Annual Report for 1981, p. 54.
5. Binhammer, op. cit., p. 374.
6. Canadian Bankers' Association, Bank Facts, 1981, p. 3.
7. Royal Bank Annual Report for 1981, p. 54.
8. Calculated from 1981 annual reports of the Big Five banks.
9. An Act to Revise the Bank Act, 1980, Section 208(1).
10. Binhammer, op. cit., p. 76.
11. Globe and Mail, Report on Business, February 15, 1982, p. B1.
12. The Bank Act, Section 2(1).
13. Ibid, Section 173(1).
14. Canadian Banking Legislation, White Paper, Minister of Finance, Ministry of Supply and Services, 1976, p. 25.
15. The Bank Act, Section 302(7).
16. Financial Post, June 20, 1981, p. 16.
17. Globe and Mail, Report on Business, February 15, 1982, p. B25.
18. Ibid.
19. Calculated from Financial Post, The 1981 Ranking of Canada's 500 Largest Companies, Toronto, 1981.
20. Ibid.
21. CBA, Bank Facts 1981, p. 1.
22. Bank of Canada Review, November, 1981.

23. Journal of Commerce. June 27, 1980.
24. The World Almanac and Book of Facts, NEA, New York, 1980, p. 88.
25. CBA, Bank Facts, 1981, p. 4.
26. Ibid, p. 1.
27. Ibid.
28. Ibid.
29. Globe and Mail, February 4, 1982, p. 1.
30. CBA, Bank Facts, 1980 and 1981.
31. Calculated from annual reports of the banks.

Chapter Two

1. Banks of the World, by Roger Orsingher, Macmillan, London, 1967, pp. 4-5.
2. Ibid, p. viii.
3. Ibid, p. 1.
4. Ibid, p. 3.
5. Ibid, pp. 6-7.
6. Money, by J. K. Galbraith, Bantam, New York, 1979, pp. 10-11.
7. Orsingher, op. cit., pp. 7-8.
8. Ibid, p. 10.
9. Ibid, p. 13.
10. Ibid, p. 14.
11. Ibid, p. 20.
12. Ibid, p. 14.
13. Ibid, p. 38.
14. Ibid.
15. Encyclopaedia Britannica, 1972, Vol. 10, p. 917.
16. Galbraith, op. cit., p. 19.
17. Ibid.
18. Ibid, p. 20.
19. Orsingher, p. 24.
20. Ibid, p. 43.
21. Galbraith, op. cit., p. 28.
22. Money and Man, by Elgin Groseclose, Ungar, New York, 1961, p. 129.
23. Galbraith, p. 29.
24. Ibid, p. 30.
25. Ibid, p. 31.

Chapter Three

1. Encyclopedia Canadiana, Grolier of Canada, Toronto, 1972, Vol. 10, p. 408.
2. Ibid.
3. A History of Canadian Wealth, by Gustavus Myers, Lorimer, Toronto, 1972, Vol. 1, pp. 183 ff.
4. A History of Banking in Canada, by B. E. Walker, Toronto, Bank of Commerce, 1909, p. 5.
5. Ibid, p. 8.
6. Martin Mayer, op. cit., p. 46.
7. Walker, op. cit., p. 10
8. Ibid.
9. Ibid, p. 11.
10. Ibid, p. 12.
11. Ibid, p. 17.
12. Encyclopedia Canadiana, Vol. 3, pp. 22-23.
13. The History of Canadian Business 1867-1914, by Tom Naylor, Lorimer, Toronto, 1975, Vol. 1, p. 108.
14. Ibid. p. 22.
15. Myers, op. cit., pp. 193 ff.

16. Naylor, op. cit., p. 127.
17. Myers, op. cit., p. 172.
18. Ibid, p. 222.
19. Ibid, p. 177.
20. But Not In Canada, by Walter Stewart, Macmillan, Toronto, 1976, p. 83.
21. Myers, op. cit., p. 208.
22. Ibid, p. 260.
23. Ibid, p. 162.
24. Naylor, p. 68.
25. Ibid.
26. Ibid, p. 150.
27. Ibid, p. 150.
28. Ibid, p. 103.
29. Ibid.
30. Ibid, p. 106.
31. Ibid.
32. Ibid.
33. Galbraith, op. cit., pp. 106 ff.
34. Naylor, op. cit., pp. 136-137.
35. Ibid, p. 119.
36. Ibid, p. 149.
37. Ibid, p. 120.
38. Encyclopedia Canadiana, Vol. 5, p. 140.
39. Binhammer, op. cit., p. 75.
40. The Canadians, 1867-1967, Edited by J.M.S. Careless and Roderick Haig-Brown, Macmillan, Toronto, 1967, p. 208.
41. Binhammer, op. cit., pp. 74-75.
42. Naylor, op. cit., p. 76.
43. Ibid, pp. 156 ff.
44. Ibid, p. 172.
45. Walker, op. cit., pp. 95-96.
46. Myers, op. cit., p. xxxii.

Chapter Four

1. Royal Bank Annual Report 1981, p. 54.
2. CBA Bank Facts 1981, p. 4.
3. Royal Bank Annual Report 1981, p. 23.
4. Don't Bank On It, by Alix Granger, Doubleday, Toronto, 1981, p. 251.
5. Notice of Changes to Service Charges, Bank of Nova Scotia, June 1, 1982.
6. Granger, op. cit., p. 44.
7. CBA Bank Facts 1981, p. 4.
8. Globe and Mail, January 5, 1979.
9. Ottawa Journal June 8, 1980.
10. Globe and Mail, December 14, 1981.
11. Letter, Eric W. Kierans to William A. Kennett, April 1, 1980.
12. Letter, W. A. Kennett to Eric W. Kierans, April 28, 1980.
13. Globe and Mail, June 11, 1980.

Chapter Six

1. Senate of Canada, Proceedings of the Standing Committee on Banking, Trade and Commerce, 20-11-79, p. 7:9.
2. Deposit-taking Institutions, Innovation and the Process of Change, by H. H. Binhammer and Jane Williams, Economic Council of Canada, Ministry of Supply and Services, 1976, p. 13.

3. Bank of Canada Review, November, 1981, p. 41.
4. Ibid.
5. Granger, op. cit., p. 41.
6. Ibid, p. 219.
7. General Information Bulletin, Trust Companies Association of Canada, September, 1978.
8. Granger, op. cit., p. 188.
9. Binhammer and Williams, op. cit., p. 4.
10. Ibid, p. 9.
11. Montreal Gazette, August 22, 1981.
12. Ibid.
13. Globe and Mail Report on Business, October 5, 1981, p. B35.
14. Granger, op. cit., p. 10.
15. Binhammer, op. cit., p. 208.
16. Naylor, op. cit., pp. 101 ff.
17. Binhammer, op. cit., p. 208.
18. Provincial Government Banks, John N. Benson, Fraser Institute, Vancouver, 1974, p. 10.
19. Globe and Mail, October 5, 1981.
20. Benson, op. cit., p. 11.
21. Ibid.
22. Bank of Canada Review, November, 1981.
23. Ibid.
24. Binhammer and Williams, op. cit., p. 42.
25. Ibid.
26. Bank of Canada Review, November, 1981.
27. Ibid.
28. Ibid.
29. Ibid.
30. Ibid.

Chapter Seven

1. The Bank Act, Section 27(1).
2. Prospectus, Unity Bank of Canada, Gairdner & Company, September 19, 1972.
3. The Bank Act, Section 28(1).
4. Globe and Mail, April 12, 1982.
5. Hansard, March 12, 1982, pp. 474-475.
6. House of Commons, Report of the Proceedings of the Standing Committee on Finance, Trade and Economic Affairs, 16-3-72, p. 3:15.
7. Ibid.
8. Ibid.
9. Chartec Limited, Letter to the Provisional Board of the Unity Bank of Canada, March 24, 1972.
10. Prospectus, Unity Bank, op. cit.
11. Returns to the Clerk of the House of Commons.
12. Ibid.
13. Press release, Investor Relations of Canada, Limited, for Unity Bank, October 16, 1973.
14. Richard Higgins, transcript of address to the First General Meeting of shareholders, January 14, 1974, p. 1.
15. Globe and Mail, January 27, 1976.
16. Annual Report, Unity Bank, 1976.
17. Financial Times of Canada, January 31, 1977
18. Ibid.
19. Globe and Mail, May 4, 1977.
20. Letter, Gordon Dryden to Isadore Levinter, December 17, 1976.
21. Toronto Star, January 26, 1977.

22. Globe and Mail, February 16, 1977.
23. Financial Post, March 19, 1977.
24. Toronto Star, May 12, 1977.

Chapter Eight

1. Globe and Mail, October 7, 1980.
2. Massey at the Brink, by Peter Cook, Collins, Toronto, 1981, pp. 263-267.
3. Business Quarterly, Vol. 44, No. 3, Brascan vs. Woolworth, by Donald N. Thompson, pp. 69 ff.
4. Globe and Mail, April 17, 1979.
5. Ibid, October 17, 1981.
6. Ibid, January 22, 1982.
7. Senate Banking Committee, Proceedings, 1-11-78, p. 1:47.

Chapter Nine

1. Globe and Mail, August 24, 1981.
2. The Canadian Who's Who, University of Toronto Press, 1980.
3. Brinco, the Story of Churchill Falls, by Philip Smith, McClelland & Stewart, Toronto, 1975, pp. 112-113.
4. Globe and Mail, October 17, 1981.
5. Financial Post, October 3, 1981.
6. The Canadian Who's Who.
7. Ibid.
8. Royal Bank, Annual Report, 1981.
9. The Canadian Who's Who.
10. Financial Post, October 3, 1981.
11. Ibid.
12. The Canadian Who's Who.
13. Financial Post, October 3, 1981.

Chapter Ten

1. Today Magazine, March 13, 1982.
2. Binhammer, op. cit., p. 36.
3. Ibid, pp. 72-73.
4. Business and Social Reform in the Thirties, by Alvin Finkel, James Lorimer & Company, Toronto, 1979, p. 117-133.
5. Binhammer, op. cit., pp. 73-74.
6. Ibid.
7. Encyclopedia Canadiana, Vol. 2, p. 304.
8. Financial Post, May 31, 1981.
9. Toronto Star, October 6, 1981.
10. Ibid.
11. Montreal Gazette, December 3, 1975.
12. Press release, Bank of Canada, January 15, 1982.
13. Bank of Canada Review, November, 1981.
14. Financial Post, May 23, 1981.
15. Globe and Mail, May 30, 1980.
16. Bank of Canada, Annual Report of the Governor, 1980.
17. House of Commons, Proceedings of the Standing Committee on Finance, October 29, 1979, p. 3:4.
18. Financial Post, March 30, 1981.
19. Binhammer, op. cit., pp. 232-233.
20. David Crane in the Toronto Star, October 13, 1979.
21. The Bank of Canada in a System of Responsible Government, by H. S. Gordon, in

Canadian Banking and Monetary Policy, Second Edition, McGraw-Hill Ryerson, Toronto, 1972.
22. Ottawa Citizen, February 2, 1973.
23. Globe and Mail, December 5, 1981.

Chapter Eleven
1. The Canadian Who's Who, 1980.
2. Granger, op. cit., p. 140.
3. Ibid.
4. Letter, November 22, 1977, Rafe Mair to Jean Chretien.
5. Granger, op. cit., p. 142.
6. Vancouver Sun, April 13, 1978.
7. Maclean's, January 23, 1978.
8. Globe and Mail, January 24, 1980.
9. Vancouver Sun, April 18, 1978.
10. The Bank Act, Section 245(7).
11. Ibid, Section 246(1).
12. Toronto Star, February 9, 1980.
13. Martin Mayer, op. cit., pp. 206 ff.
14. Ibid.
15. Montreal Gazette, October 21, 1979.
16. Globe and Mail, October 8, 1980.
17. Toronto Star, April 19, 1982.
18. The Bank Act, Section 246(2).
19. Reasons for Judgment, Mr. Justice Thomas Berger, Bank of Montreal v. Arvee Cedar Mills Ltd., June 18, 1980.
20. Ottawa Journal, June 19, 1980.
21. The Public Accounts, Volume II, 1980.
22. The Bank Act, Section 247.
23. Toronto Star, February 9, 1981.
24. Proceedings, Senate Banking Committee, Issues 3, 4, and 16, 1978 and 5, 7 and 19, 1979.
25. Toronto Star, February 9, 1981.

Chapter Twelve
1. Naylor, op. cit., p. 75.
2. Ibid.
3. Ibid, p. 76.
4. Ibid, p. 73.
5. Ibid, p. 96.
6. Counting Canada's Banks, by S. Sarpkaya, Canadian Bankers' Association, 1978.
7. Binhammer, op. cit., p. 137.
8. Binhammer and Witliams, op. cit., and Bank of Canada Review, November, 1981.
9. Calculated from Granger, op. cit., p. 23.
10. Binhammer, op. cit., pp. 136-139.
11. Ibid.
12. Benson, op. cit., p. 11.
13. Ibid, p. 13.
14. Report of the Royal Commission on Corporate Concentration, Ministry of Supply and Services, Ottawa, 1978, p. 244.
15. The Measure of Rates of Return in Canadian Banking, by Jack M. Mintz, Economic Council of Canada, Ministry of Supply and Services, Ottawa, 1979, p. 94.
16. Letter, Sylvia Ostry to Herbert Gray, M.P., February 26, 1979.
17. Granger, op. cit., p. 145.
18. Ibid.

19. Canadian Banking Legislation, Proposals issued on Behalf of the Government of Canada, Ministry of Supply and Services, Ottawa, 1976.
20. Vancouver Sun, April 2, 1980.
21. Summary of Banking Legislation, Department of Finance, 1978.
22. Proceedings, Senate Banking Committee, 1-11-78.
23. Financial Post, December 6, 1981.
24. ScotiaBank Monthly Review, January, 1981.
25. Globe and Mail, January 12, 1982.
26. Registered Political Parties, Fiscal Returns, 1979 and 1980, Office of the Chief Electoral Officer.
27. Globe and Mail, June 12, 1981.
28. Globe and Mail, October 28, 1980.

Chapter Thirteen

1. Buying Up Uncle Sam, by Mark Witter, Quest Magazine, September, 1980.
2. Transcript, Canadian Institute of Public Real Estate Companies, Toronto, February 6, 1979.
3. Ibid.
4. Toronto Star, October 2, 1981.
5. Royal Bank Annual Report, 1981.
6. Globe and Mail, January 18, 1982.
7. Ibid.
8. The Banks of Canada in the Commonwealth Caribbean, by Daniel Jay Baum, Praeger, New York, 1974.
9. Ibid, p. 6.
10. Ibid, p. 19.
11. Stewart, op. cit., p. 259.
12. Ibid, p. 258.
13. Baum, op. cit., p. 84.
14. Ibid, p. 30.
15. Canadian Annual Review, 1970.
16. Baum, op. cit., p. 103.
17. The Economist, June 21, 1980, p. 51.
18. Financial Post, January 3, 1981.
19. Globe and Mail, August 7, 1981.
20. Ibid, January 15, 1982.
21. Ibid, July 2, 1980.
22. Today Magazine, July 5, 1980.
23. Globe and Mail, January 18, 1982.
24. Toronto Star, May 31, 1980.
25. Financial Post, February 14, 1981.
26. Globe and Mail, March 29, 1980.
27. Ibid, January 18, 1982.
28. Let Us Prey, edited by Robert Chodos and Rae Murphy, Lorimer, Toronto, 1974, pp. 151-154.
29. Financial Post, June 6, 1981.
30. Washington Post, June 6, 1980.
31. Globe and Mail, January 18, 1982.
32. Financial Post, June 6, 1981.
33. Globe and Mail, January 19, 1982.
34. Ibid, January 19, 1982.
35. Financial Post, October 10, 1981.
36. Ibid.
37. Globe and Mail, October 3, 1980.
38. Financial Post, February 14, 1981.

39. Globe and Mail, August 14, 1980.
40. Galbraith, op. cit., pp. 314-315.
41. Euromoney Magazine, January, 1980, p. 41.

Chapter Fourteen

1. Bankers' Casino, by L. J. Davis, Harper's, February, 1980.
2. Modern Goldsmith Banking, by Thomas Velk, Canadian Forum, October, 1974.
3. The Behavior of the Euro-Markets and the Problem of Monetary Control in Europe, by Helmut Mayer, Bank for International Settlements, Basel, November, 1980.
4. Davis, op. cit.
5. Martin Mayer, op. cit., pp. 205-206.
6. Davis, op. cit.
7. Bank for International Settlements, Fiftieth Annual Report, Basel, 1980, p. 106.
8. Davis, op. cit.
9. Helmut Mayer, op. cit., p. 37.
10. Ibid.
11. Ibid, p. 36.
12. Davis, op. cit.
13. Velk, op. cit.
14. Davis, op. cit.
15. Ibid.
16. Ibid.
17. Globe and Mail, January 16, 1982.
18. Quoted in the Globe and Mail, February 4, 1982.
19. Globe and Mail, December 18, 1981.
20. Financial Post, October 10, 1981.
21. Globe and Mail, June 9, 1981.
22. Wall Street Journal, April 16, 1981.
23. Globe and Mail, May 29, 1980.

Chapter Fifteen

1. Globe and Mail, January 22, 1982.
2. Ibid.
3. Binhammer and Williams, op. cit., p. 25.
4. Bank of Canada Review, November, 1981.
5. IAC Annual Report, 1980, p. 2.
6. Bank of Canada Review, November, 1981.
7. Notice of Changes in Service Charges, Bank of Nova Scotia, June 1, 1982.
8. Binhammer, op. cit., pp. 374-376.
9. Toronto Star, January 7, 1982.
10. Globe and Mail, August 19, 1981.
11. Granger, op. cit., p. 195.
12. Globe and Mail, July 29, 1981.
13. Granger, op. cit., p. 206.
14. Ibid, p. 205.
15. Ibid, p. 206.
16. Globe and Mail, October 31, 1981, from a report by Gairdner, Watson Limited.
17. The Canadian Bankers' Association, Bank Profits 1981, The Year in Review.
18. Globe and Mail, January 6, 1982.
19. Financial Post, August 16, 1980, and the annual reports of the named companies.
20. Globe and Mail, November 20, 1981.
21. Ibid, January 19, 1982.
22. Sunday Morning, Canadian Broadcasting Corporation, December 13, 1981.

23. Globe and Mail, December 5, 1981.
24. Bank of Nova Scotia, Annual Report, 1981.
25. Ibid.
26. Calculated from annual reports of the named banks.
27. Ibid.
28. Globe and Mail, July 9, 1978.
29. Calculated from the annual reports.
30. Tax tables, 1981.

Chapter Sixteen
1. CBA estimate, April 16, 1982.
2. Granger, op. cit., p. 183.
3. CBA Fact Book, 1979/80, p. 8.
4. Brave New Money, by Gordon Donaldson, Quest Magazine, August, 1980.
5. Ibid.
6. Notice of Changes, Bank of Nova Scotia, June 1, 1982.
7. Granger, op. cit., p. 249.
8. Donaldson, op. cit.
9. CBA Bank Facts, 1981, pp. 7-8.
10. Granger, op. cit., p. 186.
11. Ibid, p. 188.
12. London Free Press, October 22, 1981.
13. Globe and Mail, May 5, 1981.
14. Computer Crime, Criminal Justice Resources Manual, Bureau of Justice, Washington, 1979.
15. Los Angeles Times, August 20, 1979.
16. Globe and Mail, August 5, 1981.

Chapter Seventeen
1. Orsingher, op. cit., p. 157.
2. Danish Embassy, May, 1981.
3. Banking System and Monetary Policy, Government of Austria, May, 1981.
4. Globe and Mail, November 2, 1981.
5. Embassy of Switzerland, May 12, 1981.
6. Globe and Mail, September 24, 1981.
7. The World Almanac, 1980.
8. Evidence by the Committee of London Clearing Bankers to the Committee to Review the Functioning of Financial Institutions, London, 1978.
9. World Almanac, 1980.
10. Helmut Mayer, op. cit., p. 32-38.
11. Atlanta Constitution, November 18, 1981.
12. Helmut Mayer, op. cit., p. 78.
13. Toronto Star, February 26, 1982.

Index

Abitibi-Price, 109
Acadia Life, 113
Aetna Casualty, 113
Agricultural Bank, 32
Alberta Treasury Branch, 78
Allan, Sir Hugh, 33
Allende government, 196
Anderson, Helen, 117
Apartheid, 194-96
Argus Corporation, 109
Association of Canadian
    Financial Corporations, 172
Avison, T. L., 102

Bain, Richard, 92
Balance of payments, 133
Banco Brascan de
    Investmento, S.A., 194
Bank Act, 8-9, 39, 42, 69, 73,
    78-81, 88ff., 105, 128, 131,
    155-60, 165ff., 178, 183,
    202-203, 225, 250, 262, 265
Bank Act (Jamaica), Canadian
    influence on, 191
Bank administration, 55-58, 91
Bank assets, 5-10, 182, 230-31.
    See also Big Five; Central
    banks; names of banks.
Bank auctions, 145-46
Bank Canadian National, 103
Bank consortia, 217-19
Bank errors, 55ff., 268-69
Bankers, 19ff., 26-28, 84, 118ff.
Bank failures, 38, 40, 168, 218.
    See also Unity Bank case.
Bank for International
    Settlements, 207, 212-13,
    215-16

Bank functions, suggested
    limitations on, 262-63
Banking, history of, 15ff.
Bank lawyers, 85-90, 98-99,
    106, 264
Bank Leu, 25
Bank of America, 210, 219, 258
Bank of Amsterdam, 22
Bank of British Columbia, 10,
    41, 78, 154, 171
Bank of Canada, 6, 23, 30-31,
    40-41, 88-89, 132ff., 144-46
Bank of Canada Review, 72
Bank of Commerce, 42
Bank of England, 22, 254
Bank of London and Montreal,
    191
Bank of Montreal, 2ff., 31-34,
    51, 84-86, 98ff., 119, 145,
    166, 190ff., 198, 202, 218,
    221, 231-32, 240, 268
Bank of North America of
    Philadelphia, 30
Bank of Nova Scotia, 2ff., 41,
    44, 56, 88, 91, 106, 115, 145,
    173, 181, 189-90, 195ff., 202,
    203, 221, 233
Bank of Ontario, 34
Bank of Quebec, 31
Bank of Scotland, 256
Bank of Stockholm, 22
Bank of the People, 32
Bank of Tokyo, 231
Bank of Upper Canada, 31
Bank of Western Canada,
    79, 90
Bank policy, government
    policy and, 145-48, 152-55
Bank profits, 3, 4, 9ff., 80,
    222-23, 228, 230-31, 259
Bank Rate, 144, 146, 149,

222-23, 227, 256ff., 265
Bank reform. See Bank
    Act; Porter Commission;
    Senate Banking Committee;
    White Paper.
Bank shares, 4-5, 93, 232
Banks, Canadian, 2ff., 66-68,
    70, 269-70
Banque Canadienne Nationale,
    158
Banque Europeenne de Tokyo,
    253
Banque Generale, 23
Banque Occidentale pour
    l'Industrie et le Commerce
    (Suisse), 198
Banque Ville Marie, 38
Barclays, 256
Barclays Banque, 253
Baring Brothers, 255
Basset, Doug, 109
Baum, Daniel J., 190, 192
Bayerische Vereinsbank, 252
BDM Fund, 97
Beaubien, Sen. Louis P., 117
Bell Canada, 10, 109
Bell, Gordon, 173
Bellan, Ruben, 141
Bennett, R. B., 135
Bertrand, Robert, 176
Big Five, 9-11, 13, 79, 82, 106ff.,
    117ff., 153ff., 180, 183,
    193-94, 230ff., 253, 256,
    262, 266
BIS. See Bank for International
    Settlements.
Bishop government
    (Grenada), 193
Black, Conrad, 109
Boards of directors of banks,
    106-108, 111-14, 117ff., 263.
    See also Interlocking
    directorships; Bankers.
BOLAM. See Bank of London
    and Montreal.
Bonnell, Bobby, 84ff., 98, 103
Borden, Sir Robert, 190
Bouey, Gerald, 130-31, 140ff.,
    150, 180
BP Limited, 10
Branch administration, 43,
    51, 65
Brascan, 109
Bray, Carne, 172
Brinco, 118-19
British American Bank Note
    Company, 136
British American Land
    Company, 33
Brokerage firms, 70
Brown, George, 32
Building societies, 256
Business loans, 70
Bussieres, Pierre, 162

Caisse d'entreaide, 76-77
Caisse populaires Deshardins,
    77
Caisses populaires, 70, 75, 76
Campeau Corporation, 107
Campeau, Robert, 107, 254
Canada Banking Company, 30
Canada Permanent, 71
Canada Permanent Mortgage
    Corporation, 72
Canada Permanent Trust Co.,
    72
Canada Savings Bonds, 70,
    137-38
Canada Trust, 71

Canadian Banker, 164, 165

Canadian Bankers' Association (CBA), 36, 39, 77, 91-92, 106-108, 164ff., 176-77, 231, 244, 266

Canadian banking system, 28-31, 114-16, 127-29, 251-59, 260-68

Canadian Bank Note Company, 136

Canadian Deposit Insurance Corporation, 1

Canadian Export Development Corporation, Chilean government overthrow and, 196

Canadian Export Development Bank, East European involvement of, 198

Canadian Imperial Bank of Commerce, 9, 42, 52-54, 72, 80, 107, 109, 154, 158, 191, 193, 202, 204, 220-21, 231, 233

Canadian Law Information Council, 249

Canadian Pacific, 109

Canadian Pacific Railway, 32, 41

Canadian Payments Association, 77, 180

Cantonal banks, 252-53

Capital-to-assets ratio, 7, 8

Car-leasing firms, banks' effect on, 178, 179

Cartwright, Sir Richard, 167

Castro, Fidel, 193

Castro government, 191

CBA. See Canadian Bankers' Association.

Central banks, 35-42, 69-77, 80ff., 137, 166ff., 173ff., 184, 193ff., 210, 212-13, 220ff., 230

Central banks (U.S.), 197, 258. See also Federal Reserve Banks.

Chargex. See VISA; Credit cards.

Chartec, 97

Chartered banks, 4, 8-14, 43ff. See also Big Five; Central banks.

Chartering system, 8, 34, 36, 78, 83, 89, 171, 182, 219, 231, 258, 265

Cheques, 50, 54, 238-40

Chequing accounts, 5-6, 49, 54-55, 70, 79, 143

Chretien, Jean, 131, 154, 234

Churchill Falls Corporation, 119

Citibank, 219

Citicorp, 258

City Bank, 32, 166

Clairborne Industries of Toronto, 102

Clark government, 79, 148

Clearing banks, 255

Cobus, Pat, 43, 48, 51

Coinage, 18-22

Coleman, John H., 110

Collection agencies, 59ff.

Collins, Enos, 31

Commercial banks, 144

Commerzbank, 252

Competition, 11, 69, 73, 266

Computer crimes, 245-49, 266

Computerized banking, 47-50, 207, 237ff., 252, 266. See

also Electronic Funds Transfers.
Confederation, banking practice during, 130
Conflict of interest, bank boards and, 264. See also Canadian Bankers' Association; Interlocking directorships.
Connolly, Sen. John, 69
Consolidated Bank, 33
Consolidated Revenue Fund, 160
"Constant dollars," 17
Consumer credit market, 79-81, 263
Consumer Reports, 228
Continental Bank, 81, 226
Co-operative societies, 256
Coutts, 256
Coyne, James, 79, 148
Credit bureaus, 60, 61
Credit cards, 56, 61, 64, 74-75, 228-29, 241-43
Credit Lyonnais, 262
Credit ratings, 59, 60, 62-64
Credit unions, 70, 75ff., 171
Cullen, Bud, 178
Currency, 7, 18, 133-36. See also Canadian dollar; Euro-currency; Money supply.

Danish banking law, 263
Davidson, Stanley, 169, 233
Davies, Louis, 166
Debentures, 5, 170, 233
De Blaquiere, Henry, 27
Debt, the public, 132
Debts, bad, 59

Demas, William, 191-92
Deposit insurance, 1, 42, 76, 77
Deposits, 5-6, 17, 46
Depression (1930s), 134ff.
Desjardins Canal, 27
Deutsche Bank, 252
Diefenbaker government, 148
Disclosure, 265
Discount houses, 255
Dominion Notes, 39, 132-35
Don't Bank on It (Granger), 48
Dresdner Bank, 231, 252
Dryden, Gordon, 88, 90
Duncan, Gaylen, 249
Dwyer, Dennis, 84, 90, 97, 102, 103

Eastern Townships Bank, 34
Eastgate, William A., 103
Eaton's, 109
Economic Council of Canada, 75, 229
Economic policy, Canadian, 124, 140ff., 211, 214
EEC Bulletin, 173-76
Effort Trust Company, 71
EFT. See Electronic Funds Transfer.
Egypt, banking system in, 17, 263
Electronic Funds Transfer, 241-42, 249-50, 262-64. See also Computerized banking.
Equifax Inc., 61
Euro-currency market, 216ff., 268
Euro-Money Magazine, 204
European American Bank, 217-18

Evangeline Savings &
    Mortgage, 71-72
Excelsior Life, 113

Factoring companies, 70
Family compact, 31
Federal Bureau of
    Investigation, 247
Federal Business Development
    Bank, 12
Federal reserves, 144
Federal Reserve System (U.S.),
    200, 217, 258-59
Federation des Caisses
    d'entreaide Economique du
    Quebec, 76
Finance Act, 133
Finance companies, 80, 169
Finance Minister, 88-89, 94,
    131, 166ff., 180, 191, 265
Financial Collection Agencies,
    60
Financial Post, 122, 198, 203
First Realty Company, 100
Foreign Banks, 9, 89, 177,
    180, 266
Foreign exchange market, 70,
    135-41
Foreign policy, Canadian loans
    to foreign governments
    and, 189-92, 196, 265
Foster, George, 167
FP News Service, 65
Frankfurter Bank, 252
Franklin National Bank of
    New York, 206, 217
Frazee, Rowland, 59ff., 105,
    120ff., 184, 223, 236
Frazer, Patrick, 254, 257
France, banking system in,
    23, 261
Friedman, Milton, 143-44
"Fungibility," 207-08
Fyshe, Thomas, 190

Gairdner & Company, 94
Galbraith, John Kenneth, 37
Galt, Sir Alexander, 33-34
Garin, Carlos, 100
General Motors of Canada, 10
Germany, regional banks
    in, 252
Gibbons, Edward, 109
Globe and Mail, 56, 84, 87, 118,
    184, 195, 199, 223
Goar, Carol, 162
Gold reserves, 132-33
"Goldsmith bankers," 20
Gold standard, 132-33
Goodman, Rod, 268
Gordon, Walter, 88
Government bonds, 139
Grand Trunk Railway, 32, 341
Great Britain, banking system
    in, compared with
    Canadian, 254-57
Great Crash of 1929, 133
Great Southern Railway, 26, 27
Great Western Railway, 26, 27
Gresham, Sir Thomas, 21-22
Guaranteed Investment
    Certificates, 71, 145
Guardian Trust, 74
Gulf Oil, 10

Haidasz, Stanley, 90
Hammurabi Code, 17
Harris, Cliff, 99
Harrison, Russell, 113,
    126, 220

Harvard Business School, 118
Hayden, Sen. Salter, 106, 112, 117, 169
Higgins, Richard, 84ff., 96ff., 161
Hill, Samuel, 255
Hincks, Francis, 32-33, 166
History of Banking in Canada (Walker), 29
Home Bank, 13, 40
House of Commons, 145
House of Commons Committee on Banking Trade and Commerce, 89
House of Commons Standing Committee on Finance, 90, 92, 178
Howard, Roy, 65
Hudson's Bay Company, 109

IMF. See International Monetary Fund.
Imperial Bank, 42
Imperial Oil, 10
Incorporation, Federal, 71
Inflation, 3, 4, 10, 17, 123-24, 138, 141, 144, 206ff., 216, 222-23, 228, 230, 244, 265
Inspector General of Banks, 40, 55, 69, 89, 104, 152ff., 264
Insurance companies, 70
Inter-American Development Bank, 196
Interest rates, 3-4, 11, 16-18, 20, 49, 56, 71ff., 82, 111, 127, 131, 138ff., 146, 147, 170, 179, 210, 212, 222-23, 227-28, 237
Interlocking directorships, 105-06, 111ff., 183, 263

International Banking, 207, 261, 265
International Monetary Fund, 139, 193, 203, 213
Investment houses, 70
Iron Ore Company of Canada, 119

Japan, 162-63
Jerome, James, 90

Kaplan, Robert, 90
Keeper, Cyril, 164
Kennett, William, 55, 69, 103, 152, 155, 162-63, 234
Kerr, Ian, 59ff.
Kertudo, Jean, 213
Kierans, Eric, 55
Kierans, Lena, 55
King government, 135
Kinnear, David, 109
Kinross Mortgage, 72

Labour Relations Board, 53
Lafferty, Richard, 180
La Marsh, Judy, 90
Lambert, Allen, 178
Lasalle, Dr. Gerald, 98
Lash, Z. A., 166
Laurier, Sir Wilfrid, 167
Law, John, 23-25
Lazard Brothers, 255
Ledwos, Don, 63, 64
Lending Manual, U.S.A., 202
Letters patent, 89, 177
Leverage, 5, 131
Levinter, "Bunny," 86ff., 103
Levinter, Isadore, 87, 98
Levinter, Marion, 88
Lewycky, Laverne, 164-65

Liabilities, 5
Lloyds Bank, 256
Loans, 5-6, 67. See also types of loans.
Loans officers, 54
Lobbies and lobbyists, 168, 177-79, 259, 266. See also Canadian Bankers' Association; Bankers.
Lombards, 19-32
Lombard Street, 21
Lougheed, Sir James, 167
Luck, Eaton, 97

M-1, 147. See also Bank of Canada; Monetarism; Money Supply.
Macdonald, Sir John A., 32, 167
MacIntosh, Robert, 80, 92, 165, 170ff., 178-80, 184
Maclean's, 84, 85, 87
Manhattan Bank, 35
Manley, Michael, 192-93
Mann, George, 96
Maritimes, 35, 91, 168, 260
Massey-Ferguson, 107, 114
MasterCard, 9, 71. See also Credit cards.
Mathews, David, 97
Mayer, Helmut, 206, 215-16
McCarthy and McCarthy, 106
McGill, Peter, 33
McGill University, 207
McIntosh, John, 201
McIntyre, John M., 123
McLaughlin, Earle, 52, 121, 164
McNamara, Sean, 228
McNeill, Fred, 102
Mennonite Trust Limited, 72

Mercantile Bank (N.Y.), 35
Mercantile Bank of Canada, 10, 182
Merchants' Bank, 33, 166
Midland Bank (Britain), 256
Mintz, Jack, 173, 231
Mitsubishi, 252
Mitsui, 252
Molson, Sen. Hartland, 106, 117, 169
Molson, John, 34
Molson, William, 34
Molson's Bank, 34
Monetarism, 143ff.
Monetary policy, 144ff., 259
Monetary Times, 33
"Monetizing the debt," 7
Money, 15ff., 43, 44, 132, 219
Money creation, 3-7, 16, 138, 210, 217, 222ff., 265
Money supply, 133ff., 229, 265
Money traders, 15ff., 139. See also Bankers.
Montreal (City) and District Savings Bank, 34, 79
Montreal Gazette, 158
Morgan Guaranty Trust Co., 213
Morgan Stanley, 118
Morgan Trust Co., 71
Mortgage companies, 70, 72, 81-82
Mortgage loan companies, 70, 71
Mortgage loans, 170
Mortgage market, 81-82, 225, 263
Mortgage rates, 81, 225-27. See also Interest rates.
Mortgages, 70ff., 227

Morton, Michel, 268
Morton, W. L., 40
Mulholland, William, 107, 118ff., 195, 232
Multi-branch banking, 47-48
Mutual funds, 70
Mutual Stock Savings Associations (U.S.), 257
Myers, Gustavus, 34, 42

National Bank of Canada, 10
National Girobank, 257
National Housing Act, 169
Nationalism, 191
Nationalization of banks, 261
National Savings Certificates (Britain), 256
National Trust, 71
National Westminster Bank, 256
Naylor, Thomas, 35, 36
New Democratic Party, 164
"New goldsmith banking," 207
Newman, Peter, 118
New York Times, 120, 218
Noble, William, 85, 86, 98, 100
Northland Bank, 10

Oligopolies, 127-29, 261
Ontario Savings Offices, 78
Ostry, Sylvia, 175
Ottawa Credit Bureau, 61

Parker, Donn, 249
Parliament, Members of, and CBA, 164ff., 184
Parliamentary Press Gallery, 175
Payroll management, 263
Pearse, R. L., 100, 190

Pearson government, 148
Personal finance companies, 70
Personal loans, 56, 70, 72
Petro-dollars, 216
Phoenix Assurance, 113
Poland, 218
Ponzi scheme, 208
Porter Commission (1964), 169, 264
Post Office Giro, 256
Post Office Savings Bank, 78
Prime Rate. See Interest rates.
Private banks, 41-42
Progressive Conservative Party of New Brunswick, 84
"Proofing teller," 50
Province of Ontario Savings Office, 78
Provincial Bank, 103
Provincial savings banks, 41
Prudential Assurance Co., 113

Queen's University, 150, 173

Rae, Bob, 162
Railway Act, 27
Railway speculation, 26ff.
Rasminsky, Louis, 148
Realty companies, 81
Recession (1920), 40
Regional banks, 35ff., 78-79, 168, 171, 266
Regional Trust Company, 72
Registered Home Ownership Savings Plans, 70, 263
Registered Retirement Savings Plans, 70, 72, 73, 263
Regulation manuals, 45-46, 51, 199, 201

Reserve requirements, 7ff., 38, 73, 77, 88-89, 144-45, 180-81, 207-08, 217, 226, 238
Rest Accounts, 9-10
Restrictive Trade Practices Act, 176
RHOSPs. See Registered Home Ownership Savings Plans.
Ritchie, Cedric, 125
Roseman, Ellen, 56, 242
Rotstein, Maxwell, 97
Royal Bank of Canada, 3, 5, 9, 10, 28, 43ff., 52, 53, 59ff., 65, 111, 180, 184, 190ff., 198ff., 223-25, 233, 236, 261
Royal Bank of Scotland, 256
Royal Commission on Corporate Concentration, 264-66
Royal Trust, 72
Royal Trustco, 107
RoyMor Mortgage, 72
RRSPs. See Registered Retirement Savings Plans.

Sachs, W. R., 199
Savings accounts, 5, 11, 55, 70ff., 79
Seaga, Edward, 193
Scott, W. A., 92
Scott, W. R., 161
Senate, lobbying in, 166
Senate Banking Committee, 69, 78, 90, 92, 105-06, 113, 122, 128, 168, 171, 183
Shaddick, Peter, 100
Shareholder reports, 265
Shares, 4-5, 232
Sharp, Mitchell, 169
Simpson's, 109

Sindona, Michele, 217
Slogans, 11, 30, 44, 57
Smallwood, Joseph, 119
South Africa, 194
South Africa Chamber of Mines, 195
Soviet Union, 12, 209
"Spread" of interest rates, 3-4
Stephen, George (Lord Mount Stephen), 34
Stevens, Sinclair, 79
Stocks. See Shares.
Sumitomo, 252
Swiss Bank Corporation, 252
Swiss Credit Bank, 253
Swiss Volksbank, 253

Taskforce on Churches and Corporate Responsibility, 194, 196
Taxes, 12, 141, 233-34
Tax havens, 99, 211, 219
Tellers, 46ff., 237
Term deposits, 5, 70, 74. See also Deposits.
Texaco, 10
Third World, 203
Thompson, Kenneth, 109
Thompson Newspapers, 111
Thompson, Richard M., 109, 125, 232
Toronto-Dominion Bank, 9ff., 55-56, 95, 108-09, 158, 202-03, 221, 232
Toronto Star, 162
Towers, Graham, 191
Treasury bills, 70, 134, 145
Trudeau government, 178
Truscott, Green & Co., 32
Trust companies, 70ff., 171,

192, 255-56
Turpin, Ben, 178

Underwriters, 94-96
Unemployment, 138, 139
Unicorp, 96
Union Bank of Switzerland, 253
Unions, 51, 52, 140
"Unit banking" laws (U.S.), 257
United States, 257-59
United States Banking Act (1933), 212
United States banks, 10ff., 34ff., 54, 95, 156, 257ff., 265
United States Comptroller of Currency, 209, 212
United States dollar, 209ff.
United Trust Company, 90, 96
Unity Bank case, 83ff., 161, 265
University of British Columbia, 87
University of Manitoba, 141
Upper Canada College, 87

Vancouver City Savings Credit Union, 77
Vancouver Sun, 155
Van Horne, Charlie, 84
Velk, Thomas, 207, 209, 211, 215
Venture capital, 37-38, 114, 128, 256
Victoria and Grey Trust, 71
VISA, 9, 66, 71. See also

Credit cards.

Wage and price controls, 144
Walker, Sir Edmund, 41
Walker, Leonard, 85
Weldon, Jack, 12
Welland Canal, 26
Western Canada, central banks' plunder of, 35, 36, 115
Western Economic Opportunities Conference, 171
Western European banking systems, 252-53
West Indies, 193
Wharton, Robert, 100
Whelan, Eugene, 130
White Paper on Banking (1976), 172-77
Wholesale banks, 69
Williams and Glyn's, 256
Winnipeg Free Press, 65
Women in banking, 43, 48, 52, 53, 112-13, 123-24, 268
Wood Gundy Ltd., 94
World Bank, 203
World Bank Debtor Reporting System, 213
World debt, 215

Young, Phyllis, 153

Zimmerman Bank, 26
Zimmerman, Samuel, 26-27

tional and physical distress. Dispatcher had difficulty understanding her."

"Give me a name," Anna demanded, her impatience mounting.

"Shana. Kept mentioning Melissa. What sounded like Rampart Street."

Anna and J.D. exchanged looks. J.D. turned back toward the street and began running, hearing Anna shout:

"I need backup. Now. Rampart Street!"

Shana reached Poland and Rampart with only thirty seconds to spare, parked Tyron's car half on the curb, engine idling as she rested her head back against the seat and dragged the gun onto her lap. Where the hell were the cops?

Think. Where was her cell phone? Think. She reached for her purse, dumped it out on the car seat. No phone. She must have dropped it at Honey's apartment. She couldn't remember.

The pain in her face had become a constant throb, pressure building behind her eyes. Slowly, she turned her head, did her best to focus on the empty, fog-shrouded street.

He was out there, of course. Watching her.

She fumbled for the door handle, shoved open the door, and eased from the car, moving unsteadily into the dark, toward the distant illumination of the streetlight on the corner. The moon was barely visible over the warehouses, its fog-diffused glow little more than a hazy iridescence. The rank smell of the river swam in the hot air and she could easily hear the waves lap at the old pilings of crumbling buildings jutting out over the river.

How many streetlights had she stood beneath, waiting for some nameless, faceless john to approach her, fear a hot pit in her belly, knowing that any one of them could turn into a killer.

Yet, here she stood, too weak to do more than lean against the lamppost and pray her legs didn't give out on her, knowingly waiting for a monster who fully intended to destroy her, and there was no fear. No hot pit in her belly. Only resolve.

Too damn tired to run any longer. To hide from her past. Tired of the loneliness. And the memories.

Odd that she would now allow herself to think of her mother, young, unmarried, believing she could raise a child on the little money she made working as a checker in a grocery store. Shana had only vague memories of her face, cheeks painted by the bright red and blue lights of a ferris wheel, her hand gripping Shana's one moment, then she was gone.

"Shana."

She lifted her head, her heart skipping a beat as a rush of relief swept through her. A familiar face. Oh, thank God.

"Hello, Shana."

"Eric. Thank God."

As he joined her in the pool of light, she sank against him, clutching his shirt. "The police. You have to call the police."

He removed the gun from her hand as he wrapped one arm around her. His body felt drenched with sweat.

"What happened to you?" he asked softly.

"Doesn't matter. Please, just call the police. The killer has Melissa, and . . ." She pushed away and stared into his face. "What are you doing here?"

That hot pit was back, deep in her belly, as she looked into his face, so much like J.D.'s. What was Eric Damascus doing here? No car in sight.

She backed away, realization no longer occluded by her desperate relief to find J.D.'s brother materializing out of the fog. No. Surely it wasn't possible.

She glanced down at her gun in his hand before looking back into his eyes.

"Surprise." He smiled as his hand snapped out to close around her throat.

As the car streaked down Rampart Street, the headlights bounced off the fog that moved like dingy, flimsy sheets around them. J.D. slammed his fist on the dashboard. "She could be anywhere along this damn street."

"Relax," Anna said in her infuriatingly calm voice. "We'll find her."

"Yeah, but will we find her in time?" He looked out the window at the flashes of dark, hulking warehouses along the river.

"There!" Anna shouted, drawing J.D.'s attention toward the car parked partially on the curve near the distant streetlight. Anna slammed on the brakes, causing the tires to skid on the damp street, and J.D. threw open the door, jumping from the car before it came to a dead stop. He hit the pavement, running toward the idling Viper, its driver's door open.

"Jesus God."

The car seat and steering wheel were smeared with blood. Shana's purse and contents were scattered over the seats and floorboard. He glanced toward Anna, who had remained in the car reporting the car's location to the police. Even as she spoke, the eerie wail of distant sirens filtered through the fog.

A pulse beat passed before he recognized the intruding beep of the cell phone on his belt. He glanced down at the caller ID. Christ. Beverly again. Not now, for God's sake.

The phone stopped ringing. It began again. Beverly.

Furious, he answered, "I can't talk to you now—"

"Please," she wept. "Listen to me. Patrick—"

"Dammit, Bev—"

"It's Eric. The killer—I found evidence . . ."

J.D. stared at his feet, the door of denial he had slammed the last hour blasted open with an impact that jarred his entire body.

"I found evidence," she said, her voice drowned by emotion. "In Patrick's room. The dead hookers' client books. John, he told me he found them hidden in Eric's office. Those disgusting magazines as well. He told me he'd been following Eric at night. That he followed him tonight to the old Redman warehouse where Eric has been meeting hookers. John, I'm afraid Patrick has gone back there. Eric knows. He knows I know about the books. I told him—"

J.D's gaze flashed down Poland Street and he began to

walk, his stride breaking into a run as he threw down the phone and grabbed for the gun under his jacket.

"Damascus!" Anna shouted behind him.

Down the pitted old street, beyond the boarded warehouses flanking the river that moved like a black, slithering snake with the moon tide. Sirens drifted through the hot night air, one, two, screaming from every direction as the Redman warehouse loomed ahead of him, two stories of brick and crumbling wood, boarded windows and a rusting tin roof.

Slowing, slowing, cautiously approaching the front door. Locked. Moving through the dark down the side of the building—which way? East? West? Sweat rising, the pounding of the river waves against the pilings muted by his heart slamming in his ears.

Carefully, he moved onto the walk, ancient boards skirting the building. They shuddered under him, creaked and moaned as he avoided the broken banisters that would surely turn to dust if he touched them. He headed toward the double doors at the far end of the warehouse—breathe, breathe, steady—gripping the gun in both hands.

Below, the river swirled like eddies around the mossy pilings as he reached for the door and tried it. It moved, slightly. Blinking the sweat from his eyes, J.D. squeezed through the narrow opening, stepped into the yawning black cavern.

Dim yellow light shone in the distance. J.D. inched his way through the dark, senses expanded to an excruciating level, his brain bombarded with frantic thoughts.

Was he in time? Had Eric already murdered Shana?

Could he kill his brother—his own brother, for God's sake?

Back off and let the cops take care of it.

Not enough time. Each second was precious. Since Eric knew Beverly and Patrick were aware of his crimes, he would have nothing left to lose.

Christ, oh Christ. His mother—how would he ever tell his parents?

Deep in the dark recesses of the warehouse, beyond the skeletonlike shapes of meat hooks hanging from the over-head beams, J.D. noted an old meat locker, its door ajar. His back against the wall, J.D. eased toward the door, his heart climbing his throat as he heard a woman crying.

Bracing himself, lifting the gun, finger on the trigger—

He stepped through the door, leveling the gun, his gaze streaking from one side of the locker to the other, freezing on the two women huddled on the floor together. Shana held a weeping Melissa in her arms, then Shana's head whipped around and he saw her face. Oh Jesus, her face, bloody and battered and contorted in horror—

The unexpected slam against the back of his head sent sharp shards of pain and blackness through his brain. His knees buckled. With a groan he hit the floor, the impact jarring the gun from his hand. Through a tunnel of dark agony and confusion, he heard Shana cry out, and though he did his best to scramble to his hands and knees, the dizziness in his head made him fall again. Slowly, with effort, he rolled to his back and looked up into his brother's eyes—no, not his brother's eyes, but the eyes of a madman.

"Oh, my." Eric's lips stretched into a skull-like grin.

He bent over and picked up the gun, stroked the barrel as he continued to stare into J.D.'s eyes. "Was my little brother going to shoot me?" He cocked his head to one side. His face pale and sweating, he blinked sleepily and sighed. "This is a hell of a mess, isn't it, J.D.?"

"Yeah," he said. Think. Remain calm. Where the hell was Anna?

"Now what am I supposed to do? Kill you, too? Mommy and Daddy wouldn't like that much. Would they?" He closed his eyes briefly then sat down beside J.D.

"What the hell happened to you, Eric?"

For an eternal moment, Eric stared off into space, as if he was struggling to remember, his expression shifting rapidly from madness to fear, to the pitiful semblance of a tormented child.

"It all began by happenstance. Jack . . . enjoys the company of hookers. Sherrie Shepherd. She was the first. Got a mouth on her and decided she would go public about him unless he paid her big money. He suggested that I shut her up."

Eric's smile stretched wider as tears coursed down his cheeks. "I shut her up, all right. And I liked it. For once in my life I was in control. Total control. My entire life has been dictated by Daddy. Live up to Daddy's standards. Please Daddy or he won't love me. God, I hated you for standing up to him. For refusing to kiss his ass."

"Is that why you killed my family?" J.D. said through his teeth, his sudden surge of blind fury making him clench his fists.

Eric nodded and gave him a wink. "Me and Laura . . .

it was my way of getting back at you. I'm sorry about that. The kids and all. But what could I do? She threatened to tell everyone about our affair. She was stupid to bring the kids that night. Left them asleep in the car. I had no idea they were there until I looked up and found Billy watching me cut off her head."

J.D. closed his eyes and groaned, "Ah, God."

"If it makes you feel any better, I didn't make them suffer. It was quick and clean. I'm very good with my knife.

"There was Jack, of course. Just like Daddy. Dictating my thoughts, my actions, reminding me constantly that I would be nothing without him—he held my future in the palm of his hand. I'm little more than his lackey. His pawn. I really would like to kill him, too. Him and Daddy."

The wail of sirens closed in, and Eric lifted his head, released a bone-weary sigh. "I wish I could say I hated myself for killing. But I don't. I'm quite evil, but not insane. Which brings me to the here and now. I'm going to kill you, J.D. And those whores. Then I'm going to turn myself in." He chuckled. "Imagine how humiliated Daddy will be. And Jack. He can kiss his presidential aspirations good-bye, huh?" He laughed, stroked the gun barrel again, his eyes turning as cold and lifeless as glazed glass.

J.D. grabbed for the gun, his fingers closing around the barrel as Eric swung it toward him. Throwing his body against Eric's, he slammed his brother's arm against the floor, the sudden explosion of the weapon ear-shattering in the metal room.

Then pain sliced through his ribs, driving the wind from him. From the corner of his eye he saw Eric raise a bloodied knife, prepared to plunge it into him again. He couldn't move, paralyzed by the pain, the breath rushing from his punctured lung like a deflating balloon.

Suddenly Shana was there, throwing her body over J.D.'s, her hands clawing for the knife, driving Eric back against the wall with an impact that boomed through the metal locker. As if in slow motion J.D. watched his brother fling her aside like she was little more than a weightless rag doll. She hit the floor hard on her back as Eric pointed the gun at her—

"No!" J.D. shouted, as he tried to scramble, to reach her—

Eric fired, and the bullet's impact lifted Shana's body like a stringed puppet, her hands clutching her chest, blood blooming between her fingers. Her panicked blue eyes turned toward J.D. as he clawed his way toward her, fear obliterating his pain, his hand reaching for her, reaching—

A second explosion momentarily froze him, rocking through him with such horror it seemed that his heart imploded as his gaze remained locked on Shana's.

A third shot wrenched him from his nightmare as he swung his head around to see his brother flattened against the wall, the gun sliding from his hand, his shocked eyes fixed on the shooter at the door.

Footsteps stampeding through the warehouse, then Anna's voice shouting, "Put down the gun! Down, now!"

Reality dwindled to a pinpoint as J.D. looked around,

into Patrick's tear-streaked face as the boy lowered his gun.

The world then became a blur of shouting voices, of officers exploding into the room with guns drawn, of someone shouting orders for the EMTs as J.D. gently lifted Shana in his arms.

"Hold on," he begged her as he carefully touched her battered face and did his best to smile into her eyes, refusing to look at the wound in her chest. "You're going to be okay, baby."

Her trembling lips curved slightly. "Don't . . . think so."

"Don't leave me, Shana. Please. We've got the rest of our lives to spend together."

"So tired, John."

"I know. But I'll make it good for you, honey."

"No more nightmares?"

"I swear it."

"Melissa . . . okay?"

"She's going to be okay. And so are you."

The pain left her eyes then and the fear. She lifted one hand and pressed her fingertips to his cheek. "Love you."

A sigh of breath left her. Her eyes closed. As her body grew limp, J.D. wrapped his arms tightly around her, held her to his chest as he moaned in grief.

EPILOGUE

THREE MONTHS LATER

The cluster of pink and blue balloons bounced together in the brisk breeze as J.D. held tightly on to them, Lisa's tiny hair ribbons binding each grouping together. Sitting on the marble bench, he stared at the grave markers—his family's and Shana Corvasce's. Sunlight splashed over her name and reflected off the granite like bits of gold glitter.

Sitting beside him, Anna reached into her purse, handed him the packet, and smiled.

"Everything's there. Visa. Passport. One-way ticket to Paris." She crossed her legs and tossed back her red hair. "Sure you want to do this?"

"Yeah." He nodded.

"It's a big step, walking away from your life."

"And the memories," he said. "Time to start over."

"Everything squared away with your parents?"

"Mom understands. Besides, it won't be forever. Right?"

She smiled again. "You know Jerry's offer stands. A full partnership in the firm when you're ready."

He grinned. "I'll keep that in mind."

"You're going to be missed around here. May—"

"Hey, Jerry and May deserve each other. They can aggravate the hell out of one another on an hourly basis."

She laughed. "I take it Beverly isn't pleased."

"She'll get over it. She's got her hands full with Patrick right now." He sighed. "I regret leaving him like this."

"He's got plenty of counselors helping him, J.D. He's got a tough road ahead of him, but he's a bright young man. Eventually, he'll pull it together."

She checked her watch. "Gotta run. A flight to catch."

"Back to work?"

"A nasty case in Seattle. Six priests killed—all staked to crucifixes."

As she stood, he caught her hand, smiled up into her green eyes. "Thanks, Anna."

"Be happy," she said softly, gave his fingers a squeeze, and walked away, up the meandering path toward the distant parking lot.

J.D. took a deep breath, turned his face into the sunlight, its subtle heat bringing a rise of sweat to his brow. His hand gripped the balloon strings nervously.

Christ, he felt like a schoolboy.

He watched Anna's car leave the cemetery, his gaze locking on the massive wrought iron entrance.

Where the hell was she?

A movement caught his attention.

He had not noticed the woman as she sat on a distant bench near a grouping of mausoleums. As she stood, she placed a bouquet of flowers on the ground, then turned and moved toward him, her short blond hair stirring slightly in the breeze.

She smiled.

His heart stopped.

Speechless, he swallowed, his gaze taking in the differences in her face. The plastic surgeon who had put Shana back together had done a remarkable job. She'd lost weight, her gruelling battle to survive the gunshot to her chest having taken its toll. She was still breathtakingly beautiful. It was all he could do not to sweep her into his arms and make love to her mouth. But not here. As far as the rest of the world knew, Shana Corvasce had died in his arms three months earlier—three months of not seeing her. Hearing her voice. The only communication between them coming through Anna.

As she joined him, Shana glanced at her name on the grave marker and shuddered before drawing back her shoulders and looking at him again, her blue eyes sparkling.

Extending her hand, she said, "Hello. The name is Karen. Karen Keiler. I've missed you," she said, her smile growing.

"We have the rest of our lives to make up for it."

"Are you sure about this, John? You think we can make it together?"

"I think we won't know unless we try."

Her gaze moved to his children's grave markers, as did his. Less pain now at the thought of letting go. The grief no longer unbearable.

"You're sure?" she asked softly.

He nodded. "It's time to move on. A new beginning. For us both."

His fingers trembling, he tugged Lisa's hair ribbon from the strings and released them.

As the spheres lifted in the air, J.D. reached for Shana's hand. Together, they watched the splashes of color swirl above their heads, pink and blue shimmering with angelic light.

And with a sudden gust of wind they rose, fanning across the bright blue November sky . . . dancing their way toward heaven.